CONSCIOUSNESS
REVOLUTION IN
SOVIET PHILOSOPHY

How does matter become meaningful?

This is the first critical history of the philosophical culture of
the USSR, and the first substantial treatment of a modern Soviet philosopher's work by a Western author. The book identifies a significant tradition within Soviet Marxism that has produced powerful theories exploring the origins of meaning and
value, the relation of thought and language, and the nature of
the self.

   The tradition is presented through the work of Evald Ilyenkov (1924–79), the thinker who did most to rejuvenate Soviet
philosophy after its suppression under Stalin. Professor Bakhurst sets Ilyenkov's contribution against the background of
the bitter debates that divided Soviet philosophers in the 1920s,
the "sociohistorical psychology" of Vygotsky, the controversies over Lenin's legacy, and the philosophy of Stalinism. He
traces Ilyenkov's tense relationship with the Soviet philosophical establishment and his passionate polemics with Soviet opponents.

   This book offers a unique insight into the world of Soviet
philosophy, the place of politics within it, and its prospects in
the age of *glasnost'* and *perestroïka*.

CONSCIOUSNESS AND REVOLUTION IN SOVIET PHILOSOPHY

From the Bolsheviks to Evald Ilyenkov

DAVID BAKHURST

Department of Philosophy
Queen's University, Ontario, Canada

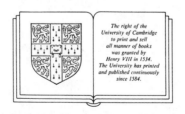

The right of the
University of Cambridge
to print and sell
all manner of books
was granted by
Henry VIII in 1534.
The University has printed
and published continuously
since 1584.

CAMBRIDGE UNIVERSITY PRESS

CAMBRIDGE

NEW YORK   PORT CHESTER   MELBOURNE   SYDNEY

Published by the Press Syndicate of the University of Cambridge
The Pitt Building, Trumpington Street, Cambridge CB2 1RP
40 West 20th Street, New York, NY 10011, USA
10 Stamford Road, Oakleigh, Melbourne 3166, Australia

First published 1991

Printed in the United States of America

Library of Congress Cataloging-in-Publication Data
Bakhurst, David.
Consciousness and revolution in Soviet philosophy :
From the Bolsheviks to Evald Ilyenkov / David Bakhurst.
p. cm. – (Modern European philosophy)
Includes bibliographical references and index.
ISBN 0-521-38534-2. – ISBN 0-521-40710-9 (pbk.)
1. Philosophy, Russian – 20th century. 2. Consciousness.
3. Revolutions – Philosophy. 4. Il'enkov, Eval'd Vasil'evich.
I. Title. II. Series.
B4231.B35 1991
197 – dc20 90–21015

British Library Cataloguing-in-Publication Data
Bakhurst, David
Consciousness and revolution in Soviet philosophy :
From the Bolsheviks to Evald Ilyenkov
1. Russian philosophy
I. Title II. Series
197

ISBN 0-521-38534-2 (hardback)
ISBN 0-521-40710-9 (paperback)

An earlier version of Chapter 3 appeared in
Studies in Soviet Thought, 31 (1986), 103–29,
© 1986 by D. Reidel Publishing Company,
and reprinted by permission of Kluwer Academic Publishers.

FOR MY PARENTS

CONTENTS

ACKNOWLEDGMENTS

This book could not have been written had I not had the opportunity to discuss the Soviet philosophical tradition with some of its living representatives. I am grateful to Keele University and the British Academy for funding a number of short visits to Russia, and to the British Council for granting me a scholarship to study in Moscow for the whole academic year 1982–3. I should like to thank Moscow University, the Institute of Philosophy, Moscow, and the Institute of General and Pedagogical Psychology, Moscow, for receiving me so warmly on these occasions. Above all, I thank the philosophers and psychologists who made me welcome and who devoted so much time to helping my work.

The book began its life as a doctoral dissertation, which I had the pleasure of writing in Oxford, first at Balliol College, where I was a graduate student for two years, and then at Exeter College, who did me the honour of electing me to a Junior Research Fellowship. Both colleges are splendid places in which to work. I am especially grateful to my colleagues at Exeter, Michael Hart and Gregory Hutchinson, for their friendship and support. John McDowell and Michael Inwood supervized the thesis, and Katherine Wilkes and Robert Service examined it. I thank them all for their criticisms and suggestions. I am also grateful to Stephen Blacklocks, Andrew Chitty, Hanjo Glock, and Paul Snowdon, with whom I enjoyed many fruitful philosophical discussions in Oxford. And I must not forget to thank Mrs. Carol Menzies of the Bodleian Library for her expert help in locating obscure Russian sources, and for suppressing with her rule of steel the loquacious tendencies of the Slavonic Section.

I completed this book during my time as an Assistant Professor in the Department of Communication at the University of California, San Diego. I am obliged to my former colleagues and students there for making the department such a congenial place, and particularly to Carol Padden, Michael Cole, and Ellen Watson for their helpful suggestions on my work. I am also indebted to Raymond Geuss and Mary Tiles, editors of the Modern European Philosophy series, for their useful comments on the original manuscript, and to Terence Moore of Cambridge University Press for his patience and advice.

Finally, I should like to mention four people who have followed this project from its beginnings. I owe a great debt to Genia Lampert, whose masterly works on Russian intellectual history first prompted me to think about that country's philosophical culture. Had he not kindled my interest in Soviet philosophy while I was an undergraduate at Keele, I should never have begun this work. I was also fortunate to be taught at Keele by Jonathan Dancy, who first made me interested in philosophy, and who has been a constant source of ideas and encouragement ever since. Many of my philosophical insights, such as they are, have emerged in the course of conversations with Jonathan. Another philosopher who has greatly influenced me is my friend Felix Mikhailov, whom I first met in 1980, and who has since entertained me with his marvellous philosophical skills on so many occasions. Our conversations in Moscow are among the most enjoyable I have known. Finally, Christine Sypnowich helped me define this project, and offered incisive criticisms and fruitful suggestions at every stage of its development. Thanks to her, the work is much better than it otherwise would have been. In composing these acknowledgments, I realize how many friends I have made in the course of my work on this book. I very much hope they will take pleasure in the result.

A NOTE ON TRANSLATION, TRANSLITERATION, AND REFERENCES

Except where I cite a published translation, quotations from Russian sources appear in my own translations. Where Russian words are cited for clarification, nouns are given in the nominative singular, adjectives in the masculine nominative (except where cited with the noun they qualify, in which case they agree with the noun), and verbs in the imperfect infinitive. In quotations, words enclosed in square brackets are my own insertions, except where otherwise indicated.

To avoid a proliferation of transliterated or translated titles in footnotes, references are given in the text by the author/date method. Many Soviet publications are collaborative works whose authors are not specified, and for which no editor is nominated. In such cases, the work is cited in the text by the first word of its title. I have usually identified works by their date of first publication, rather than that of the edition I have used.

1

INTRODUCTION

Why study Soviet philosophy? The best reason to study another philosophical tradition is that philosophy itself will benefit; there could be no stronger incentive to consider the work of Soviet philosophers than the prospect of enlarging the compass of philosophical knowledge in general. The study of Soviet philosophy, however, is rarely advocated on these grounds. On the contrary, the prevailing opinion in the West is that philosophers in the Soviet Union have produced nothing of intellectual substance. It is usually believed that what has passed for philosophy in the USSR is merely the elaboration of Marxist–Leninist doctrine, a mixture of platitudes and non sequiturs that, at least until recently, formed the ruling ideology of the Soviet Communist Party. "Soviet philosophy," it is sometimes joked, must be a contradiction in terms.

The prevalence of such views explains the character of the small body of Western literature on Soviet philosophy. The study of Soviet philosophy has traditionally fallen to scholars of a "sovietological" orientation, who have envisioned their primary task as the analysis of an alien superpower's ideology. They have thus sought to codify the official philosophy of the Soviet establishment, avoiding lengthy discussion of any

particular Soviet thinker's ideas.[1] The writings of the more inventive Soviet philosophers are sometimes cited to show how
Marxist–Leninist dogma can be cleverly interpreted to preserve a semblance of intellectual activity, but it is seldom argued that these writings make a contribution to philosophy as
a discipline.[2] It is hardly surprising, therefore, that the deliverances of philosophical sovietology have had little more than
curiosity value for Western philosophers.

When in the early 1980s I spent a substantial period of time
among philosophers in Moscow, I came to feel that the typical
Western conception of Soviet philosophy was inadequate. It is
true that I encountered many an ideologue peddling a crude
and dogmatic Marxism. Furthermore, it seemed that everyone was expected to show allegiance to this "textbook" doc-

1 The founding fathers of philosophical sovietology are Gustav Wetter
   (see esp. 1958) and J. M. Bocheński (see esp. 1961, 1963a–c). The discipline is celebrated in Dahm, Blakeley, and Kline (1988).
2 Commentators often claim that Soviet philosophy is interesting "in
   its own right," but their presentations rarely lend this claim any
   plausibility. For example, it is hard to see how Bocheński can say of
   Soviet philosophy that "much of it is philosophically interesting"
   (1963b: 2) when he also claims that its "main doctrines are nothing
   but a robust and slightly systematized expression of simple common
   sense," that its "techniques, the range of its problems, and its formulations are abysmally primitive," and that "no true philosophical
   problem is ever set out clearly and correctly – let alone solved"
   (1963a: 116–17). Recently, authors of a more sympathetic persuasion
   have attempted to challenge this impression, but with little success.
   For example, James Scanlan's *Marxism in the USSR* (1985) expressly
   aims to show that Soviet philosophy is more fertile and intellectually engaging than is commonly believed. However, the book in fact
   paints the familiar picture of a philosophical community predominantly concerned with the elaboration of an incoherent dogma. Scanlan stresses the plurality of views among Soviet philosophers, but he
   finds the source of this pluralism not in the logic of philosophical
   debate but in the fact that official Soviet philosophy is either so vacuous that philosophers may hold a variety of positions while main-
   taining verbal allegiance to orthodoxy, or so inconsistent that they
   are free to opt for either side of a contradiction. Yet to establish that
   Soviet thinkers do not all endorse the same monolithic doctrine because "ambiguities, misunderstandings, and other impediments to
   unanimity will arise in any intellectual community" (Scanlan 1985:
   28) and because "Orwellian devices of thought control" have not
   been applied thoroughly and effectively in the USSR (313–15) is by
   no means to show that Soviet philosophy is "marked by fundamental
   searching and dispute" (9). On the contrary, the overall impression
   of Scanlan's book is that Soviet philosophy is intellectually bankrupt.

trine and to pursue research compatible with its tenets. Yet this was far from the whole story. For all the dogma, there was also a real philosophical culture alive in Moscow. Moreover, the representatives of this culture were by no means dissident figures. On the contrary, they were united by a commitment to a critical Marxism, informed by the philosophy of Hegel and the German classical tradition. These philosophers saw the renewal of such "genuine" Marxism in Soviet political culture as an essential prerequisite of the rejuvenation of Soviet society.

Although the ideas of these "critical Marxists" (as we may call them) seemed to form part of a distinctively Soviet philosophical tradition, it was a beleaguered one. Its present generation had done its most challenging work in the early 1960s, but had lost momentum when the "thaw" of those years began to refreeze. These philosophers now held an uncomfortable relationship to a philosophical establishment that often viewed critical thinking and scholarly erudition with distrust. Relations were also strained with those Soviet thinkers who believed German classical philosophy to be obscurantist and reactionary, inhibiting Marxism's desired alliance with the natural sciences. Such thinkers turned away from dialectical philosophy and sought a more progressive framework in the rigours of the analytic tradition. Thus, paradoxically, the critical Marxists' call for a "return to Marx" appeared too radical for the dogmatists who deemed themselves true guardians of Marxist doctrine, yet too orthodox for those who sought to animate Soviet philosophy by opening it to Western debates. Beset by such opposition, few philosophers of this critical persuasion held positions of institutional strength.

For all this, however, it was the ideas of the critical Marxists that appeared most original and that seemed to bear in interesting ways on debates within the Anglo–American tradition. Moreover, their ideas evidently had a long history in Soviet philosophy; to master them demanded an understanding of the development of Soviet philosophy since the 1917 Revolution. The study of these critical Marxists therefore promised to reveal much about the character of the Soviet philosophical tradition and the forces, intellectual and political, that had driven its development.

It was clear, however, that these thinkers could not be

studied by traditional sovietological methods. Philosophical sovietology is written almost entirely from the perspective of the external observer. The sovietologist summarizes Soviet positions, but does not engage with them in a way that reveals how their philosophical content might matter to those who hold them, let alone how it might matter to us. In contrast, an *internal* perspective is what is required if one is to understand a philosophical culture that appears so distant from our own, both in its approach to philosophical inquiry and in its vision of the role of philosophy in public life. This book therefore rejects the sovietological method in favour of a form of "philosophical ethnography," which attempts to convey how Soviet philosophical culture appears from the inside.

To achieve such an internal perspective, I propose to focus on a particular thinker whose work brings together many of the dominant themes within the Soviet tradition: Evald Vasilevich Ilyenkov. Ilyenkov is widely esteemed in the USSR as a scholar of great integrity who made an important contribution to the renewal of Soviet Marxism after Stalin. Many who worked with him personally (such as Batishchev, Lektorsky, Lifshits, and Mikhailov, and the psychologists Leontiev, Meshcheryakov, and Davydov) describe him as the leading philosopher of his generation, a brilliant orator, and inspiring teacher. Some would say his finest writings are unparalleled in Soviet philosophy.[3]

To reconstruct Ilyenkov's philosophy as a meaningful whole and to locate it within the tradition to which it is a contribution requires an exercise of sympathetic identification: I explore the philosophical motivation for his position by working with his ideas, defending and developing them where necessary. Such a project demands sensitivity to the social and historical context of Ilyenkov's contribution, not simply as a catalogue of background facts, but as a live influence, stimulating or bridling his ideas. It is hoped that by entering

---

3 An indication of the esteem in which Ilyenkov is held is the moving gathering of friends and colleagues that takes place every year on the anniversary of his birth. After a morning meeting at Ilyenkov's graveside, an afternoon devoted to the discussion and evaluation of his work ensues at the Institute of Philosophy. In the evening, a more bacchanalian celebration of his contribution is held at the Ilyenkov family home in Gorky Street.

the position of a participant in the debate, we shall attain a vantage point from which Soviet philosophical thought, as well as its tangled social and political setting, fall into perspective.

This chapter sets the scene. The upcoming section offers a biographical sketch of Ilyenkov. This is followed by a description of the character of "official Soviet philosophy" at the time he was writing, and an account of the position of his contribution in the history of Soviet philosophy. I then briefly discuss the relevance of Ilyenkov's project to debates current in the Anglo–American tradition. The chapter concludes by considering the significance of Ilyenkov's work in the age of *glasnost'* and *perestroĭka*.

Introducing Ilyenkov

Ilyenkov was born in Moscow in 1924. His first article appeared in 1955, and he continued to publish widely until his untimely death in 1979. Several works have been published posthumously, and more are due to follow. Like many of his contemporaries, Ilyenkov was most inspired in the early 1960s as he strove to inject new life into Soviet philosophy after the stale orthodoxy of the Stalin era. In this period, he produced works that would lay the foundation for all his later thought.

It may seem remarkable that the time in which Ilyenkov was educated produced any serious philosophers at all. By the end of the 1930s, the Bolshevik intelligentsia established by the Revolution had been virtually wiped out in Stalin's purges. Whether from opportunism or prudence, the new generation of academics placed their disciplines in the service of the state ideology. At Moscow University, for example, where Ilyenkov studied after World War II, philosophy seems largely to have been reduced to the exposition and interpretation of Stalin's writings, focusing on his synopsis of dialectical and historical materialism in the *Short Course* of 1938 (see Yakhot 1981: 208, and the opening of Chapter 4). University life in the Soviet Union had reached its lowest ebb.

Despite this, however, the discipline of philosophy survived. This was due in part to the presence of a number of distinguished and inspired individuals, such as Asmus, Losev, and Lifshits, who managed to continue teaching in Moscow. In addition, some isolated centres of scholarship remained in existence, such as the Moscow Institute of Philological and Literary Studies (MIFLI), where Ilyenkov was fortunate to study philosophy for one year before he was called up for active service in 1942. (Sadly, MIFLI was disbanded immediately after the war.) Moreover, ironically, thoughtful philosophy students found an incentive for intellectual inquiry in the contrast between the dogma they were taught and the texts they were assigned. Such students sought each other out and returned together to the classics of philosophy – above all, to Marx. Thus, with the passing of Stalinism, there emerged a new generation of young philosophers, eager to reestablish a scholarly and discerning approach to their Marxist heritage.

Accordingly, in 1960, Ilyenkov produced a significant book on Marx's method, *The Dialectics of the Abstract and the Concrete in Marx's "Capital."* This work is a landmark in Soviet Marxist scholarship. Two years later, he published a remarkable article on Marxist philosophy's account of nonmaterial phenomena, "The Ideal," which appeared in the five-volume *Philosophical Encyclopedia,* a tour de force of the cultural renaissance after Stalin. Ilyenkov's writings had a significant influence on his contemporaries, and in 1965 he was awarded the Chernyshevsky prize "for research into vital questions of the theory of knowledge of dialectical materialism."

However, official recognition of Ilyenkov's work was limited. The reforms of the Khrushchev era, which had promised so much, failed to remove the old guard of philosophers. This was a disaster for thinkers like Ilyenkov, who, in their efforts to challenge the legacy of Stalinism, quickly made enemies among senior academics. Immediately after Stalin's death, Ilyenkov lost his position at Moscow University after an unsuccessful attempt to persuade his colleagues that Soviet philosophy should rethink itself.[4] In 1953, he was appointed at Moscow's Institute of Philosophy. Though he continued to hold a position there until his death, his regular clashes with the Institute's directorship ensured that his situation was far from happy.

---

4   This he did by reading a number of "Theses on Philosophy" at a meeting of the *kafedra* (chair) of dialectical materialism at Moscow University. Sadly, the theses are now lost.

An illustration of the difficulties Ilyenkov encountered is given in the editorial preface to Ilyenkov's "Marks i zapadnyĭ mir" ("Marx and the Western World") (1965), an article recently published for the first time in Russian by the journal *Voprosy filosofii (Questions of Philosophy)*. In this preface, A. G. Novokhat'ko explains how, in 1965, Ilyenkov was invited to contribute to an international symposium at the University of Notre Dame. The symposium, which focused on Marx's contribution to the "Western World," was organized principally to foster dialogue between communist and noncommunist intellectuals. Although Ilyenkov's paper was discussed at the symposium, he was unable to participate in person, ostensibly because he was "hospitalized" at the time (Lobkowicz 1967: xii). Novokhat'ko's preface implies, however, that the reason Ilyenkov failed to attend was that the Institute of Philosophy opposed his participation (Novokhat'ko 1988: 98). Furthermore, soon after his paper was published in the conference's proceedings (Ilyenkov 1967c), Ilyenkov was subjected to a "campaign of political accusations," with his article being attacked for its "anti-Marxist" orientation (Novokhat'ko 1988: 98).

Interestingly, Ilyenkov's piece is one of the few he devoted exclusively to political philosophy. As such it offers a window on to the complex relations between philosophy and politics in the world he inhabited. In this article, Ilyenkov argues that the most basic feature of the communist worldview is a commitment to the social ownership of property; thus what divides "Western" and "Eastern" worlds is their different forms of ownership (1967c: 392). Turning to Marx's critique of private property, Ilyenkov stresses that Marx fully appreciated the positive influence of private ownership on the development of the "technological and scientific culture of Europe and North America," recognizing its power to stimulate personal initiative and free human resources "from the surveillance of bureaucratic regimentation" (1967c: 395 [1965: 102]). Accordingly, the socialization of property does not mean that everything is owned and administered by a central state apparatus. On the contrary, state ownership is merely a transitional phase: Under fully developed communism, however, social property is, at the same time, "the property of each person, of each separate individual" (1967c: 400). The socialization of property thus requires the disappearance of the state, which in turn demands the abolition of the division of labour, so that each individual can achieve the all-round development essential for popular sovereignty.

It may be hard for a Western observer fully to comprehend the criticism Ilyenkov's piece provoked. To the uninitiated, it seems a model of Soviet orthodoxy. Its central ideas can all be found in the Marxist classics, it is unreservedly optimistic about the eventual flourishing of Soviet communism, and it wastes few opportunities to criticize Western interpretations of Marx. How could such an article be thought "anti-Marxist"?

There are several reasons why Ilyenkov's colleagues may have found fault with his position. The first is Ilyenkov's radical antistatism, which, though formally consistent with official Soviet ideology, is not sweetened by an apologetic portrayal of the existing Soviet government as an "all people's state." On the contrary, the article implies that Soviet state ownership (particularly its appropriation of property through collectivization) is not even an embryonic form of communist organization, but is actually incompatible with popular sovereignty properly understood. Second, in his discussion of the employment of Marx's "Western" ideas in the Russian setting, Ilyenkov offers more than the standard view that the backwardness of the Russian economy inhibited the application of Marxist theory. The text also implies that the peculiar character of the Russian context has sometimes led to "a mass of illusion" about Marxist ideas (400) and even to their wilful misinterpretation (394). Finally, the tone of Ilyenkov's article may have provoked hostility. Ilyenkov writes not as a Soviet delegate presenting an official line, but as an autonomous scholar addressing the specific concerns of the symposium in his own voice. We are left, therefore, with the paradoxical conclusion that the essay that provoked accusations of anti-Marxism was a work of Marxist scholarship, sympathetically addressing issues of paramount importance to Soviet reality.[5] Such para-

---

5 An interesting feature of Ilyenkov's article is its far-sighted rejection of the idea, then so influential in Western Marxism, of a "break" between the early "humanistic" Marx of the *Manuscripts of 1844* and the mature "economic" Marx of *Capital* (Ilyenkov 1967c: 401–6). Ilyenkov insists that, since communism's vision of popular sovereignty demands human as well as economic transformation, Marx's political economy is incomplete unless it is seen to preserve the philosophical anthropology of the early Marx.

doxes are all too familiar in the Soviet academic world. As Novokhat'ko confirms (98), the controversy over "Marx and the Western World" was by no means an isolated incident in Ilyenkov's career.[6]

The constant danger of provoking controversy did not, however, diminish Ilyenkov's resolve to make his philosophy relevant to the political and social issues of the day. Its effect was rather to cause Ilyenkov to redefine his audience. As the brief renaissance in Soviet scholarship gradually lost impetus, Ilyenkov turned away from academe to address a wider readership. In 1968, he published *Of Idols and Ideals,* a book that pursues many of the themes of "Marx and the Western World" in a more popular vein. Once again, Ilyenkov's focus is the

---

6 Ilyenkov's writings were, of course, subject to the kind of editorial interference that was, until very recently, ubiquitous throughout the Soviet academic world. At present, however, we must rely on hearsay to gauge the effect of such censorship. For example, it was once suggested to me that Ilyenkov's last work, *Leninist Dialectics and the Metaphysics of Positivism* (1980, 1982), was intended to show that the positivism of Lenin's supposedly discredited opponent, Alexander Bogdanov, continued to persist within Soviet politics and philosophy, but that Ilyenkov's message was obscured when his discussion of modern Soviet positivism was excised from the work. (Ilyenkov's essay is discussed in Chapter 4.)

Another rather different example of editorial interference is illustrated by the publication of an excerpt from Ilyenkov (1977a) in *Sputnik,* a popular journal similar to *Readers' Digest.* In this excerpt, Ilyenkov writes, "As the ancients put it: 'Don't cite the name of your teacher, present your own arguments.' But since the dogmatic mind is incapable of independent conceptualization of a fact or event that has provoked a controversy, such a person attempts to take cover behind a 'standard solution.' This leads him to follow trodden paths. If he fails, he starts behaving hysterically" (Ilyenkov 1978: 78). In the original, this remark figures as a criticism of the Soviet education system. Published in the West, however, the passage has the opposite effect. Ilyenkov appears as a spokesman *for* Soviet education policy, his words evidence of the undogmatic character of a Soviet education.

However, we should also note that, for all the suspicion of his work within the Soviet academic world, Ilyenkov sometimes enjoyed considerable publishing privileges. He had a friend, L. K. Naumenko, on the editorial board of *Kommunist,* the principal theoretical journal of the Soviet Communist Party, and he twice published significant articles on its pages. Ilyenkov is also one of the most translated of Soviet philosophers. Many of his major works have appeared in European languages. (Ilyenkov [1960a] was also published in Japanese.) Unfortunately, some of the English translations do violence to his prose; Ilyenkov (1967c, 1977c, 1982b) are the best.

relation between popular sovereignty and the self, but rather than promoting the scholarly interpretation of Marx, his aim here is to stimulate discussion of the Soviet education system's duty to create individuals capable of participating in communist self-government. In this context, *Of Idols and Ideals* introduces a theme that was to preoccupy Ilyenkov for the rest of his career: the critique of crude reductionist conceptions of the individual. Ilyenkov suggests that Soviet philosophers and psychologists, in their euphoria about the "scientific-technical revolution" of the 1960s, were becoming captivated by cybernetic models of the mind that portrayed human individuals as no more than sophisticated self-regulating machines. This regression to "pre-Marxist materialism," Ilyenkov argued, encouraged the view that, since psychological activity is simply a function of the "mechanics" of the brain, each individual's intellectual capabilites are principally determined by biological considerations. In consequence, it threatened to reinforce a dangerous trend toward specialization in Soviet education: If some children are "hard-wired" with an aptitude for mathematics, others for music, and some for manual labour, why squander resources on their "all-round" development? Such specialization would, Ilyenkov argued, only perpetuate the division of labour and hence postpone the realization of popular sovereignty. Ilyenkov and other "critical Marxists" began a war against reductionism, conducted in a series of popular and polemical pieces, which sought to counter its influence in popular culture as well as the academic world (e.g., Arsen'ev, Ilyenkov, and Davydov 1966; Ilyenkov 1968b, 1970).

Ilyenkov saw this popular writing as a means to convey to a wide audience how a literate form of Marxist philosophy could be brought to bear on important issues of public life. It was not, however, a forum that facilitated the development of his philosophical views. His only theoretical book of the 1970s was *Dialectical Logic* (1974a; trans. as 1977e; revised and expanded 2nd ed. 1984a), a collection of essays that develop a materialist "phenomenology of mind," tracing the mind's evolving conception of itself as a phenomenon essentially embodied in a material world. Although the book is by no means a failure, the arguments at its heart recapitulate positions Ilyenkov had forged a decade before. His environment no longer demanded innovation, nor offered him new heights to reach. In marked contrast to his early work, Ilyenkov now sought principally to find acceptence for an old message.

At the end of his career, Ilyenkov returned once more to the "problem of the ideal," the subject of his most innovative work in the early 1960s. The result was a long article (1979a), grudgingly published by *Voprosy Filosofii* after Ilyenkov's sudden death. The essay is one of Ilyenkov's finest writings, elegantly composed and compellingly argued. Once again, however, it essentially represents a reiteration of his earlier stance. It thus provides a sad commentary on the intellectual climate of the Brezhnev period, underlining how little those years had facilitated the development of Ilyenkov's thought.

Orthodoxy and history

It is difficult to appreciate Ilyenkov's contribution without understanding the social and political context in which it was made. At the time he was writing, however, this context was not a possible object of debate in the Soviet philosophical literature itself. Given that philosophers were reluctant until recently even to cite the names of their Soviet opponents, it is not surprising that they failed to discuss critically the role of philosophy in public life or the machinations of the Soviet academic world. Hence, there is little documentation from which to construct the fine detail of Ilyenkov's situation.

One feature of his world that is evident from the Soviet literature is, of course, the "official" Marxist–Leninist doctrine said to comprise the shared premises of all Soviet philosophers. Throughout Ilyenkov's career, this doctrine was a constant presence in Soviet debate. It dominated the philosophical textbooks, the many philosophical dictionaries and encyclopedias, and the introductions to Soviet philosophy published in the West.[7]

According to this "textbook" Marxism–Leninism, philosophy is the science of the universal (*vseobshchii:* lit. "common

7 See, for example, *Filosofskii slovar'* (1975); Afanasyev (1980); *Fundamentals of Marxist–Leninist Philosophy* (1982; a collective work [*sbornik*] written under the general editorship of F. V. Konstantinov); *Filosofskii entsiklopedicheskii slovar'* (1983); and Spirkin (1983). Scanlan 1985 is the best commentary on the textbook doctrine as it was in the late 1970s and early 1980s (see the first section of each chapter).

to all") laws (*zakonomernost'*: "regularity" or "law-governed-ness") that govern both "being" (i.e., nature and society) and "thinking." Thus the "basic question" of philosophy is conceived as the relation of being to thinking, matter to consciousness. Philosophy is said to answer this question at the highest level of generality, invoking the most general laws of the development of nature, society, and thought, expressed by means of universal concepts or "categories." Such a general account of the relation of being and consciousness constitutes a "worldview." It is argued that a philosophical worldview is distinguished from religious or traditional worldviews as it offers rational, theoretical grounds for its principles. As Marxist–Leninist philosophy alone is able to justify its conclusions adequately, it is said to be the first truly scientific worldview.

The textbook doctrine maintains that answers to the basic question of philosophy come in only two forms: materialist and idealist. While materialism holds that being is prior to and primary over thinking, idealism holds the opposite, arguing that the world is (in some sense) identical to, or a consequence of, thought, consciousness, or idea. Soviet philosophers are said unanimously to endorse a materialist standpoint. The priority of being over thought has two dimensions. First, being is primary over thought in the sense that while the material world exists prior to and independently of thought, thought cannot exist independently of matter. Consciousness, and indeed all nonmaterial properties, are held to issue from states of the material world. Second, the materialist argues that consciousness is determined by the material conditions in which the thinking subject lives: That is, the contents of each subject's mind are formed in the process of his or her interaction with the material world, and are explicable only in the light of that interaction.

Soviet materialism draws its conception of matter from Lenin (1909a). Matter forms an objective reality existing independently of thinking subjects and presented to them in sensation. This objective reality is said to be in principle fully cognizable; that is, the material is not a realm of unknowable "things in themselves." In addition to its independence and its cognizability, matter is held to have a number of other general properties: motion, space, time, infinity, and "inexhaustibility in depth."

Soviet philosophers stress that their materialism is *dialectical.* In the textbooks, the dialectical character of Soviet philosophy is expressed as a commitment to certain principles and laws. The principles of dialectics are as follows:

(a) The phenomena of reality are interconnected.
(b) The world is in a constant state of change and development.
(c) This development proceeds via the resolution of contradictions.

In its commitment to these principles, dialectical materialism is contrasted with *metaphysical* materialism, which is said to view phenomena in isolation from each other and to offer an ahistorical conception of reality as changeless and static.

On the basis of these principles, Soviet materialism endorses three dialectical laws said to govern all development, be it in the realm of nature, society, or thought:

1. *The law of the transformation of quantity into quality:* In any process the gradual accumulation of quantitative changes eventually results in a qualitative change in the developing phenomenon; such qualitative changes take the form of an abrupt "leap" to a new stage of development.
2. *The law of the unity and struggle of opposites* (an elaboration of (c)): All phenomena and processes are unities of opposites; that is, they contain internal contradictions, the struggle and resolution of which constitutes development.
3. *The law of the negation of the negation:* Development is a process of the "negation" of one stage by the next. In "dialectical" negation, however, a special relationship holds between stages of a process such that part of an earlier stage (its "progressive content") is preserved in later stages. The law of the negation of the negation is sometimes taken to entail that development proceeds in spiral fashion: Stage p is "negated" by q, but reappears in transformed mode in stage r.

The study of dialectics falls into two subdisciplines: *objective* dialectics, the application of the principles and laws of dialectics to the development of objective reality, and *subjective* dialectics, the dialectics of cognition or "gnoseology" (epistemology). Once again, textbook dialectical materialism draws its epistemology from Lenin (1909a). It is argued that our knowledge of the world is an accurate reflection of it: Objective truth is therefore possible. However, although our knowledge is objective it is not absolute, for absolute knowledge would be knowledge of "everything in the world." Human beings are capable of such knowledge in principle, but in practice human knowledge contains only a part of what would figure in an absolute account of the world. Thus, at any stage in the development of human knowledge, our picture of the world is only relatively true.

An important notion in Soviet epistemology, also drawn from Lenin, is the elusive concept of *partiĭnost'* (lit. partyness). The lack of consensus among Soviet philosophers about the nature of the "partyness" of philosophy is reflected in the textbooks themselves, which offer a variety of overlapping interpretations. Philosophy is said to be "partisan" in either one or more of the following senses:

(a) Because there are only two answers to the basic question of philosophy, any philosopher is either a member of the "party" of materialists or the "party" of idealists.

(b) What philosophers believe is determined by their class position, so that we can associate certain philosophical positions with the worldview of certain classes. (Combined with (a), this yields the view that idealism is the worldview of the bourgeoisie, materialism the worldview of the proletariat.)

(c) Philosophical theories not only reflect class interests, but can be made to serve them: Philosophy is a weapon in the class war.

(d) There is no unprejudiced standpoint (i.e., a "god's-eye view" or Archimedean point) from which the philosopher may construct and assess philosophical theories: Our understanding of reality is always formed, and is only intelligible within, the perspective of a community, society, tradition, or class.

The first three interpretations have traditionally prevailed. While the concept of *partiĭnost'* is sometimes developed to suggest that objective truth may be discernible only from a certain cultural perspective, it has more often been invoked in arguments designed to discredit philosophers by showing that their work serves the interests of the bourgeoisie. In this, the vagueness of the concept has contributed to its political menace.

These are the basics of dialectical materialism as it was presented in the Soviet textbooks at the time Ilyenkov was writing. As a discipline, dialectical materialism addresses issues that, in the Anglo–American tradition, fall within metaphysics, epistemology, and the philosophy of mind. Problems of moral and political philosophy come under the rubric of "historical materialism," which is construed as the application of the concepts, principles, and laws of dialectical materialism to social and historical phenomena. Dialectical and historical materialism, thus understood, jointly constitute the philosophical dimension of Soviet Marxism–Leninism.

As the official position of the Soviet philosophical "establishment," this textbook doctrine has formed the common currency of debate. To be supported by universities and other institutions of higher education, and to gain access to philosophical journals and academic publishing houses, Soviet philosophers have had to represent their work as in harmony with the state-endorsed view. No academic five-year plan would meet approval if it challenged the official position in any substantial way. The existence of this doctrine thus represents a crucial institutional factor affecting not only the course of philosophers' careers, but the very formation of their philosophical interests and the way in which they express their ideas.

However, though the influence of this "official Soviet philosophy" should never be ignored, its relevance to our present project may easily be overestimated. The textbook orthodoxy has enjoyed such institutional dominance that it is tempting to try to understand any Soviet philosopher's views with reference to it, analyzing the degree to which his or her thought conforms to or departs from the official doctrine. Such an approach would be tedious and uninformative. Rather than the star around which the whole of Soviet philosophy turns, the official doctrine must be seen as only one element of the Soviet philosophical world, and, moreover, one that recedes into the background once other significant elements enter the picture. For example, Ilyenkov drew many of the problems he considered, and the resources with which he addressed them, not from the textbook orthodoxy but from the complex history

of the Soviet tradition. We have already observed that Ilyenkov's work must be seen, at least in part, as a reaction to Soviet
philosophy under Stalin. Significantly, however, his response
to Stalinism re-creates themes from still earlier periods of Soviet philosophy, themes that had become lost or distorted during
the 1930s and 1940s. For example, Ilyenkov's work reintro-
duces issues central to the debate between the "Mechanists"
and "Deborinites," which dramatically rent the Soviet philosophical world in the 1920s. Furthermore, Ilyenkov's conception of the mind, the culmination of his research, may be
seen as a descendant of the position conceived by the psychologist Vygotsky in the late 1920s and early 1930s, and developed further by the thinkers of the "sociohistorical" school.
Finally, Ilyenkov's constant emphasis on the significance
of Lenin's contribution to philosophy returns us to the pre-
revolutionary period when the foundations of Soviet philosophy were laid by Lenin and his "Empiriocritic" opponents.
Ilyenkov's work, then, forms a prism through which a variety of themes from the history of Soviet philosophy are refracted.

The project of grasping the "internal perspective" on Ilyenkov's philosophy thus coincides with the project of reconstructing the history of Soviet philosophy. We should observe,
however, that Ilyenkov's writings do not directly address any
of the historical continuities that are so crucial to understanding his thought. Since the 1930s, Soviet philosophers have
been reluctant to write, not only about the political context of
their work, but also about the history of their own tradition.[8]
Thus, in marked contrast to the Western literature, the published corpus of Soviet philosophy cannot be seen as the tradition's memory. Instead, the tradition is preserved in a complex oral culture: in anecdotes and reminiscences, in ways of
reading texts and of recounting positions, and in the manner
that each generation of philosophers has understood and ra-
tionalized its concerns.

This book therefore seeks to make explicit the historical
antecedents of Ilyenkov's contribution. The discussion of Il-

---

8 Although some periods have received interesting treatments (e.g.,
   Joravsky [1961] and Yakhot [1981], both on the Mechanist–Deborinite controversy), no adequate, comprehensive history of Soviet philosophy has yet appeared from either a Soviet or Western author.

yenkov's ideas is thus prefaced with three historical chapters, which explore the Debornite–Mechanist debate, Vygotsky's philosophical psychology, and Lenin's contribution to philosophy. This historical material is not intended as an encyclopedic rendition of "how things were." Rather, my treatment seeks to highlight aspects of these topics that Ilyenkov himself would have thought salient, and that later emerge in his own contribution. The result is a history of Soviet philosophy written from an Ilyenkovian perspective.

Ilyenkov and the Anglo–American tradition

Ilyenkov's contribution can illuminate not only the history of Soviet philosophy, but also contemporary debates in Anglo–American philosophy. The past fifteen years have witnessed a growing disillusionment in the analytic tradition with a set of ideas inherited from the philosophy of the Enlightenment. Theories of mind and language with their roots in the eighteenth century have drawn strong criticism, and the powerful influence of such theories on our ethical and political thought has been widely recognized. Ilyenkov shares this hostility to the philosophy of the Enlightenment, though the roots of his critique lie in Hegel and Marx rather than in the Wittgensteinian ideas that have inspired so much of the recent Western debate.

Ilyenkov's principal target may be described as a form of "empiricism," though one that represents far more than the view that all knowledge is ultimately derived from sense experience. For Ilyenkov, empiricism (or "positivism" as he sometimes calls it) forms a package of interrelated ideas, each reinforcing the others, many of which derive ultimately from a thinker who was not himself an empiricist: Descartes. These ideas present a picture of the individual thinking subject and its relation to the world, the object of its thought. According to this picture, each individual mind or "self" is a discrete entity, a self-contained world of thoughts and experiences. Such "atomic" selves are thought to enjoy a special independence from all other selves and from the external world itself. While, as a matter of fact, they exist in constant interaction with other minds and external objects, their existence is held to be "logically independent" of the existence of other entities; that is, it is conceivable that such selves could exist even if there were neither other minds nor an external world.

The admission of the logical independence of the self sets the agenda for this philosophy, determining both the problems the philosopher must address and the methods that may be used to solve them. For example, the self's independence raises the spectres of solipsism and skepticism. If the self could operate independently of everything else, how can we be sure that it does not in fact do so? How can we be certain that there really are entities beyond the mind and that, if there are, they are the way the mind supposes them to be? In such a setting, the philosopher can aspire to answer these questions only through an analysis of the contents and operations of the individual mind itself.

Within this framework, the relation between "subject" and "object," mind and reality, is thus a relation between two distinct realms: the self-contained mental world of the individual self and the external world of things beyond the mind. As a result of the interaction between the two realms, the subject receives ideas by means of the senses, ideas that he or she weaves into a conception of the object world. Ilyenkov's empiricist opponent identifies the project of understanding the nature of the world as it is independently of our minds with *science*. Anything that is not included in a scientific account of reality ultimately owes its origin to our minds. Since the scientific picture of the world makes no reference to meanings or values, the empiricist concludes that neither are constituents of reality in itself; minds are the source of meaning and value. It thus transpires that the world of the self and the external world are realms that are utterly different in kind. (Indeed, they are so different that some empiricists lose confidence that an external world, so conceived, is something that could stand in a relation to a mind. Thus, there emerge idealist variants of the empiricist theme that eschew the idea of mind-independent reality, representing the external world as a "construction" of the mind.)

This sketch of Ilyenkov's principal opponent is no more than a rough caricature. In subsequent chapters, we shall refine our understanding of this position as we consider the forms it has taken in the history of Soviet philosophy and the criticisms it has provoked. For the present, however, we need only observe that several features of the picture Ilyenkov opposes have also been challenged recently by members of the Anglo–American tradition. For example, a renewed interest in the possibility of "moral realism" has led a number of philosophers to attack the idea that science provides the only legitimate criterion of objectivity, denying that the only properties that are constituents of objective reality are those that are intelligible without reference to us (e.g., Wiggins 1976; McDowell 1978, 1983; Lovibond 1983; McNaughton 1988). Attacking this criterion of objectivity has opened the prospect of admitting not only moral values, but further anthropocentric properties (such as aesthetic qualities and colours) into "the fabric of the world" (see, e.g., McDowell 1983, 1985). In addition, Wittgenstein (esp. 1953), Davidson (1985), Quine (1960, 1961), and many philosophers inspired by them have challenged the idea that meanings are "in the head," arguing that meaning cannot be understood as an intrinsic property of mental entities, or as a relation between the subject and the contents of his or her mind. The idea that meaning is a "public" phenomenon sustained by the activity of a community of speakers has provoked the further suggestion that, since the meaning of propositions is determined by communities and mental states are attitudes to propositions, the community is (in some way) essentially involved in the determination of the contents of each individual's thoughts (Kripke 1982; Davidson 1985). This suggestion represents a bold challenge to the empiricist's idea of the discrete, self-contained self. Further criticism of the empiricist's "atomistic" conception of the individual has come from the domain of political philosophy, where its deleterious influence on our political thought can be seen as a theme in the work of Taylor (e.g., 1979), MacIntyre (1981, 1988), and Sandel (1982, 1984). Although Ilyenkov expresses himself in an idiom far removed from analytic philosophy, his work anticipates many of these criticisms and suggestions.

Moreover, while the coincidence between Ilyenkov's concerns and the interests of some analytic philosophers is interesting, the contrast between them is equally significant. In Anglo–American philosophy, the refutation of the Enlightenment picture has been a "death by a thousands cuts." Although each aspect of it has been separately challenged in different areas of philosophy by different thinkers, philosophers have seldom sought to attack the picture as a whole. Further, even among those who have (e.g., Rorty 1980), it is rare to find a substantive philosophical theory advanced as an alternative. Since, as we observed, the Enlightenment framework sets an agenda for philosophical inquiry, some philosophers conclude that its refutation spells the death of philosophy itself. In contrast, Ilyenkov's work is concerned both to challenge the Enlightenment picture as a whole and to articulate a positive alternative in the form of a holistic theory of the relation between nature, society, and the thinking individual. For Ilyenkov, though the creation of such a theory is indeed a departure from philosophy as it is traditionally understood, it represents not the demise of philosophy, but its elevation to a new "scientific" stage (though Ilyenkov's account of the scientific differs radically from his empiricist opponent's).

While Ilyenkov's criticisms are often more roughly hewn than the arguments of his counterparts in the Anglo–American tradition, his positive vision is bold and challenging. Ilyenkov rejects the fundamental dualism at the heart of the Enlightenment picture, arguing that the relation between subject and object is not a relation between two worlds, but a unity realized within a single world: the material world in which the individual thinking subject is embedded. However, the unity of subject and object can be understood, Ilyenkov argues, only if we bring to the centre of the philosophical stage a concept that has so far been neglected by the analytic tradition: the concept of *activity*. Thus, while Ilyenkov has enough in common with some members of the Anglo–American tradition for a dialogue between Western and Soviet philosophy to be possible, his approach remains sufficiently foreign to suggest that the dialogue would be a provocative and rewarding one.

Finally, we must observe that analytic philosophy is not the only area of Western academe to which Ilyenkov's views are relevant. In recent years there has been a growing interest in the West in the legacy of the sociohistorical tradition of Soviet psychology. In England and America, this interest has centred largely on Vygotsky's significance for developmental psychology, while in Continental Europe attention has been focused more on the application of Alexei Leontiev's "activity

theory," not only to the theory of education, but also to the
psychology of work. Ilyenkov's writings help to articulate the
philosophical premises of this most theoretical of psychological schools.

Ilyenkov's legacy in the age of *glasnost'* and *perestroĭka*

At the time of writing, the Soviet Union under Gorbachev is
engaged in a process of massive social and political change.
Far-reaching attempts to reorganize the economy have been
accompanied by governmental reforms almost unthinkable
only a few months ago. In consequence, the notion of a ra-
tionally planned economy administered by a single-party
state has been completely undermined, and almost all Soviet
thinkers now look to "the free market" for a solution to the
country's growing economic problems. Freedom of speech is
becoming a reality, and the Soviet people are beginning to
confront the character of their country's past. Many republics
are clamouring for independence.

Yet more dramatic are the reforms that Gorbachev's initiatives have precipitated in the countries that were formally
Soviet "satellites." With Germany now reunified, and free
elections everywhere resulting in the rejection of the former
communist regimes, all the old certainties of the relation between "the Western world" and "the Eastern bloc" have evaporated. It remains unclear what we shall find in their place.

As we might expect, the Soviet philosophical world has
moved with these changes. The philosophical journals contain many "roundtable" discussions of the future course of Soviet philosophy, and, for the first time, works are appearing
that openly discuss the character of the philosophy of the Stalin era (e.g., Kapustin 1988). There is now a passionate interest
in republishing the works of Russian philosophers who had
been dismissed as idealist (e.g., Solov'ev, Fedorov, and Shes-
tov) and a new willingness to take non-Marxist philosophy
seriously. Furthermore, the teaching of philosophy in the
USSR is being gradually reformed. It is no surprise that an
immediate effect of *glasnost'* in Soviet philosophy was to bring
about the critical reevaluation of the official doctrine and, significantly, the production of a major new textbook designed to
convey the open-endedness of philosophical dispute and to

promote a balanced and undogmatic assessment of both Marxist and non-Marxist philosophical positions (the work is pre-
viewed in Frolov, Stepin, Lektorsky, and Kelle [1988]). Philosophy students are now encouraged to think for themselves
and to view their subject as a resource for the discussion of
both social and personal issues.

It might be considered strange, with such events in progress, to devote this book to a philosopher who produced much
of his work in the Brezhnev years, the time now known as
"the period of stagnation." Ilyenkov may appear to be a thinker of a bygone era whose work can reveal little about the character of Soviet thought today. In reply, we may observe that
the mood of much recent Soviet philosophical literature has so
far been one of rebuilding, not abandoning, Soviet Marxism.
The classics of Marxism are once again being addressed
anew, the positive contributions of Soviet philosophers are being publically distinguished from the hackwork of the ideologues, and Soviet Marxism is opening itself to critical debate
with other traditions. Moreover, this project of rebuilding Soviet intellectual and political culture is argued to be essential to
the wider process of democratizing the state and reforming
the economy.

If the rejuvenation of Soviet philosophy is conceived in this
way, then Ilyenkov is an entirely appropriate figure on which
to focus discussion. His legacy represents a powerful resource
for the Soviet Marxist tradition, and one that the tradition has
never fully appreciated or developed. Moreover, as I have argued, it is impossible to recover Ilyenkov's contribution without confronting the history of Soviet philosophy, and it is difficult to comprehend the limits and disappointments of his
career without addressing the character of the environment
in which he worked. Indeed, this is precisely why *Voprosy
filosofii* has sought to renew discussion of Ilyenkov's life and
work by the publication of "Marx and the Western World"
and, still more recently, a powerful personal reminiscence by
his friend and colleague Felix Mikhailov (1990).[9]

Such a diagnosis of the contemporary philosophical scene
in the Soviet Union may, however, be met with some skepti-

---

9 Sadly, Mikhailov's article appeared too late for me to incorporate his
   many insights into this account.

cism. Surely, it might be argued, the deliverances of such journals as *Voprosy filosofii*, which have always served as bastions of Marxist orthodoxy, can no longer be taken as an index of the mood of the Soviet philosophical community. Whatever we may find on their pages, the reality of the present situation in the USSR is that *glasnost'* and *perestroĭka* will eventually bring, not the revitalization of socialism in Russia, but its wholesale rejection. When this occurs, the present developments within the Soviet philosophical world will come to be seen not as gropings toward a new beginning, but as the final chapter of the history of Soviet philosophy.

This stark possibility, however, makes the presentation of Ilyenkov's thought no less important. If Soviet socialism were finally to collapse, the work of philosophers like Ilyenkov might be lost forever, particularly given the Soviet propensity to begin a new phase by obliterating the past. It would be a tragedy if the best of Soviet philosophy was never considered and the history of the Soviet tradition never written from the perspective of the philosophers who worked within it. It is too soon to say for certain what *perestroĭka* means. Whatever it means, however, we have much to learn from the life and work of Evald Ilyenkov.

2

DEBORINITES, MECHANISTS, AND BOLSHEVIZERS

In Chapter 1, I suggested that Ilyenkov's contribution may appeal to those philosophers of the Anglo–American tradition who share his hostility to the "logic of empiricism." However, as we saw, the roots of Ilyenkov's philosophy lie deep in a terrain very foreign to the "analytic" tradition: Soviet dialectical materialism. For Ilyenkov, to be a dialectical materialist is to hold that a scientific understanding of reality can be attained only through the materialist transformation of Hegel's dialectic. Accordingly, he vehemently denied the "positivist" principle that the natural sciences alone can give a complete account of objective reality.[1]

---

1 The Russian language permits Ilyenkov to argue that a scientific account of reality cannot be achieved by the natural sciences alone without appearing to create a paradox. The Russian for "science," *nauka*, like the German *Wissenschaft*, denotes a broader class of disciplines than the natural sciences, which are denoted by the terms *estestvoznanie* and *estestvonauka* (see Alekseev 1983). What makes a practice scientific (*nauchnyĭ*) in this wider sense is an important question, particularly in the light of Soviet claims that Marxism is the only truly scientific theory of "man, nature, and society." It admits, however, of no simple answer. As a working definition we can say that a discipline is "scientific" in the broad sense if it offers a comprehensive explanation of its object of inquiry by the application of a systematic and rigorous method. We shall return to this is-

Ilyenkov was not the first Soviet Marxist to champion what he thought was true dialectical materialism against a scientism deemed theoretically disastrous and socially pernicious. Nor was he the first to find sustained opposition to his views from within Soviet philosophy itself. Debates between dialectical and positivist versions of Marxism, each laying claim to orthodoxy, have a long history in Soviet thought. This chapter takes us back to the birth of Soviet philosophy in the 1920s, to the first and most famous of these debates: the Deborinite–Mechanist controversy.

The influence of this controversy on the course of Soviet philosophy is often underestimated or misconstrued. While the Soviets themselves now rarely refer to it, Western commentators are usually preoccupied with the debate's historical significance as the prelude to the rise of the "Bolshevizers," who formed the "new philosophical leadership" under Stalin.[2] In consequence, the philosophical substance of the Deborinite–Mechanist controversy is usually given only a supporting role in a primarily political drama. This is a mistake because, first, the philosophical content of the debate is itself a significant component of the historical and political story and, second, the arguments of the 1920s are essential to understanding later developments in Soviet philosophy. Unless we take the philosophy seriously, we shall fail to understand fully how the emergence of the Bolshevizers was possible, and how the next generation, in reacting to Stalinism, reopened issues very similar to those that divided Soviet philosophers in the 1920s. Although contemporary Soviet philosophers may not see themselves as re-creating the early controversy, the continuity is undeniable. This is particularly so in the case

Footnote 1 (*cont.*)
   sue in Chapter 5, when we examine Ilyenkov's conception of dialectical method.

2 The two book-length treatments are Joravsky (1961) and Yakhot (1981); both are excellent pieces of scholarship. As the latter has been published only in the West, I consider it part of the Western literature, even though Yakhot is an émigré who conducted much of his research in Moscow. Shorter accounts are Hecker (1933: chaps. xiii–xv), interestingly written from the perspective of the Bolshevizers; Wetter (1958: chaps. 6–8); Ahlberg (1962); Kolakowski (1978: vol. 3, chap. 2); Lecourt (1983); Zapata (1983b); and Bakhurst (1985a). The best Soviet accounts are Ksenofontov (1975), and the recent first book of the fifth volume of *Istoriya filosofii v SSSR* (1985: 204–69).

of Ilyenkov, who can be seen as heir to the Deborinites' project.[3]

The beginnings of Soviet philosophy

Soviet philosophy began in a spirit of great optimism. In the intellectually fertile years soon after the Revolution, *Under the Banner of Marxism* (*Pod znamenem marksizma*), the newly founded journal of Soviet philosophy, impressed upon philosophers the importance of their task. The programmatic articles in its early issues, by such authorities as Lenin (1922) and Trotsky (1922), urged Soviet philosophers to explore and develop Marx's materialism, so crucial to his method, yet so enigmatically presented in his writings. This was deemed a task of more than merely scholarly significance: The very success of the revolution was argued to be at stake. The Bolsheviks held that the dissemination of the materialist worldview would overthrow the superstitious, religious ideology that threatened to stand between the Russian masses and the recognition of their true interests. They also believed that only a solid theoretical foundation would protect young revolutionaries in the "vanguard of the proletariat" from the disorienting effects of the rapid shifts of Bolshevik policy as it adapted to the changing demands of the young revolution (Trotsky 1922: 6). Finally, Bolshevik policy itself was to be constantly guided by Marxist philosophy. A comprehensive philosophical materialism, allied to the rapidly developing natural sciences, was to form the theoretical basis of the new order. By deepening this materialism and raising it to self-consciousness, Soviet philosophers were to enable a new unity of theory and practice.

The excitement, however, was quickly tempered. Severe organizational obstacles stood before the development of Soviet philosophy. In particular, the shortage of "red specialists" forced newly founded institutions, like the Communist Academy and the Institute of Red Professors, reluctantly to invite non-Bolsheviks to teach courses in Marxism.[4] Consequently,

3 The parallel between Ilyenkov's contribution and the Deborinites' work is noted in both Yakhot (1981: 195–6) and Scanlan (1985: 121).
4 The new philosophical institutions established by the Bolsheviks are described in Zapata (1983b: 323–7) and in the course of Joravsky (1961) and Yakhot (1981). The literature of the early years of the 1917

many of those charged with forming the "philosophical leadership" took up their posts in an atmosphere of suspicion. For example, there was considerable opposition to the appointment of former Mensheviks A. M. Deborin and Lyubov Akselrod to posts at the Communist (Sverdlov) University in 1921, and while Lenin himself intervened to secure their appointment, he ominously advised that "an eye should be kept on them" (Lenin 1958–69: vol. 52, 393). Furthermore, *Under the Banner of Marxism* was no sooner founded than its programme was attacked on the grounds that the very idea of Marxist philosophy was a confusion. This charge came not from opponents of the regime, but from within Soviet Marxism itself.[5] Thus, Soviet philosophers were forced to defend their discipline against those holding that Marxism could achieve the desired unity of theory and practice without the help of philosophy.

The most significant "liquidationist" trend was led by S. K. Minin.[6] The polemical thrust of Minin's argument was this: Marx's theory of ideology invites us to ask what functional role any aspect of the ideological superstructure plays. If we ask this of philosophy, we find it to be an intrinsically bourgeois phenomenon that functions exclusively to preserve capitalist economic relations. The need for philosophy derives from capitalism's uneasy relation with science. The capitalist welcomes the technological innovation science brings, but fears the power it offers his class enemy, the proletariat. He thus turns to the philosopher to obscure the liberating potential

Footnote 4 (*cont.*)

Revolution abounds with heated debates about how the new generation of Soviet philosophers was to be trained. Examples of such articles are Akademik (1922), Materialist (1922), and Partiets (1922).

5 By the beginning of 1922, the principal non-Marxist Russian philosophers, such as Berdyaev and Lossky, had already been estranged from the Soviet philosophical scene. They were expelled from the Soviet Union later in the same year.

6 Minin's initial article (1922a) appeared first in an obscure provincial journal, *Army and Revolution* (*Armiya i revolyutsiya*). It was later republished in *Under the Banner of Marxism*. When Minin objected that the editors had butchered his text, he was allowed a further appearance in the latter journal (1922b). Both articles were published with replies by Rumii (1922a,b). See Joravsky (1961: 93–6) and *Istoriya filosofii v SSSR* (1985: vol. 5, 218–21) for details of other liquidationist trends, such as Enchmann's "New Biology" and Lyadov's campaign to strike philosophy from the syllabus of the Communist University, where he was Rector.

of science and to legitimize the ruling class's monopoly over the dissemination of ideas. Philosophy achieves this by fostering religious and moral views that justify the division of society into mental and manual labourers, a division reproduced in the consciousness of the ruling classes as the division between philosophy and science. Minin argues that communism has no need either for philosophy's coercive, legitimizing role or for the division between positive and speculative knowledge it perpetuates. If the Soviets aspire to a new synthesis, they must end this absurd "foreplay" with philosophy.

Liquidationist slogans – "Science to the bridge, philosophy overboard!" and "Science is its own philosophy!" – gained considerable currency, particularly among students, and the establishment moved to nip "Mininism" in the bud (see Rumiĭ 1922a,b). Minin's opponents denied that philosophy can only be a "spiritual weapon" in the class war. Just as philosophy predates the emergence of capitalism, so philosophy can survive its exploitation by the bourgeoisie and serve the proletariat. After all, Minin's critics continued, Marxists are agreed that materialism is an essential component of both natural science and Marxism itself. But materialism is a "worldview," and what is that if not a philosophical position? It is therefore Soviet *philosophers* who must defend and develop materialism. At the same time, Minin's opponents sought to undermine the support that his position might seem to draw from the classics of Marxism. They argued that it was only *idealist* philosophy that Marx and Engels scorned; dialectical materialism, though the opposite of idealism, remains nonetheless a form of philosophy.

Minin's opponents concentrated on attacking his hostility to philosophy and ignored the positive dimension of his theory, his vision of the role of science under communism. For Minin, science under capitalism is monopolized by a small minority, and its development dominated by class interests. Our theories of the world thus remain fragmented and dislocated. True science, however, would be the cognition of the material world in its unity, a picture of reality as a seamless whole. Marx's theory, for the first time, has provided the "broad and solid fundament" for such a science, which, Minin argues, can flourish only in communist society (Minin 1922b: 195). Gradually, as the obfuscating layers of bourgeois ideology are stripped away and science becomes the province of all, reality will become transparent to humanity. Thus science will bridge the gulf between human beings and nature, a gulf that finds both its reflection and its legitimation in philosophy. In this way, the development of science is of massive emancipatory significance, and of a piece with humanity's political liberation from capitalism. Having harnessed the "external forces" of both nature and society, the communist individual will be a truly self-determining subject, at one with the environment. Thus communist science has no need to be complemented by other disciplines, it is as "unified and whole," as "all-embracing and self-sufficent," as reality itself (Minin 1922b: 195). Indeed, ultimately it will make no sense to talk of "science" at all, for there will no longer be other forms of understanding to contrast with science. Minin writes:

> Science begins with the proletariat and culminates (*zavershat'*) in communist society on the basis of collective production and the liquidation of social classes. It "culminates" ... not in the sense that the quantity of the material for cognition runs out – it is inexhaustible – but in a qualitative sense, that is, in the sense that the vast majority (and then all) of humanity acquires the skill, the ability and the boundless desire to grasp (both practically and theoretically, *begreifen*) the world both as a whole and in each of its minutest component parts, materially, dialectically, scientifically.
>
> Culmination means the end. And in communist society (although not soon) the *end of science,* the original (*svoëobraznyi*), *highest negation of it,* will, in the well-known sense, really come to pass.
>
> Science will cease to be an object of assault, and a weapon of battle. Science, in the practice of work and of cognition, will become as natural and obvious to us as the air we breathe. (Minin 1922b: 195)

As science becomes all, so it withers away.

This side to Minin's contribution is hard to square with the picture of a philistine antiintellectual painted by his opponents and adopted by his successors (e.g., Deborin 1961: 11). Rather, he appears as a child of his time, caught in the fervour of the age and striving to give sense to the liberating power of science within a tradition that includes not only Saint Simon and Comte, but also strands in the writings of Marx and Engels.[7]

Minin threw down a challenge to make sense of the relation of philosophy and science. To deny his positive conception, his opponents were required to articulate the sense in which philosophy has a role, and preferably an indispensible one, to play alongside science. It is significant that they did not rise to this challenge, choosing to attack Minin from behind a smoke screen of quotations from Marxist classics rather than to address the real issue. For while Minin disappeared, the question he raised did not: It returned with a vengeance two years later at the centre of the Mechanist–Deborinite debate.

The composition of the two camps

The Mechanists and Deborinites contested their differences in the philosophical literature, and at gatherings in scholarly institutions, between 1924 and 1929. The Mechanists comprised a variety of thinkers with constrasting backgrounds and interests. They included the party activist and antireligious propagandist I. I. Skvortsov-Stepanov, a group of scientists based at the Timiryazev Institute led by A. K. Timiryazev (son of the distinguished biologist after whom the Institute was named), and various philosophers, including the émigré Hungarian activist S. Var'yash, the Ukrainian S. Yu. Semkovsky, and V. N. Sarab'yanov. Also associated with Mechanism were Alexander Bogdanov and the Bolshevik luminary Nikolai Bukharin.

It is hard to identify the common position that these diverse thinkers shared. Most Mechanists adopted the view that the explanatory resources of science are able to provide a complete account of objective reality. They held that science employs reductive procedures able, in principle, to reveal exhaustively the nature not only of physical objects, but also of living or-

7 Minin must have enjoyed Marx and Engels's remark in *The German Ideology* that "philosophy and the study of the actual world have the same relation to one another as masturbation and sexual love" (1845–6: 103). In many respects, his positive vision of science anticipates Marx's *Economic and Philosophical Manuscripts of 1844* (especially the third manuscript), which were not published until 1927.

ganisms and psychological phenomena. While Minin had operated with a vague conception of science as all "positive" knowledge, contrasting this with supposedly speculative methods of understanding, the Mechanists adopted a more familiar idea of science. For them, science was natural science. Also unlike Minin, the Mechanists wished not to abolish philosophy, but only to preserve the autonomy of science. They held that the proper domain of philosophy is the elucidation of the most general concepts and laws employed by science, and that dialectics is "general scientific methodology," drawing its conclusions by generalization from scientific practice. They therefore denied that philosophers can adopt a standpoint independent of science from which to pass judgment on its claims: Philosophy leaves science where it is.

Not all the Mechanists, however, held so radical a position. Some, like Lyubov Akselrod, were drawn to Mechanism more by suspicion of the Deborinites than by confidence in the global explanatory power of natural science. But the Mechanists welcomed all those sympathetic to their cause and, though Deborin mocked them as a "mechanistic assembly" of eclectics, they saw disagreement within their ranks as a potential source of productive debate rather than a weakness (Deborin 1926a: 315).

In contrast to the Mechanists, Deborin's group was remarkably homogeneous. Almost all its leading lights, including Ya. E. Sten, N. A. Karev, and I. K. Luppol, were products of Deborin's seminar at the Institute of Red Professors. They were united both in their fidelity to Deborin's philosophy and in their admiration for him as their leader. Perhaps in virtue of their greater homogeneity, the Deborinites were able to consolidate control over *Under the Banner of Marxism* and the major philosophical institutions, and they came to see themselves as representatives of the Soviet philosophical establishment and spokesmen of Marxist orthodoxy.

The Deborinites held that Soviet philosophy's principal project was to undertake a materialist reworking of Hegelian dialectics. Only a materialist understanding of Hegel's conception of the relation of thinking and being would, they argued, explain the categories under which human beings cognize reality and the relation in which those categories stand to reality itself. Since, on their view, dialectical philosophy seeks to understand the very *possibility* of scientific methods of cognition, the Deborinites held that such an understanding could not be achieved by generalization from actual scientific practice. They therefore dismissed the Mechanists' optimism about the global explanatory potential of natural science. Without philosophy, they argued, science would not be able to understand itself.

The diversity of the Mechanists made them a moving target, and Deborin and his group strove to identify a definitive Mechanist position to attack. In so doing, the Deborinites were often guilty of distorting their opponents' views. In return, the Mechanists refused to interpret the Deborinites sympathetically. Consequently, the debate was conducted in an atmosphere of deceit and bad feeling. The tone of the debate has greatly influenced the way that it has been perceived. Such, indeed, was the degree to which the two camps misrepresented each other that some commentators have suggested that the dispute was really only "a war of words" (Yakhot 1981: 139). It is argued that while there was a difference between each camp's position and the views it attributed to its opponents, the contrast between the *actual* positions of the two schools was negligible (see Yakhot 1981: chap. 5). To assess this interpretation we must examine the details of the debate.

The substance of the debate

As we have seen, the point of departure of "mainstream" Mechanism is the view that the explanatory resources of the natural sciences can in principle yield a complete account of objective reality. For many Mechanists, the basis of this claim was the principle:

M: All phenomena are, or can be reduced to, entities the nature of which can be explained by appeal to the laws of natural science.

They held that M simply followed from the materialist view that reality was matter-in-motion, and that M had to be true if Marx's vision of a single holistic science of reality was well-founded. Nonetheless, the Mechanists were divided about how M was to be interpreted. Some pressed for a very strong reductionism, holding:

M_8: All phenomena are, or can be reduced to, physical phenomena, the nature of which can be exhaustively explained in physical terms.

Although the scope of this reductionism was intended to be genuinely universal, its adherents usually restricted discussion to the psychological and the sociohistorical:

> Science is certainly on the way to revealing psychological processes to be the transformation of energy from one form into another. (Stepanov 1928: 9)

> *Theoretically and in the last analysis,* social phenomena too are open not only to qualitative (sociological) analysis, but also to quantitative (physico-chemico-biological) analysis . . . [U]nsuccessful attempts in the past *do not prove* the impossibility *in principle* of building a quantitative dialectical materialist mechanical foundation under sociology. (Bosse 1925: 63–4)

There was no univocal Mechanist view about the vocabulary in which science would express its reductive explanations. While most talked vaguely about explanation in "physicochemical" terms, some thought the class of natural-scientific laws broader than the physicochemical (because they were, say, suspicious of the reduction of the biological to the physicochemical), and some thought it narrower (because the physicochemical would ultimately be reduced, say, to the thermodynamic). The Mechanists were not perturbed by this uncertainty, believing that science itself would eventually decide which terms were basic. Despite the way they were portrayed by their opponents, few Mechanists believed that the laws of mechanics would prove to be the basic physical laws (cf. Deborin 1926a: 340–1). They did, however, sometimes misleadingly adopt the term "mechanistic" to describe the terms, whatever they may prove to be, in which science will finally explain all phenomena. (I shall simply call them "physical" terms.)

Some Mechanists, however, could not accept this extreme reductionism, adopting the weaker position that, while some phenomena cannot be strictly reduced to the physical, they can be understood *on the model* of physical phenomena. On this view, social events and psychological phenomena can be explained by laws analogous to physical laws.[8] We can formulate this weak variant of M thus:

M_w: All phenomena EITHER are reducible to phenomena that can be explained in physical terms OR are phenomena that can be understood on the model of physical phenomena under the influence of physical laws.

An example of such "analogizing" thought is Bukharin's application of the notion of "equilibrium" to Marx's theory of history. For Bukharin, social unrest and revolution must be understood as a consequence of a "disturbance in equilibrium" caused by a dislocation between a society's level of technology and its relations of production. On this view, history is a process of the constant disturbance and restoration of equilibrium until communism establishes a stable correspondence between technology and production relations (Bukharin 1921; see Kolakowski 1978: vol. 3, 56–63; for disapproval of Bukharin's position by another Mechanist, see Sarab'yanov 1922: 70).

Bukharin's "Marxist sociology" is quite crude compared to the sophisticated theories of Bogdanov on which it was based. Bogdanov took the fact that the operation of natural laws can be fruitfully projected onto not just social but also *psychological* systems (belief sets, conceptions of the world) as evidence that the natural, the mental, and the social are all aspects of a single self-organizing structure governed by the same set of organizing principles. He attempted to express these principles in a new science: "tektology," a precursor of such modern generalizing sciences as systems theory and cybernetics (see Ilyenkov 1980: 85n; *Istoriya filosofii v SSSR* [1985: 207–8]). Bogdanov looked to the pure quantitative science of mathematics as the ultimate basis of tektology:

> My initial point of departure consists in the fact that structural relations can be generalized to the same degree of formal purity as the relations of magnitudes in mathematics, and on this basis organizational problems can be solved by methods that are analogous to the methods of mathematics. (Bogdanov 1925–9: vol. 3, 209)

8 Vasil'ev (1927) describes the use of such analogy by the Soviet Mechanists, and by their seventeenth-century predecessors. Though he published in *Dialektika v priroda*, the Mechanists' "annual," Vasil'ev, an expert on Hegel, was very critical of "mainstream" Mechanism.

Adopting an extreme empiricist epistemology, Bogdanov held that the material to which tektology's organizational principles ultimately apply is *experience;* reality, the "external world," is simply "socially organized experience." He therefore was seen as a supporter of a version of M_s rather than M_w: All phenomena are treated as constructions out of experience analyzable by appeal to the single science, tektology, the laws of which are those governing the organization of experience. This position provoked the objection that, for Bogdanov, reality was mind-dependent. His views were thus widely held to be incompatible with materialism and he was frequently denounced as an "idealist," "relativist," and "subjectivist."

The fact that Lenin himself had attacked Bogdanov in these terms as far back as 1909 encouraged most Mechanists to distance themselves from Bogdanov's position.[9] The Deborinites, however, claimed their opponents suffered from idealist and subjectivist propensities similar to those Lenin had discerned in Bogdanov. At first sight, this claim is surprising, for many Mechanists appear to accept a simple realism, holding that science aspires to a picture of the world as it is in itself, independent of human minds. Few Mechanists shared Bogdanov's passion for epistemology, instead unreflectively subscribing to a basic Lockean empiricism according to which we are acquainted with a mind-independent reality through the ideas it causes in us. How could the Deborinites argue that, despite these assumptions, the Mechanists found themselves committed to the view that reality (or at least too much of it) is mind-dependent, that since truth is "an ideological form, ... a reflex in our heads ... there is no truth outside of man himself, no non-subjective truth" (Hecker 1933: 172, citing the Mechanist Sarab'yanov)?

The basis of the Deborinites' charge was an argument of the following kind. The scientific picture of reality, which mainstream Mechanism takes to capture all that is real, represents the world "in itself" to be very different from the way we or-

9 Bogdanov, who maintained that the "mechanistic world view" was the basis of his "tektology" (Bogdanov 1921: 52–5), described his relation to the Mechanist group thus: "You won't find people so stupid as to cite me; it's disadvantageous ... There is unity, but they won't cite me" (quoted in Joravsky [1961: 136]). A fuller treatment of Bogdanov's philosophy is given in Chapter 4.

dinarily take it to be. For example, while science treats reality as a collection of discrete, qualitatively indistinct, miniature particles in motion under the influence of physical forces, our everyday conception of the world takes it to be composed of solid objects possessing a range of qualitatively diverse properties that have no place in the scientific picture (e.g., colours, values, meanings). Therefore, Mechanists are obliged to give an account of the relation between scientific and everyday conceptions that explains how the world appears to have the properties the everyday conception attributes to it. The Deborinites assumed the Mechanists would appeal to a Lockean theory of secondary qualities to explain the status of those properties included in the everyday conception but excluded from the scientific one.[10] On this view, such properties are not constituents of reality as it is in itself, but only appear to be so in virtue of the nature of our minds: Our everyday or "prescientific" way of seeing reality is a consequence of the interaction of an independent reality with the kinds of minds and sense organs that we have. This Lockean approach already makes too much of our world mind-dependent for the Deborinites' taste. Moreover, the Deborinites would have held that such a theory is destined to collapse into idealism. They would have doubted whether the theory leaves enough in reality as it is "in itself" to explain how that reality could interact with our minds in a way that would produce our everyday conception of it. Thus, the Deborinites thought that the Mechanists would ultimately be forced to deny that the contrast between scientific and everyday conceptions is one between reality as it is and reality as it seems to us in virtue of the particular character of our perceptual and cognitive mechanisms. Instead, in the sway of their basic empiricism, they would come to hold that the scientific and everyday conceptions are just two different constructions out of the data of sense.

The Deborinites, then, held that the Mechanists were committed to blatant reductionism and tacit subjectivism, and they set out to attack both. They argued that M, whether in its strong or weak version, was false for large classes of phenomena. In particular, they denied that comprehensive accounts

10 The theory of secondary qualities is part of the empiricist position sketched in the penultimate section of Chapter 1.

of the nature of either the sociohistorical or the psychological could be given in purely physical terms. Though the existence of psychological and sociohistorical phenomena is in some sense consequential on the physical, neither can be reduced to physical phenomena, nor explained on the model of physical phenomena:

> To reduce the mental to the physical is to erase the specific, special quality of the mental. Between the mental and the physical there is no unpassable metaphysical opposition; they have the same root, one and the same source, in the unity of matter. Nevertheless, the mental comprises an original [*svoëo-braznyï*]) property, a special quality of matter, which is distinct from what we call the physical.[11] Between the mental and the physical there is unity, there is likeness [*skhodstvo*], but there is also difference, qualitative particularity ... In our opinion, thought is a particular quality of matter, the subjective side of objective, material, i.e., physiological processes, with which it is not identical and to which it cannot be reduced. (Deborin 1926a: 320–1)

Thus, for the Deborinites, mental and sociohistorical phenomena are genuine constituents of objective reality.

This "objectivism" about the sociohistorical and the mental was one expression of the Deborinites' strong realism. While the Mechanists' reductionism committed them to the view that there is less in reality than our everyday conceptions suppose, the Deborinites denied that objective reality could be radically different from the way in which our concepts represent it as being. Rather, our historically evolving conceptual scheme (thought of as a system of concepts and universal categories) mirrors the objective structure of reality itself: We are compelled to organize our thoughts under its categories because they reflect what reality is like. Thus it is not that our conceptual scheme contributes all kinds of properties to our picture of the world that a scientific understanding must dis-

---

11 There is no satisfactory way to render "*svoëobraznyï*" in English. Literally, it means "of it own (*svoi*) form (*obraz*)," though "-*obraz-*" conveys more than "form," meaning also "image" and "icon." The term expresses novelty and particularity, "prototypicality." "*Svoëobraznyï*" is the adjective of the noun "*svoëobrazie*" and the abstract noun "*svoëobraznost'*." The latter is one of the categories of the dialectic.

pose of. Rather, our picture of the world (of which the natural sciences are part) can and does reflect reality as it is. Therefore, science exists not to overthrow our "everyday" conception, but to deepen it (see Deborin 1925, 1926b: 167–8).

The Deborinites' idea that the mental constitutes a realm of "original" (*svoëobraznyĭ*) properties provoked the objection that they were guilty of "vitalism," that is, of introducing into their supposedly materialist account peculiar nonmaterial phenomena – strange superphysical entities and forces – that science was powerless to explain.[12] The Deborinites, however, were adamant that this was not so. They argued that the genesis of the mental is part of the development of the material world. Thus an account of the origin of the mental need make no reference to strange, nonnatural entities. The mental is irreducible to the physical not because it is some special substance, but because mental phenomena, while resultant from, or "supervenient" on, physical phenomena, emerge as properties "qualitatively distinct" from physical entities and thus cannot be captured by a purely physical vocabulary. As Deborin cryptically put it, the mental reduces to the physical "in genesis, but not in form" (1926a: 319).

At this point in the exposition of the debate, many commentators begin to lose patience, for the Deborinites' position here seems no different from the stance of many Mechanists. At least some of the Mechanists who endorse M_W rather than M_S hold theories of the mental similar to the Deborinites'. For example, Sarab'yanov's view that "higher levels of the organization of matter rise out of the lower ones, but each level has a special quality that is not entirely reducible to the levels below it" seems identical to the position developed by the Deborinite Karev (1926; quoted in Joravsky 1961: 146). Thus it may seem that, at most, the two camps disagreed about whether we can understand mental phenomena *on the model* of physical phenomena. Since neither side addressed that question very di-

---

12 The charge of "vitalism" was originally made against the Deborinites' suggestion that reductive accounts are incapable of capturing the phenomenon of life (see, e.g., Stepanov 1925: 51). However, the charge was soon made against any theory suspected of invoking strange forces and entities beyond the compass of natural science. It became one of the Mechanists' favourite objections (see, e.g., Akselrod 1927b: 156).

rectly, should we not conclude that this aspect of the controversy was indeed just a war of words?

This judgment would be premature, for although particular representatives of the two camps may have agreed on whether reductive explanations of some class of phenomena were possible, they strongly disagreed about how this could be decided. The Mechanists wanted to let science do the talking: The test of whether reductive explanations were possible in a particular domain was whether science could actually produce them. The Deborinites, however, thought the possibility of reduction was always a "question of principle" ("*printsipial'-nyĭ vopros*") that could be settled only by philosophical argument (Deborin 1925: 224). Therefore, the conflict was not only about whether explanation by reduction is possible, but also about the legitimate grounds for deciding whether it is.

The Mechanists were alarmed not only by the idea that philosophy could settle in advance whether certain species of scientific explanation can succeed, but also by the kind of philosophical arguments the Deborinites produced to show this. The Deborinites did not advance considerations to show that, for each particular domain under discussion, the specific nature of the phenomena in question necessarily makes their reduction to the physical impossible. Instead, they launched very general arguments that appealed to the "laws of dialectics," in particular, to the "law of the transformation of quantity into quality."

We encountered this law in our discussion of orthodox Soviet dialectical materialism in Chapter 1. Based on the categories of quality, quantity, and measure in Hegel's *Logic*, it holds that "qualitative" changes in an object (i.e., changes in its "nature") are consequential upon "quantitative" changes in its component parts (i.e., changes describable in purely quantitative terms – e.g., changes in its mass, volume, or the distribution of its parts). An object will tolerate quantitative changes within certain limits without qualitative change. These limits circumscribe the "measure" of the object. At the limit, or "node," further quantitative change will result in the qualitative transformation of the object. Thus, development must be seen as a process of abrupt qualitative transformations precipitated by gradual quantitative changes: Development proceeds in "leaps." The example of a liquid is often given as an illustration. Water, for instance, will tolerate quantitative changes in temperature between (under normal conditions) the limits of 0 °C and 100 °C; but further quantitative change in either direction results in the sudden qualitative transformation of the liquid into a solid (ice) or a gas (steam). Thus, changes in quantity produce changes in quality.[13]

The Deborinites based their antireductionism on the application of this supposed law to the development of the material world as a whole. They argued that we can conceive of the development of the world purely quantitatively by describing the movement of matter with scientific and mathematical formulae. However, at certain nodes in this quantitative development, qualitative transformations occur that introduce properties into the world hitherto not present (e.g., mental and sociohistorical properties). These new properties require a new vocabulary and new laws to describe and explain them: Quantitative methods of analysis alone are insufficient to capture reality qualitatively transformed. The qualitative diversity of nature is, therefore, not a projection of mind onto matter, but a genuine property of objective reality itself. It is explained not by appeal to strange, extraphysical entities, but by the evolution of the physical world itself: In the course of its development, brute nature has, in virtue of changes that can be portrayed purely quantitatively, undergone qualitative transformation into a world abounding with mental, sociohistorical, and other "ideal" (nonmaterial) properties.

The Deborinites thus appealed to the law of the transformation of quantity into quality, conceived as a "universally valid law of nature, society, and thinking," to establish a picture of reality as a unity of qualitatively diverse realms that, though unified in their origins in the physical, are governed by specific laws and demand a specific vocabulary. They then invoked this picture to quash any putative attempt at the reduction of one realm to another:

---

13 This and other examples of the transformation of quantity into quality are given in Hegel (1812–16: bk. 1, sec. 3; 1830a: 107–11) and Engels (1873–83: 61–8). Most illustrations of the supposed law in the "diamat" canon do not withstand scrutiny. The silliest is Plekhanov's attempt to discern qualitative changes in arithmetic: After the digit "9" we supposedly make a "leap" into double figures! (Cited in Kolakowski [1978: vol. II, 341].)

The emergence of new forms is always connected with a break in continuity, with leaps. The new form emerges from the old, and we can establish qualitative equivalents and often even *measure* them. Nevertheless, the new form is a new quality that, as such, is not identical with the old, and represents something distinct from it and often even opposed to it. This is what we call unity in diversity and diversity in unity. The category of quality serves to mark the originality [*svoëobrazie*] of things. (Deborin 1926a: 318)

The Deborinites supported their antireductionist theory of the mind almost exclusively by such general considerations.

For their part, the Mechanists dismissed the idea that philosophy can determine what reality is like independently of science as the purest a priorism. Such speculative constructions, they argued, could never constitute a rival to the natural sciences' conception of reality, for how could a philosopher preaching the constructive unity of philosophy and science – as the Deborinites did – argue that a scientist should reject theories established by the application of his or her procedures in favour of the philosopher's picture, if the evidence by the scientist's own lights tells against the philosopher? In short, either the philosophical conception of reality conflicts with the scientific picture or it does not. If it does, then the scientific picture wins. If it does not, then philosophy leaves science where it is. Either way, science should proceed without interference from philosophers.

The Mechanists were particularly critical of the Deborinites' conception of the role of dialectics. The Deborinites maintained that "without the cultivation of a materialist dialectic there will be stagnation in science" (Deborin in *O raznoglasii* 1930 [*OR*]: I, 38). They based this view on the claim that, unaided, natural science yields only a partial, one-sided, and dislocated picture of the world (Deborin 1926a: 341). Since synthetic thought is alien to science, scientists will always be prone to idealist speculation to achieve a unified vision of reality. This, they argued, put science in grave danger, for the widespread acceptance of idealism within the scientific community would impede its further development. They concluded that only a materialist dialectic, based on a reworking of the categories of Hegel's *Logic,* could offer a synthetic vision of reality that would not impugn the integrity of science.

The Mechanists replied that it was not science that gave a fragmented picture of reality, but the Deborinites themselves. They argued that the Deborinites' obsession with "synthesis" was simply a reflection of the lack of real unity in their own speculative vision of reality as an amalgam of qualitatively diverse realms. But since this vision was in fact a consequence of the Deborinites' own dubious conception of dialectics, they were invoking dialectics to solve a problem dialectics had itself created! It was not true, the Mechanists continued, that science was incapable of synthesis. The Deborinites were looking for synthesis in the wrong place. They turned to abstract philosophical speculation to produce what science achieves *in practice*. Akselrod writes:

> Sten reproaches contemporary natural science on the grounds that synthetic thought is foreign to it. "Where's the synthesis?," he exclaims time and again. Let me be bold enough to answer like this: The synthesis is in the aeroplane, in the radio receiver, and in all the great practical results of contemporary natural science. I can be so bold because I have not forgotten Marx's great rule, that one can explain the world in one way or another, but the most important thing is to change it. (Akselrod 1927b: 162)

Science achieves a synthetic picture of nature not in metascientific theory but by bringing nature ever more under human control.

The Mechanists did not deny that dialectical "laws" had *some* application to nature, but they were frustrated by the Deborinites' failure to produce arguments in support of their view. When challenged, Deborinites would typically just appeal to authority: It was "axiomatic" for a Marxist to believe that the laws of dialectics were true and reflected reality as it is (see Deborin 1926b). The Mechanists therefore accused them of arbitrarily imposing Hegelian categories onto nature. This, the Mechanists argued, was a dangerous practice, for since the universality of Hegel's categories invited their application to any subject matter, the Deborinites thought themselves licensed to pronounce on matters of which they had no concrete knowledge. As Akselrod put it:

> And so, thanks to the universality of the laws of dialectics, it is possible to talk about everything while knowing nothing, to

talk in abstract terms, imparting a scholarly appearance to
pure contentlessness. Observing this process, one can say that
no one can hide his ignorance so well and so carefully as an
abstract philosopher. (Akselrod 1927b: 159)

The Deborinites were thus "formalists," spinning dialectical
webs from empty phrases, constructing theories in a vacuum.

For the Mechanists, the laws of dialectics acquired what
truth they had as empirical generalizations from the findings
of science; but, as such, they could hardly be used to overthrow natural science's conception of the world, or to challenge its explanatory procedures. While the Deborinites were
adamant that dialectical laws had enormous heuristic significance, the Mechanists thought it was an open question
whether the conscious apprehension of such laws would help
scientists in their research. The onus of proof was on the dialecticians, who, as A. F. Samoĭlov put it, must show

> that, by applying dialectical thought, dialectical method, they
> can go further, more quickly and with less effort, than those
> who take another path. If they can show that, then dialectics
> will win its place in science without a superfluous, fruitless,
> and offensive polemic. (Samoĭlov 1926: 81)

Samoĭlov, who was not a Marxist, was pessimistic about the
possible contribution dialectics might make to science. Other
Mechanists, however, like Lyubov Akselrod, saw great potential in dialectics. She argued, however, that this potential could
be realized only if dialectics was not conceived as a set of abstract laws or categories. Instead, dialectics must be seen as a
method, as a way of rendering our understanding of some specific subject matter more "concrete." Akselrod contrasted her
"historicist" dialectics with the "formalist" approach of her
Deborinite opponents:

> Dialectical method must be a tool for the cognition of reality,
> but the dialectic must not intrude upon reality, it must not pre-
> scribe to objective reality from its formal laws. Hegel himself,
> despite his absolute idealism, is incomparably more empirical
> than the "orthodox" and "militant" materialist Deborin.
> Because of his *historicism* ... Hegel had to realize his method
> in concrete domains. Therefore, in Hegel, we do not find en-

tirely abstract categories of dialectics, but the application of dialectics to concrete material, albeit in an idealist form: to the philosophy of history, to the philosophy of law (*Recht*), religion, art, etc. It is just this side of Hegel . . . that makes him the ancestor of materialist dialectics . . .

 . . . Dialectics is only given its true significance when it is intimately and indissoluably tied to concrete content . . . [I]n each separate sphere it manifests itself in different forms precisely as a result of the different concrete content of these spheres. But if one approaches each sphere with the general, abstract formulae "the negation of the negation," "thesis–antithesis–synthesis," then as Engels justly notes, it is impossible to do anything in any sphere. Such a formal understanding is nothing but a resurrection of the old metaphysics. (Akselrod 1927b: 148–9, referring to Engels 1878: 49–56)

Thus, for Akselrod, the dialectical method is highly *particularist;* we cannot, on the basis of its application to one domain, formulate principles that we can automatically apply elsewhere. Rather, how dialectics will guide us depends on the particular contours of the subject under study.

I conclude therefore that the Deborinite–Mechanist controversy did turn on an issue of real substance. Though, in some cases, their views on reductive explanation may actually have converged, Mechanists and Deborinites disagreed violently about whether it was philosophy or science itself that ultimately determined the plausibility of such explanations. In the course of this argument, the two camps expressed radically different conceptions of the nature and role of dialectics.

The defeat of the Mechanists

Soon after the controversy began, it became clear that neither side had the theoretical might to defeat its opponents. Appeal to authority, abuse, and accusations of heresy came to substitute for argument, and the promise of philosophical progress evaporated. In 1929, the Deborinites used their institutional supremacy to force victory at the Second All-Union Conference of Marxist–Leninist Institutions of Scientific Research. The Mechanists were officially condemned.

Mechanism was defeated not by new philosophical arguments, but by the charge that it was a revisionist trend and, as such, a *political* danger. The Deborinites had long tried to develop such a case against their opponents. In 1926 Deborin had argued that, by attacking the Soviet philosophical establishment (i.e., the Deborinites), the Mechanists had created a climate of "free criticism" of Marxism, opening the floodgates to all kinds of reactionary elements. Since the Mechanists had not taken up arms against these "Western European liquidators of Marxism," they were accused of tacitly forming a "bloc" with them (see Deborin 1926a: passim).

Deborin complemented these implausible accusations with the charge that Mechanism provided a theoretical rationale for "gradualist" politics. He based this criticism on his opponents' suspicion of the law of the transformation of quantity into quality:

> The emergence of new qualities is the sphere in which the quantitative is transformed into the qualitative and "continuous change" leads to "leaps." Thus the recognition of only quantitative changes and the negation of the category of quality leads to reformism.
>
> ... [For Mechanism] all qualities are only the result of gradual, continuous growth or the regrouping of quantitative elements, of their sum. There are no interruptions, no transitions to new qualities produced by, but essentially different from, the old. Therefore socialism *grows* within capitalism, representing only a quantitative change from it. (Deborin 1926a: 339)

Although Deborin's case was highly dubious, by 1929 his accusations had come to carry a special threat. Given the backwardness of Russia's economy, Russian Marxism had always been concerned with the problem of whether, as Marx had argued, the possibility of communism presupposed the full development of capitalism. While the Menshevik faction had aspired to replace tsarism with a bourgeois democracy that would stimulate capitalism and eventually grow into socialism, Lenin's Bolsheviks pressed for socialism's immediate inauguration. The Bolshevik seizure of power did not settle this issue. After almost four years of the centralized economics of "War Communism," the Bolsheviks were forced to retreat to the mixed economy of the "New Economic Policy" (NEP), which offered a gradualist path to communism through controlled capitalist relations of production in restricted parts of the economy. In 1929, with the failure of the NEP, the party broke with this gradualist policy and began Stalin's "Great Leap Forward"; the drama of collectivization commenced. With this, the party conducted a campaign against the "Right Deviationism" that counselled perseverence with the old gradualist strategy. As Mechanism was associated with Bukharin, the principal theorist of NEP and the leader of the "Right Opposition," its supposedly gradualist and determinist metaphysic made it an easy target as the ideological basis for Right Deviationism. This sealed Mechanism's fate.[14]

The aftermath of the debate:
The defeat of the Deborinites

Deborin's triumph was short-lived. Throughout the 1920s, the Deborinites had been accused of reneging on their promise of a synthesis of theory and practice, cultivating instead an abstract Hegelian philosophy divorced from the problems of real life. As the party began the Great Leap Forward, even the Deborinites' own students began to express impatience with their tutors' "academism." In April 1930, a band of young activists at the Institute of Red Professors complained that the "philosophical leadership" had shown insufficent "party spirit." Two months later, three of such activists, M. B. Mitin, V. N. Ral'tsevich, and P. F. Yudin, expressed their grievances in print (Mitin, Ral'tsevich, and Yudin 1930). The fact that this article – the infamous *stat'ya trëkh* ("article of the three") – was published in *Pravda* with an endorsement from the editors showed that the Party hierachy was behind the young "Bolshevizers." A campaign against the Deborinites was underway. At a meeting of the Presidium of the Communist Academy in October 1930, the Deborinites' grip on Soviet philosophy was finally broken.

At this meeting, fascinatingly transcribed in the Academy's bulletin (*O raznoglasii* 1930 [*OR*]), the Mechanists' cry of "formalism" was resurrected with a vengeance: The Deborin-

14 To be fair to the Deborinites, they stressed the link between Mechanism and Right Deviationism only after the Mechanists themselves had, very implausibly, tried to use the same argument against them (see Joravsky 1961: 51).

ites were accused of divorcing theory from practice. Having identified the dialectic of "Marx–Engels–Lenin–Stalin" with Hegel's, the Deborinites were said to have made "philosophical theorising ... a procession of ideas completely torn from their concrete, historical, social-class setting." Because they had turned "dialectic from a living method of cognition into a set of *abstract* formulae externally imposed on material," philosophy had been unable to pull its weight in the construction of socialism (Mitin in *OR:* I, 59). The Deborinites had not even posed, let alone solved, any of the problems of the transition from capitalism to communism. Although they had tackled the Mechanists, the theorists of Right Deviationism, the Deborinites had failed to realize that the party now fought a "battle on two fronts." Consequently, they had ignored the party's other enemy, Trotsky's "Left Deviation." Thus they had not adhered to the principle of *partiĭnost'*, which required philosophy to defend the general line of the party against those who deviated from it. Indeed, since Sten and Karev had been associated with Trotskyism, their opponents even mooted the idea that "the theory of Trotskyism had found its reflection" in the Deborinites' work (Milyutin in *OR:* I, 18). Finally, the Deborinites were accused of underestimating Lenin's significance as a theorist. Blind to the organic relation of theory and practice, they had supposedly treated Lenin only as political actor, failing to understand how his work inaugurated a "new stage" in Marxist philosophy.

At first Deborin (*OR:* I, 14; I, 23–89), S. Novikov (*OR:* I, 72–6), Karev (*OR:* I, 105–17), and Sten (*OR:* I, 183–97) offered a vigorous defence. They claimed that their opponents' charge of "formalism" was really a form of contempt for theorizing per se:

> Soon it will be impossible to write a single theoretical article – everything will be called formalism. This is a terrible danger which we must fight. (Deborin in *OR:* I, 35)

The Deborinites expressed their amazement at the idea that Bolshevik philosophy needed to be "bolshevized," and held that the suggestions about how this was to be done were lifted from their own programme (see Hecker 1933: 181–2 for the Bolshevizers' programme). Finally, the charge that they had undervalued Lenin was, they argued, based only on a few unfortunate quotations torn out of context. Deborin concluded that he would willingly undertake "self-criticism" if he could only understand what he had done wrong.

What Deborin had done wrong soon became clear. As the debate reached its climax, Skrypnik (in *OR:* I, 87ff.) and Yaroslavsky (in *OR:* I, 126–8) reminded the assembly that Deborin had, in his days as a Menshevik, criticized the Bolshevik line in philosophy. Deborin angrily replied that his criticism had been directed at Bogdanov, who in 1908 was widely regarded as the philosopher of Bolshevism, and who Lenin himself was attacking at that very time. When this response fell on deaf ears, Deborin finally realized that rational argument was not going to win the day. In a speech in striking contrast to his initial offensive, Deborin conceded defeat to the Bolshevizers. (He gave them every point but one: He refused to admit that he had misunderstood Lenin's contribution to philosophy [*OR:* II, 73–83].) The Deborinites' reign was over. Once he had embraced the spirit of self-criticism, Deborin never again challenged the cogency of the case against him. Even thirty years later, in the preface to a collection of his writings, he wrote in praise of "the Central Committee's well-known resolution of 26 January 1931 on the journal *Under the Banner of Marxism*" (Deborin 1961: 18). That was the resolution that finally took the journal out of Deborin's control.

The Deborinites had fallen in Stalin's campaign for discipline on the "ideological front." In all spheres theoreticians were called upon to justify the party's "general line" as it embarked on the Great Leap Forward. It is therefore fitting that it was Stalin himself who finally crushed the Deborinites when, at an interview with the party executive of Institute of Red Professors in December 1930, he dubbed the Deborinites "Menshevizing Idealists," an epithet embodying a suitable blend of political and philosophical heresy. Throughout the 1930s, an extraordinary mythology was spun around Menshevizing Idealism. It was "discovered" that Menshevizing Idealism had developed from the petit-bourgeois elements of the NEP to provide "an ideological cover for Trotskyite double-dealers, spies, traitors, and Trotskyite agents on the philosophical front." The trials were said to have revealed how "the majority of Menshevizing Idealists [had] turned into participants

in mean bands of Japo–German Trotskyite Terrorists, sabo-
teurs, spies, and agents of the fascist secret services" (Berestnev 1938: 828–30). Of the Deborinites, only Deborin himself
and a handful of others survived those trials.

The Deborinites' defeat was a turning point in the history
of Soviet philosophy. With the rise of the Bolshevizers, Soviet
philosophy's conception of itself underwent a radical change.
Under Mitin's "new philosophical leadership," philosophy's
mission was no longer seen as the systematic theoretical understanding of reality. Philosophy was to exist not to interpret
the world but to change it. To this end, philosophy entered a
symbiotic relationship with the party. Philosophy would uphold the "general line" of the party, and in return, the party
would sponsor all philosophy that came to its support. On this
basis, Mitin could taunt Deborin that whether the Bolshevizers' criticisms were "full of mistakes" was irrelevant: The fact
that the Bolshevizers supported the party and that the party
supported them was evidence of the cogency of their position
(Mitin in *OR:* I, 40). Thus, for the Bolshevizers, the unity of
theory and practice meant that philosophy was to be a "weapon in our class war" (Skrypnik in *OR:* I, 84). The reign of the
Bolshevizers therefore stands as a curious expression of Minin's supposedly discredited idea that philosophy is and only
can be such a weapon – except now it was the proletariat, not
the bourgeoisie, that sought to wield it.

How were the Bolshevizers possible?

Although the "great turn on the philosophical front" was designed by the party, the Bolshevizers' triumph cannot be attributed to political machinations alone. On the contrary, the
nature of their rise to power owed much to the debate between
Mechanists and Deborinites that preceded it.

The Bolshevizers were possible because the Deborinite–Mechanist controversy was a philosophical stalemate. In a tradition where the development of Soviet philosophy was deemed
essential to the success of the revolution, an atmosphere of intellectual uncertainty was intolerable. For this reason, the Deborinites felt compelled to force victory by extraphilosophical
measures. However, in defeating the Mechanists on political
grounds, the Deborinites did nothing to resolve the philosoph-

ical issues at the root of the deadlock. Consequently, they left themselves open to the Bolshevizers' charge that, in the first decade of Soviet philosophy, nothing had been achieved except stagnation. Worse than this, the tactics the Deborinites employed against the Mechanists undermined what philosophical culture they had created. By accusing the Mechanists of political heresy, by denying them access to print and deliberately distorting their views, and by behaving as if philosophical disputes can be instantly resolved by a quotation from Marx or, failing that, by a vote, the Deborinites themselves created the methods of "argumentation" which the Bolshevizers were quick to use against them. Thus, the Bolshevizers' reasons to overthrow the Deborinites, and the means they employed to do so, are intelligible only in the light of the stalemate of the earlier controversy.

Some commentators may suggest that the stalemate between Deborinites and Mechanists was the result of the vacuity of their debate. I want to challenge that interpretation. As we have seen, the core of the Mechanist–Deborinite controversy is a dispute about explanation. The Mechanists set down global criteria for successful explanation: Genuine explanation was natural-scientific explanation, and science itself was to determine which explanations were successful. The Deborinites thus found it impossible to convince Mechanists that their criteria were inadequate, for any supposed counterexample to Mechanism was, from the Mechanists' perspective, *ex hypothesi* not explanatory. This problem is double-edged, for Deborinism similarly invoked rigid, global criteria for successful explanation. When two such theories meet in head-on conflict, theoretical stalemate is to be expected, since from the perspective of one theory the explanatory force of the other is invisible.

Thus, the Deborinite–Mechanist controversy was a clash of "two logics," a seemingly intractable opposition of two global philosophical positions, one grounded primarily in the procedures of natural science, the other in Hegelian Marxism. The Bolshevizers, however, did nothing to resolve the philosophical stalemate that had brought them to power. Despite the severity of their criticisms of Deborin, most of the Bolshevizers' philosophical views differed from the Deborinites' only in their greater crudity. For example, they inherited the Deborinites' strong realism about the material world, but they treated the contentious idea that the material world is a self-developing unity of qualitatively diverse realms utterly uncritically. The Bolshevizers attributed any problematic entities to the rich diversity of the material world and appealed to the "autodynamism" (*samodvizhenie*) of matter as the source of everything and as the justification of everything progressive (see Berdyaev 1933: 237–8). They also championed the Deborinites' idea that dialectical materialism must guide the scientist in his or her research. The result was that the autonomy of science suffered in exactly the way the Mechanists had feared.[15]

The philosophical deadlock between Mechanists and Deborinites thus helps explain how the Bolshevizers were possible. I have argued that to understand the deadlock, we must understand the nature of the philosophical dispute between the camps. Taking the philosophy seriously is a condition of writing the history correctly.

The philosophical significance of the controversy

Even the most skeptical of commentators might agree that the Deborinite–Mechanist controversy is philosophically significant in the sense that its philosophical content is relevant to the explanation of how the Bolshevizers came to power. To conclude this chapter, I want to ask whether the debate was philosophically important in a more substantial sense. As we are concerned ultimately with the debate's significance for Ilyenkov, I shall address this question by examining how Ilyenkov himself might have answered it.

Although Ilyenkov never wrote about the early controversy, I believe he would have found in it two issues of the utmost importance.[16] The first is the question of the role of Marxist philosophical theory in the construction of the new society of which the Bolsheviks dreamed. In the light of subsequent

15 The best known examples are the party's support for Lysenko's genetics and the dismissal of cybernetics in the 1940s as a "bourgeois science."

16 My discussion is based on Ilyenkov (1965), his criticisms of positivism in Ilyenkov (1980), his writings on "militant materialism" (1979b,f), and his critique of the Soviet neo-Mechanism of his day (e.g., Ilyenkov 1968a,b).

events, it is easy to be cynical about Soviet philosophers' early plans for a grand synthesis of theory and practice. It should be remembered, however, that the Bolsheviks believed they were the first self-conscious historical agents. The Soviet Union was to be the first society to develop not spontaneously, but by design. Theorists in the USSR were no longer to follow passively in the wake of events, interpreting them after the fact; rather, theory was to dictate the course of history. Informed by Marxism's account of the forces that govern society's development, human beings would be able to harness those forces in practice. This was the climate in which the Deborinites and the Mechanists accepted the responsibility of developing Soviet philosophy. Their success or failure as *philosophers* is thus important not only to those who, like Ilyenkov, think the Bolsheviks' hopes justified and realizable, but to anyone who seeks to understand and assess the original Bolshevik ideal.

Second, Ilyenkov would have argued that the issues that divided the two camps were philosophically profound. In particular, despite the inadequacy of the Deborinites' philosophy and its disastrous consequences, Ilyenkov would have disagreed with Yakhot's recent verdict that the Deborinites' arguments against the Mechanists

> do not have serious foundation. They have been refuted by the further development of science. There is only one reason to repeat them today: if one has a deep interest in preventing the truth about the events of those years from coming to light. (Yakhot 1981: 151)

In spite of Soviet philosophy's sordid history of opportunistic political attacks on philosophical positions, the relation between philosophy and political beliefs (or, as he would have put it, between "logic" and "worldview") remained a real issue for Ilyenkov. He shared the Deborinites' abhorrence of "positivism" (taken as the view that natural science can provide an exhaustive account of objective reality), and throughout his career he struggled to articulate its incompatibility with Marxist politics. Ilyenkov identified two principal dangers in positivism. First, he feared that its obsession with the explanatory power of natural science led to a naïve confidence that science and technology would ultimately yield the solution to all social problems, and, more sinisterly, that organizational, and ultimately political, responsibility should be delegated to "scientific experts" or technical systems. Such ideas, he felt, were especially pernicious when applied to a society characterized by a rigid, centrally planned economy. For example, the Bolsheviks endorsed Marx and Engels's thesis of the "withering away" of the state: Under communism, "the government of persons is [eventually to be] replaced by the administration of things," by rational and harmonious planning in all spheres of social life (Engels 1878: 341; see Sypnowich 1990: chap. 1). This thesis is so radical that it is essential for us to have a clear conception of its rationale. Marx gives a functional account of capitalist forms of government: Under capitalism, it is argued, the state exists to mediate conflict between the interests of competing individuals; thus, as communism gradually abolishes the basis of conflict, the state withers away. This argument is usually taken to depend on the premise that all social conflict derives from the struggle of egoistic wills for scarce resources. Its validity is thus usually held to turn on whether communism can abolish scarcity and whether, if it can, egoism will give way to altruistic decision making characterized by agreement and harmony (see, e.g., Campbell 1983; Sypnowich 1990: chap. 5). However, in its classic form, the argument contains another premise that is rarely made explicit. This is the idea that rational planning will be possible because there will be no dispute about *facts*. Science will, in the absence of psychological barriers to consensus, guarantee agreement on issues of organization by rendering transparent which of the competing strategies is most efficient. This idea is often implicit in the Mechanist's image of the power of science.[17] For Ilyenkov, who struggled against the resurgence of such conceptions in the "scientific-technological" revolution of the 1960s, such a view was utopian. He believed that truth can be reached only through intellectual conflict (see Ilyenkov 1977a: chap. 3). Science will never be able simply to read the truth from the facts; truth becomes evident only from the struggle of conflicting perspectives, and only then in a way that may yet remain

17 It emerges graphically in Bogdanov's science fiction utopia, *Red Star* (1908), discussed in Chapter 4.

opaque to the occupants of some of them. Thus, the withering away of the state cannot depend on the assumption that the "administration of things" will proceed without conflict. Insofar as the Soviet positivism of the 1920s upheld that assumption, it encouraged a perilous political utopianism that sought the abolition of the state for the wrong reasons.

For Ilyenkov, the second political danger of positivist philosophy is that it tends to reduce human capacities to objects that can be understood exclusively by natural science. This tendency is clear in the Mechanists' concept of the human individual. Mechanism treats the individual as a complex machine, a machine somehow capable of self-development and self-organization. According to Ilyenkov, the consequences of such a view extend beyond psychology and the philosophy of mind into the political arena. First, this conception encourages crude political theory; but second, and more important, are its consequences for our idea of human perfectibility. On the Mechanist picture, human capacities are represented as functions of our *physical* organization. A person's intelligence, for instance, is seen as a consequence of how well his or her brain works. This view may, in turn, be thought to support two related theses:

1. Human perfection may be achieved by altering individuals' physical makeup.
2. Facts about the physical constitution of human beings may place constraints on their perfectibility and on the perfectibility of the societies in which they live.

Ilyenkov, who held that human capacities were socially constituted in some very strong sense, thought both these ideas theoretically baseless and politically pernicious.

In subsequent chapters, we shall see how Ilyenkov developed these ideas in his critique of Alexander Bogdanov (who was, as we have seen, a fellow traveller of the Mechanist camp), and in discussions with the "neo-Mechanists" of the modern era. I present them here, however, to illustrate that the Deborinite–Mechanist controversy was by no means just an empty squabble between warring factions of Soviet communists. It is a testimony to the reality of the issues raised by the early controversy that they reemerged at the heart of Soviet philosophy in the post-Stalin period.

Conclusion

In 1966, the Italian Marxist Sebastiano Timpanaro wrote of a polarization in Western Marxist thought between

(a) a positivism that holds that the task of philosophy is to systematize science's methods and to generalize its results and

(b) a Hegelian Marxism that, critical of the agnosticism and idealism of positivism, insists on the necessity of a dialectical materialist *Weltanschauung* to combat eclecticism and to guide the development of science.

Timpanaro argues that both positions are fundamentally unsound. While positivism collapses into a "narcissistic theorization of the activity of the scientist," whom it conceives as "the legislator of nature," the Hegelian alternative represents "an ostentatious archaism ... whose conception of nature was regressive at birth," an archaism that devalues "not only how much is new in Marxism by comparison with Hegel, but also of how much in pre-Hegelian culture, and in particular in the Enlightenment, is more advanced than Hegel" (Timpanaro 1975: 36–7).

The polarization Timpanaro describes in modern Western Marxism strikingly recalls the divide between Mechanists and Deborinites. Indeed, the criticisms he advances are identical to those the Deborinites and Mechanists made of each other. This suggests that the relevance of the Soviet controversy is not confined to the specific context of Russian Marxism. If Timpanaro's diagnosis of the crisis in Western Marxism is correct, then the Mechanist–Deborinite debate must be seen in a wider context, as the expression of a deep and recurring tension within the Marxist intellectual tradition.

Some would suggest that the polarization of Marxist philosophy into positivist and dialectical schools is the inevitable consequence of the uneasy alliance between the science of the Enlightenment and the philosophy of Hegel in the theories of Marx himself. Ilyenkov, however, maintained that the tension between these influences on Marx's thought need not prove irreconcilable. He believed that the clash of two logics found its resolution in a social theory of consciousness, a theory that would allow Marxism to avoid both the Scylla of positivism and the Charybdis of idealism. While the Deborinites and Mechanists were enmeshed in their controversy, the psychologist Vygotsky was at work on just such a theory.

3

VYGOTSKY

It is hard to believe that Lev Semënovich Vygotsky's impressive contribution to Soviet psychology began in the same year and in the same city as the turgid controversy between the Mechanists and the Deborinites. From his debut on the Soviet psychological stage in 1924 until his death from tuberculosis only ten years later, Vygotsky produced a series of works that abound with creative insights.[1] In contrast to his philosophical contemporaries, Vygotsky's career was marked by theoretical achievements that have had a direct and enduring influence. It is now common to talk of a "Vygotsky School" in Soviet psychology (sometimes known as the "sociohistorical" or "cultural-historical" school), which includes A. N. Leontiev and A. R. Luria, who both worked under Vygotsky in their youth, and a younger group of educational psychologists, of whom A. I. Meshcheryakov and V. V. Davydov are

1 Vygotsky first appeared on the Soviet psychological scene in January 1924, making a spectacular contribution to the Second Russian Psychoneurological Congress in Leningrad (see Luria 1979: 38–9). Later that year he took up a position at the Institute of Psychology in Moscow. He continued to work in Moscow until his death in 1934, although his research group moved the base of its activities from the capital to the Ukrainian city of Kharkov in 1931, as the political climate in Moscow became intolerable (see Bakhurst 1990: 212–16).

best known.[2] In addition, Vygotsky has a growing following in the West, where Jerome Bruner, Michael Cole, James Wertsch, and others have suggested that his ideas speak to the quandaries and confusions that haunt Western psychology today. Now that a Russian edition of his collected works has at last appeared, Vygotsky's influence is set to grow still further.[3]

Vygotsky's approach to psychology is remarkable both for its theoretical intensity and its sense of mission. Vygotsky believed that the psychology of his day bore the characteristics

2 Karl Levitin presents an engaging account of the Vygotsky School through pen-portraits of its principal members in *One Is Not Born a Personality* (1982). Levitin, who is a journalist, draws on a variety of materials including interviews, correspondence, and personal reminiscences. The result is a work rich in detail, offering a rare insight into how, in the late 1970s, the school saw itself and its history. The book contains (in chap. 1) the best biographical sketch of Vygotsky to date.

3 Vygotsky's masterpiece, *Myshlenie i rech'* (*Thought and Speech*), appeared posthumously in 1934, but after the Central Committee's resolution of 4 June 1936 against pedology, Vygotsky's writings were backlisted in the Soviet Union until 1956, when an edition of selected writings was published (see *Psikhologicheskii slovar'* 1983: 254–5; Valsiner 1987: 104–5). Since then, his works have been slowly appearing, culminating in the recent six-volume *Collected Works* (*Sobranie sochinenii*), containing much previously unpublished material (1982a,b, 1983a,b, 1984a,b).

   Western interest in Vygotsky dates from the early 1960s, with the appearance of Hanfmann and Vakar's abridged translation of *Myshlenie i rech'* as *Thought and Language* (1962). Although an English edition of *The Psychology of Art* was produced in 1971, the Hanfmann–Vakar *Thought and Language* remained the principal Western source of Vygotsky's thought until the publication of *Mind in Society* in 1978, a patchwork composition skillfully constructed by Michael Cole and colleagues from a number of Vygotsky's writings. Since then the amount of translated material has been steadily growing. Articles by Vygotsky are included in Wertsch 1981, and in many issues of the journal *Soviet Psychology*. Recently, not only has Alex Kozulin produced an enlarged version of the 1962 *Thought and Language*, but Norris Minnik has provided the first complete translation of *Myshlenie i rech'*, in the first volume of a projected English edition of the *Collected Works*. The critical literature on Vygotsky and the socio-historical school is also growing fast, and a number of Western psychologists now see themselves as working within a Vygotskian framework (see, e.g., Kozulin 1984: chap. 5, 1986; Rogoff and Werstch 1984; Lee 1985, 1987; Werstch 1985a,b; Bakhurst 1986, 1990; Valsiner 1987: chap. 4; Cole 1988; and *The Quarterly Newsletter of the Laboratory of Comparative Human Cognition*, especially vol. 9, no. 3 [July 1987] and vol. 10, no. 4 [Oct 1988]).

typical of any young science: It was composed of a fragmented hodgepodge of competing schools employing different,
and often incompatible, methods. He argued that if psychology was to forge a scientific understanding of consciousness –
its principal object of analysis – it was imperative that a unifying theoretical framework be developed to integrate its dispa-
rate branches. However, like the Bolsheviks, Vygotsky was
not interested in theory for the sake of theory alone. He believed that psychology should seek not just to understand the
mind, but to make possible its perfection.

In the late 1960s, when Ilyenkov came to Vygotsky's work
through his association with Leontiev and Davydov, it was
thus both the theoretical and practical dimensions of Vygotsky's psychology that attracted him. Ilyenkov recognized Vygotsky as an ally whose ideas strengthened his own theory of
the mind. Before long, Vygotskian concepts, particularly the
notion of *internalization,* entered Ilyenkov's writings, and he
began to play the role of the philosophical spokesman of the
Vygotsky School (e.g., Ilyenkov 1970). In this role, however,
Ilyenkov stressed not only the philosophical importance of
Vygotskian ideas, but also their clinical, educational, and political significance. His enthusiasm for the practical dimension of Vygotskian psychology is evident in his passionate
defence of Meshcheryakov's work with the blind-deaf, which
he championed throughout the 1970s (see Chapter 7).

This chapter presents Vygotsky's theoretical perspective via
an account of the main tenets of his work that reveals their
mutual relations. The features of his contribution that have appealed to Soviet philosophers – such as Ilyenkov and his lesser-
known contemporary Felix Mikhailov – are especially salient
in my account. We shall begin by considering Vygotsky's
views on method, and then turn to the method's application to
the relation between thought and speech, the relation that Vygotsky considered the key to the nature of consciousness.

The critique of the prevailing climate

Vygotsky was particularly concerned with the question of
how psychologists' methodology (including general theoretical suppositions) can infect the object of their analysis, and in
all his major works he sought to make psychology conscious

of its own methods by constantly exploring the subject's short history. Vygotsky believed that, since psychologists must seek a method appropriate to the specific nature of their object, to address methodological issues is at the same time to inquire into the nature of the object itself. He writes:

> The search for method becomes one of the most important problems of the entire enterprise of understanding the uniquely human forms of psychological activity. In this case, the method is simultaneously prerequisite and product, the tool and the result of the study. (Vygotsky 1978: 65)

Vygotsky's concern with methodology grew in response to what he called the "crisis in contemporary psychology." In the 1920s, psychology was a battleground of warring schools. Vygotsky believed that Gestalt psychology, psychoanalysis, Stern's personalism, and the "reflexological" theories of Pavlov and Bekhterev had all made insightful contributions to our understanding of the mind. He argued, however, that the different explanatory principles employed by these theories made it impossible to integrate their results, posing a threat to the unity of psychology as a science. In response to this threat, each theory sought to establish unity by ousting its rivals. Yet these colonial ambitions came to nothing, for as each theory grew in scope, so its explanatory principles became vacuous.

> Each of these four approaches is, in its own place, extremely contentful, valuable, fruitful, and full of significance and meaning. But when they are raised to the rank of world laws, they are worth just as much as each other, they are as absolutely equal as round and empty noughts. (Vygotsky 1927a: 308)

Vygotsky held that the emptiness of these four theories, and of the behaviourist and "subjective-empirical" approaches also then prominent in Russia, was most evident when they applied their explanatory principles to the analysis of the "higher mental functions."[4] And so long as psychology lacked a

---

4 The notion of the "higher mental functions" (*vysshie psikhologicheskie funktsii*), now a basic concept of Soviet psychology, owes its origin to Vygotsky (see *Psikhologicheskiĭ slovar'* 1983: 65). Vygotsky holds that only human beings possess these functions. They include those men-

plausible theory of these functions, the nature of consciousness would remain a mystery.

Vygotsky proposed that psychology respond to this "crisis" in three ways. The first was that it must radically revise its understanding of the mental and of the methods appropriate for its analysis. Vygotsky believed that psychology was trapped between two approaches to the mind that, though they appeared to be the only alternatives, were both unsatisfactory. Russian psychology, for example, was divided between the "objectivist" approach of the behaviourists and reflexologists, and the introspectionism of the "subjective–empirical" school. The former sought to explain all human behaviour in "stimulus–response" terms, which made no essential reference to mental phenomena. They held that talk about the mental, insofar as it is relevant to the explanation of behaviour, can be reduced to talk in terms of responses. In contrast, the subjective–empirical school, while recognizing the significance of the stimulus–response framework for the explanation of behaviour, argued that no purely objective account can capture consciousness, the inner dimension of mental life. They insisted that this inner realm remains a legitimate object of psychological investigation even though it is in principle beyond the reach of scientific method, accessible to the psychologist only through the introspective reports of the subject.

Vygotsky, though, saw these apparently opposite approaches as two sides of the same coin. He argued that both treated behaviour as bodily movement explicable on the stimulus–response model, and that both held that psychology is scientific only insofar as it employs such mechanistic explanations. Their disagreement was over whether psychology should concern itself with anything beyond the explanation of behaviour so understood. And even on *this* point objectivists were prepared to compromise: Bekhterev, the champion of Russian reflexology, admitted that his theory of human behaviour left open the question of the existence of "souls" or "minds." Thus

tal operations that Anglo–American philosophy typically treats as "propositional attitudes," i.e., thought, belief, desire, logical memory, intention, etc., as well as other psychological capacities, such as speech, attention, and the higher forms of classification. For Vygotsky, these functions form an interrelated system of psychological capacities that constitutes human consciousness. (What makes them "functions" is discussed in the next section.)

both sides held the same dualistic premise that it is in principle possible to give an account of human activity without reference to consciousness; the human mind and the operations of the human body are separable realms of inquiry.

> The most important thing is that the exclusion of consciousness from scientific psychology maintains to a significant degree all the dualism and spiritualism of the subjective psychology of the past. V. M. Bekhterev asserts that reflexology does not contradict the hypothesis of the "soul." The basic premise of reflexology – the supposition that it is possible to explain without remainder all of human behaviour without recourse to subjective phenomena – is the dualism of subjective psychology (its attempt to study a pure, abstract mind) turned inside out. It is the other half of the old dualism: There we had mind without behaviour, here behaviour without the mind, and in both, "mind" and "behaviour" are understood as two distinct phenomena. (Vygotsky 1925b: 80–1; see also 1931a: 15)

For Vygotsky, the way forward is to reject the assumption that the stimulus–response model is the only means to a scientific understanding of human activity. This model is inadequate, he argues, because it construes "the relation between human behaviour and nature as unidirectionally reactive" (1978: 61). The distinguishing feature of *human* behaviour, however, is that, by the use of tools and, especially, language, human beings are able to *mediate* between stimulus and response. Human beings can conceive of an object or situation as demanding a certain course of action, to question the correctness of their conception in the light of previous experience, and to project and evaluate alternative procedures. The subject's self-conscious or "reflexive" understanding of his or her relation to the world undermines the idea that some particular parcel of experience, considered in itself, can be seen as a stimulus that *necessitates* some particular response. Thus, in the case of human beings, it is impossible to establish lawlike correlations between states of affairs conceived as psychological stimuli and the activities those states of affairs precipitate. The stimulus–response model's scientific pretentions, however, rest on the possibility of such lawlike correlations.

For Vygotsky, this objection to the stimulus–response model itself suggests how psychology must rethink its conception of the mind (see 1925b). Vygotsky argues that the psychologist's task is to understand how human activity is mediated by language and other psychological tools. He proposes that psychology retrieve the concept of consciousness to understand this mediation. Consciousness, conceived as the totality of higher psychological capacities, must be understood neither as something reducible to activity nor as something logically distinct from it, but as its "organizing principle." Psychology thus overcomes the "old dualism" with the view that human activity and consciousness, though distinct, are not independently intelligible.

For Vygotsky, the second response that psychology must make to the crisis is to eschew purely a priori methods of investigation; pure "conceptual analysis" cannot reveal the nature of psychological capacities. At the same time, however, Vygotsky criticizes those, like Piaget, who rejected the a priori in order to concentrate on the documentation of facts (1934: 25 [1986: 14]). For Vygotsky, psychology knows neither pure facts nor pure concepts; the difference between conceptual and empirical inquiry is only "a matter of degree" (1927a: 315). Since we cannot disentangle the facts from their presentation in our concepts and theories, we cannot drive a wedge between the assessment of facts and the analysis of concepts. Psychology, therefore, must carve a path between a priorism and naked empiricism.

Vygotsky also attacks a second form of a priorism: the idea that psychological faculties themselves exist prior to experience. He denies that the child enters the world naturally equipped with embryonic forms of the higher mental functions that subsequently develop under the influence of the environment. Rather, he argues that psychology must show how these functions are *created* through the child's intercourse with his or her surroundings (1978: 45ff.).

Third, Vygotsky argues that psychology must not attempt to build up a theory of the higher mental functions from an understanding of more basic psychological mechanisms (of the kind, perhaps, with which animals and human children are endowed by nature). The higher mental functions, he claims, are irreducible to their primitive antecedents, either phylogenetic or ontogenetic. He thus criticizes Pavlov and the "zoopsychologists" for trying "to reproduce [in theory] the path that nature herself has taken" (1927a: 295). In contrast, Vygotsky maintains that the complex is the key to the comprehension of the simple. He argues that a proper understanding of elementary mental capacities rests on a grasp of the higher mental functions and not vice versa. Quoting Marx, Vygotsky reminds us that "the anatomy of man is the key to the anatomy of the ape" (1927a: 294).

Vygotsky's functionalism

The best way to understand Vygotsky's critique is to consider the alternative he advances. On the opening page of *Thought and Speech* (*Myshlenie i rech'*), the work that represents the culmination of his research, Vygotsky remarks that psychologists typically pay lip service to the unity of consciousness and then proceed to treat the functions that constitute consciousness as isolated and self-contained processes (1934: 10 [1986: 1–2]). In contrast, Vygotsky argues that to understand the unity of consciousness we must conceive of the various psychological capacities – thought, memory, speech, volition, attention, and so on – as standing in interfunctional (*mezhfunktsional'nyi*) relations of mutual determination. Psychological capacities are to be analyzed functionally. Each capacity is to be characterized in terms of what it does: It is thought of as being employed, or employing itself, for some purpose in some activity, and its nature is said to lie in why and how it comes into play as it does.[5] This basic functionalism is spiced by the following consideration. We determine what function a particular capacity fulfils by observation and experiment. However, when we come to consider, say, the child's ability to classify objects, we see that the activity we want to call clas-

---

5 The idea that a function "employs itself" is meant to convey only that, for Vygotsky, the higher mental functions do not require a "self," existing over and above them, to exercise them. (Note that Vygotsky's functionalism should not be confused with the brand, recently fashionable in Western philosophy of mind, that (a) analyzes mental states in terms of the causal relations their instances bear to the subject's environment and to other mental states, and (b) represents instances of those causal relations as realized by the physical states of the brain [see Smith and Jones 1986: 152–89].)

sification changes according to the level of development of the child (Luria 1979: 67–8). Vygotsky claims that we can explain this familiar truth only if we concentrate on how developments in other faculties have brought about changes in the child's capacity to classify. Here Vygotsky is offering more than a simple interactionism between already existing capacities: He holds that the nature of each capacity is transformed through the developing relations it bears to other changing capacities. The idea is that each psychological function does not possess its own immanent logic of development, for we can only identify behaviour at different stages of development as manifestations of a *single* function by attention to the way in which developments in *others* make possible changes in the one under investigation. The essence of each capacity lies outside it: What it is and what it may become are determined by the development of the other psychological functions.[6]

Vygotsky's functionalism has two immediate and important consequences. First, he argues that, if the mind is conceived as a totality of evolving interfunctionally related capacities, then its nature can only be captured by a *historical* theory. He writes:

> We need to concentrate not on the *product* of development but on the very *process* by which the higher forms are established ... To encompass in research the process of a given thing's development in all its phases and changes – from birth to death – fundamentally means to discover its nature, its essence, for "it is only in movement that a body shows what it is." Thus the historical study of behaviour is not an auxiliary aspect of theoretical study, but rather forms its very base. (1978: 64–5)

Psychology, therefore, must produce a historical, or "genetic"

6 What is at issue here is, to use a Wittgensteinian expression, "the criterion of sameness" for manifestations of particular capacities at different stages of their development. It is often difficult to see this criterion as problematic. This is because the mind projects its mature psychological capacities onto the earlier stages of its development: We see the higher mental functions in the infant's behaviour even when they are not yet present. Although this projection is crucial in child development (Vygotsky holds that treating children *as if* they had abilities they do not yet possess is a necessary condition of the development of those abilities), it can have damaging consequences for psychology, encouraging the view that children possess higher mental functions from birth.

(*geneticheskiĭ*, from "genesis"), reconstruction of the mind's development that reveals the changing relations its functions bear both to each other and to the world in which the individual is located.

Second, Vygotsky's functionalism grounds his claim that the mature psychological functions are irreducible to their primitive antecedents. On Vygotsky's account, the development of each psychological capacity is mediated by developments in the other capacities to which it is interfunctionally related. Thus, the development of any capacity represents not a linear process of steady growth but a "dialectical" series of abrupt qualitative transformations precipitated by changes in other capacities. These qualitative changes (or "leaps") between stages in the development of a function mean that its nature cannot be reduced to the form in which it first appears (Vygotsky 1978: 57).

Thought, speech, and "unit analysis"

Vygotsky proposes that psychology begin its "genetic" account with an analysis of the central relation in the development of consciousness, the relation between *thought* and *speech*. Vygotsky's treatment of this relation in the first chapter of *Thought and Speech* offers important insights into his understanding of interfunctional relations and of the methods appropriate for their analysis. We must be clear about the reference of the terms "thought" and "speech" in this opening discussion. By "thought" (*myshlenie*), Vygotsky means the process of thinking, the cognitive activity whereby the subject forms a conception of the world and learns to solve problems within it. By "speech" (*rech'*) or "word" (*slovo*), he means overt linguistic behaviour, the intentional production of *noise* or movement to elicit a response from another through *meaning*. Prior to the investigation of the relation between thought and speech, it would beg the question to offer detailed definitions of the two relata. Vygotsky's aim is simply to draw attention to a basic contrast from which the psychology of consciousness must begin: the contrast between the individual, mental activity of thought and the external, physical activity of our linguistic and communicative practices.

Vygotsky begins by noting that psychologists typically employ either of two erroneous approaches to the relation of thought and speech. The first treats the relation as one of *identity*. Such a view might hold, for instance, that thought can be conceived as "speech minus sound." Vygotsky dismisses this reductionist stance on the grounds that

> He who runs thought and speech together closes the road to the question of the relation of thought and word and thereby makes the problem insoluble in advance. The problem is not solved, but simply avoided. (1934: 12 [1986: 2–3])

The second misguided strategy treats thought and speech as two logically independent phenomena, representing "the connection between them as a purely external, mechanical dependence between two distinct processes" (1934: 12 [1986: 3]). Here the psychologist attempts to explain the relation between thinking and linguistic behaviour in terms of the interaction of the properties of two independently intelligible components. Vygotsky calls this procedure "analysis into *elements*" and, using an analogy prompted by Marx, he argues that to try thus to explain the relation between thought and speech is like trying to explain why water extinguishes fire in terms of the fire-quenching properties of the substances that compose it: hydrogen and oxygen. Such an attempt obviously fails, since hydrogen burns and oxygen sustains fire (Marx 1865: 206–7).

Vygotsky contrasts "analysis into elements" with an alternative procedure: "analysis into *units*." A "unit" (*edinitsa*) is "a product of analysis which, unlike elements, retains all the basic properties of the whole and which cannot be further divided without losing them" (1934: 15 [1986: 5]). Therefore, in the chemical analogy, the H_2O molecule, and not hydrogen and oxygen considered separately, should be taken as the unit of analysis of water's capacity to extinguish fire. Vygotsky argues that the psychologist must seek the appropriate unit of analysis of psychological phenomena – in this case, of the interrelation of thought and speech.

It might be objected that Vygotsky's recommendations regarding unit analysis, celebrated though they are by his followers, are no more than quasi-scientific speculation. He offers unit analysis as a universal method, but why should such a procedure work in all cases? And how, for example, is the scientist to decide what is to count as the unit? Independently of Vygotsky's functionalism, unit analysis provides no criterion for the determination of the relevant units, and read in the light of that approach it seems to amount only to the platitude that we must not go "below the functional level," deconstructing the system under study to the extent that we can no longer see how its parts contribute to the whole.

However, this objection is unfair.[7] To grasp his idea, we must return to the fallacy committed in analyzing thought and speech "into elements." For Vygotsky, this method fails because it treats thought and speech as two distinct processes in purely "mechanical" interaction. In contrast, Vygotsky argues that the relation between thought and speech is an "*internal*" (*vnutrennyĭ*) relation. This metaphor of "internality" implies we must recognize a *logical* dependence between thought and speech. Their logical dependence is expressed in the fact that the criteria by which we individuate the two faculties are inextricably interwoven. That is, we cannot identify something as an expression of (developed) thought without appeal to considerations about the way in which that thought is made manifest to others, the way it is expressed in behaviour; and conversely, we cannot identify linguistic expressions independently of considerations about what they express, without seeing them as manifestations of thought. It is this logical dependence that inclines us to construe the relation of thought and speech as one of identity; but we do so against a powerful intuition that thought and speech represent two distinct capacities, two quite different processes.[8] The psychologist must be

7   The objection is encouraged by some Soviet discussions of unit analysis. For example, V. P. Zinchenko proposes a list of criteria that any unit must satisfy ("The unit must be a living part of the whole," "the unit . . . must be capable of development, including self-development," etc.), but no reasons are given why these criteria are appropriate. The reader is left to wonder if we are being offered hard principles, presumably grounded in some kind of dialectical logic, or very obscure rules of thumb (see Zinchenko 1985: 97–9).

8   The tension between (a) the temptation to reduce thought to speech and (b) the desire to preserve the autonomy of thought is reflected in the early sections of Wittgenstein (1980): "The word 'thinking' can be used to signify, roughly speaking, a talking for a purpose, i.e., a speaking or writing, a speaking in the imagination, a 'speaking in the head' as it were" (sec. 9). "It isn't true that thinking is a kind of speaking, as I once said (cf. [Wittgenstein's] *Philosophical Notebooks* 12.9.1916). The concept 'thinking' is *categorically* different from the

able to preserve the "reflexive," "internal," "private," and distinctively mental domain of thought, and contrast this with the "external," "public," and communicative nature of the physical expression of speech. In a dialectical mood congenial to Vygotsky's universe of discourse, we might say that the psychologist strives to give sense to a *unity of opposites.*

Thus, to understand the nature of thought and speech, we must analyze their "internal" relation. How may we do so? Since this relation has been described as a "logical" relation, and logical relations are thought to hold exclusively between concepts, it may seem appropriate to analyze the relation a priori, by inspecting the concepts of thought and speech. As we have seen, however, Vygotsky is hostile to conceptual analysis, and here that hostility seems well placed; for the conceptual analysis of thought and speech would require a superior grasp on the two concepts than is available to the psychologist at this stage in the inquiry. It is not that the content of the concepts is simply given, leaving us only to trace the relations between them; the investigation must determine both the scope of the concepts and the nature of their relation. Further, the conceptual analysis of thought and speech implies not only that we can individuate the related concepts successfully, but also that the relation between them always remains constant (or "static"), a claim that Vygotsky would deny.

We presented the logical interdependence of thought and speech as a fact about the criteria of individuation of the two functions. How we feel compelled to individuate their manifestations, however, is itself a fact that requires explanation. For Vygotsky, this explanation must be sought not in purely conceptual space, but by attention to the way in which thought and speech are related in the actual development of the individual. The psychologist turns to the world. The investigation begins with a hypothesis: that the internal relation between thought and speech is a relation of mutual determination. That is, it is only *within* this relation that the two faculties can develop. If we wish to treat them as two *distinct* processes, we may do so not as a prior condition of the relation between them, but as its consequence. *Thought owes its independence to*

concept 'speaking.' But of course thinking is neither an accompaniment of speaking nor of any other process" (sec. 7).

speech and vice versa. Vygotsky holds that to tell the story of the development and mutual determination of the two relata is to give an explanation of their nature. To do this, we must ask what factor explains the very *possibility* of the relation between thought and speech. To grasp this would provide a perspective from which the identity of the two opposites is visible, from which their "unity in diversity" is expressed. This factor is the "unit." It is not invoked as a dialectical recipe for instant explanation, but as a response to the problem of the analysis of internal relations.

In *Thought and Speech*, Vygotsky proposes the notion of *meaning* (*znachenie*) as the unit of analysis of thought and speech. This proposal too is a hypothesis. There is no decision procedure for determining the appropriate unit in advance: The choice is grounded simply in a strong intuition. Meaning is clearly a necessary condition of both thought and speech, in all but their most primitive forms; and it is the power of meaning and representation that transforms primitive mental operations and speech behaviour into human intellectual and communicative activity as we know them. However, the choice of this unit is not backed by any logical guarantee. The selection is vindicated only by the fruitfulness of the genetic explanation in which the proposed unit is to figure.

Vygotsky's discussion of method thus leads inexorably to the "substantive" issue of how the genetic account of the relation of thought and speech in the history of human consciousness is to be constructed. We turn now to Vygotsky's proposals for this account.

The independence thesis

On Vygotsky's genetic account, thought and speech initially exist as independent faculties that, in the course of their development, eventually converge. The concept of meaning (the unit) enters at the point of contact of the two lines of development, for convergence occurs when the child comes to employ speech as an aid in intellectual activity; that is, when he or she begins to exploit the symbolic power of speech to solve problems. Thus, at the point of convergence it becomes possible to think of noises or movements the child makes as actions directed at another person with the aim of influencing

that other's behaviour in virtue of their meaning. This, for Vygotsky, is the crucial moment in ontogenesis, making possible the subsequent mutual determination of the two faculties
and facilitating the development of the other higher mental
functions.

Vygotsky puts his position thus:

(1) In their ontogenetic development, thought and speech
    have different roots.
(2) In the speech development of the child, we can with cer-
    tainty establish a preintellectual stage, and in his thought
    development, a prelinguistic stage.
(3) Up to a certain point in time, the two follow different lines,
    independently of each other.
(4) At a certain point these lines meet, whereupon thought be-
    comes verbal and speech rational. (1986: 83 [1934: 105])

Clauses (1)–(3) form Vygotsky's "independence thesis"; (4)
raises the issue of the convergence of the two hitherto independent lines of development. Before treating the problem of
convergence we must ask what grounds the independence
thesis.

In the independence thesis, by "prelinguistic thought"
Vygotsky means primitive forms of problem-solving activity
that can be described in intentional terms, however crudely,
while by "preintellectual speech" he has in mind any form
of noise making or gesturing directed toward some audience,
however indeterminate, that commonly elicits some response
from that audience, however general in kind. Vygotsky
claims to be able to discern these functions in the earliest
stages of the child's development.

If Vygotsky eschews a priori definitions of psychological
functions, on what does he base these definitions? Some of the
discussion in *Thought and Speech* suggests Vygotsky would appeal to an analogy between human and animal development.
First, we establish the independence thesis in the case of apes.
We can show experimentally that, while chimpanzees possess both primitive intellect and preintellectual "speech" in
the senses defined above, their speech plays no significant
role in intellectual (i.e., problem-solving) activity. Next, we
suggest that the relation between thought and speech in the
early stages of the human child's development is analogous to

the relation between thought and speech in apes. This analogy is deemed to hold on the grounds that the level of development of thought and speech in apes reflects the level of development attained by these functions at a primitive stage of *human* phylogenesis, and that the development of each human individual recapitulates the stages of the phylogenesis of the human species.[9]

However, the second step of this argument begs the question. For Vygotsky, an understanding of the relation between human and animal mental functions should be a *consequence,* not a precondition, of his analysis of thought and speech in humans. That analysis cannot, therefore, commit itself from the outset to the specific analogy between animal and human

9 Vygotsky's view of the relation between phylogenesis and ontogenesis is unclear. While Wertsch denies Vygotsky held that ontogenesis recapitulates phylogenesis, a few pages later he argues that Vygotsky "tried to incorporate results from phylogenetic research into his account of ontogenesis by using findings from [Köhler's] research on higher apes' problem-solving activity. His assumption was that apes' problem-solving activity approximates what elementary mental functioning would be in human ontogenesis if this functioning were not influenced by cultural development" (Wertsch 1985a: 41–5; cf. Scribner 1985: 129–30). I believe that Vygotsky did think that there was an important symmetry between ontogenesis and phylogenesis, between the development of the individual and the development of the human race. However, he denied (against Hall) that the repetition of phylogenesis in ontogenesis was a matter of *biological* inheritance, that the child's development is conditioned by an inherited causal process defined by the course of evolutionary development of the species (Vygotsky 1927b). Rather, the symmetry has to be understood as follows: The crucial achievement in the history of the human species is the development of the ability to use tools in problem-solving activity, and most important, the emergence of language as human beings' most sophisticated tool. The genesis of meaning marks the transformation of *Homo sapiens* from animal to human. Likewise, the point at which the child grasps conceptions of significance and representation is the vital stage in ontogenesis precipitating the child's development into a self-determining subject of knowledge and morality. However, children do not inherit the phylogenetic achievement biologically, but *socially.* It is preserved not in the physical structure of their bodies but in the practices of the community into which they are born. Each child must then make these practices his or her own, must internalize them. The significant *asymmetry* between onto- and phylogenesis is that, whereas the former presupposes a prior community that socializes infants into its form of life, the latter obviously cannot be represented as the appropriation of already existing practices.

intellectual development. Appeal to such an analogy, however, is not the only means to support the independence thesis. It is perhaps more fruitful to see Vygotsky as occupying a standpoint similar to that of the "radical interpreter," who figures so prominently in the philosophy of Quine, Davidson, and their followers.[10] However, the Vygotskian radical interpreter is concerned not only to attribute particular psychological states to speakers as part of a theory of translation designed to render intelligible their activity as a whole. The Vygotskian also has to determine which manifestations of the subject's behaviour are to count as manifestations of the same type. He or she must decide what it is to think of *these* phenomena as deliverances of, say, belief, *these* of memory, and so on. On such a model, accepting the independence thesis is just good radical interpretation. The definitions of prelinguistic thought and preintellectual speech must be seen as hypotheses marking out minimal behavioural criteria for the presence of these primitive functions. These hypotheses, however, are backed by no guarantee: They will ultimately be vindicated only retrospectively, by the contribution they make to a full-blown theory of the higher mental functions.

However, this reconstruction of Vygotsky's argument must not be allowed to obscure his recognition of the continuity between animal and human development, both phylogenetic and ontogenetic. He asserts that

> It is my belief, based upon a dialectical materialist approach to the analysis of human history, that human behaviour differs qualitatively from animal behaviour to the same extent that the adaptability and historical development of humans differ from the adaptability and historical development of animals. The psychological development of humans is part of the gen-

10 The "radical interpreter" (or "radical translator" as Quine has it) is pictured as attempting to develop a theory of translation for a language *from scratch*, based on observations of the behaviour of the community he or she is interpreting. The example reveals that determining what speakers mean requires us simultaneously to determine what they believe, desire, hope, intend, etc. This is taken to hold equally when we seek to understand speakers of our own language. Thus, the device of the radical interpreter provides a fruitful framework in which to consider the grounds on which we attribute psychological states, or the exercise of psychological functions, to human subjects (see, e.g., Quine 1960: chap. 2; Davidson 1985).

eral historical development of our species and must be so understood. (1978: 60)

Since Vygotsky holds that the qualitative leap between animal and human development is a consequence of the developmental horizons opened by the convergence of thought and speech in human beings, he therefore sees strong parallels between the mental life of animals, infants, and "primitive man." Thus, it would not be surprising if he bolstered the independence thesis with the kind of argument we considered and rejected above. But although such arguments, properly understood, may help persuade those already sympathetic to the cause, they will clinch nothing, for their "proper understanding" rests on the Vygotskian theory we are trying to establish.

Internalization and the convergence of thought and speech

Having established the initial independence of thought and speech, Vygotsky turns to their convergence. He writes:

> The most significant moment in the course of intellectual development, which gives birth to the purely human forms of practical and abstract intelligence, occurs when speech and practical activity, two previously independent lines of development, converge. (1978: 24)

Vygotsky claims that the point of contact between thought and speech occurs when speech becomes a *tool* in problem-solving activity; that is, when the child's words or gestures take on a representational character and may therefore be employed to realize desired ends. Thus, Vygotsky's genetic account is obliged to explain the *genesis of meaning*, to say how the child comes to relate to noises and movements as *significant* objects.

Vygotsky proposes the following account. He argues that the symbolic relation between noise or gesture and object or action is set up only in the context of the child's relations with other people. From birth, the child participates in situations in which his or her behaviour is significant for others. The child's movements (or utterances) are attributed meaning by the surrounding adults. However, though the adults treat some of the child's movements as signs, the sign does not enter the situation as something that has meaning for the child: It acquires its significance only in virtue of the function the movement takes on for the adult participants. This function is then said to undergo a process of "internalization" in which the movement (utterance) through which it is realized becomes endowed with meaning *for the child.*

Vygotsky illustrates his position with the example of the development of the child's ability to point:

> We call the internal construction of an external operation *internalization.* A good example of this process may be found in the development of pointing. Initially, this gesture is nothing more than an unsuccessful attempt to grasp something, a movement aimed at a certain object which designates forthcoming activity. The child attempts to grasp an object placed beyond his reach; his hands, stretched toward that object, remain poised in the air. His fingers make grasping movements. At this initial stage pointing is represented by the child's movement, which seems to be pointing to an object – that and nothing more.
>
> When the mother comes to the child's aid and realizes his movement indicates something, the situation changes fundamentally. Pointing becomes a gesture for others. The child's unsuccessful attempt engenders a reaction not from the object but *from another person.* Consequently, the primary meaning of that unsuccessful grasping movement is established by others. Only later, when the child can link his unsuccessful grasping movement to the objective situation as a whole, does he begin to understand this movement as pointing. At this juncture there occurs a change in that movement's function: From an object-oriented movement it becomes a movement aimed at another person, a means of establishing relations. *The grasping movement changes to the act of pointing.* As a result of this change, the movement itself is then physically simplified, and what results is the form of pointing that we may call a true gesture. It becomes a true gesture only after it objectively manifests all the functions of pointing for others and is understood by others as a gesture. Its meaning and function are created first by an objective situation and then by people who surround the child. (1978: 56 [1931a: 143–4])

Thus, in this process of "internalization," an activity of the child that, in a given context, is significant for others, becomes significant for the child. Following Benjamin Lee, we could say that, through internalization, the significance of the child's action becomes part of the cause of the action and not just its effect (Lee 1985: 81). Internalization is therefore the key to understanding the possibility of the convergence of thought and speech, the process in which the representational powers of speech are harnessed to serve as a tool in problem-solving activity.

Vygotsky argues that internalization must be seen as "a long series of developmental events" in which "an operation that initially represents an external activity is reconstructed and begins to occur internally" (1978: 56–7). This internal reconstruction of external activity represents the process in which all the higher mental functions come into being. Thus, he argues, it is through participation in, and internalization of, social forms of activity that the child's mind is *created:*

> Every function in the child's cultural development appears twice: first on the social level, and later, on the individual level; first *between* people (*interpsychological*), and then *inside* the child (*intrapsychological*). This applies equally to all voluntary attention, to logical memory, and to the formation of concepts. All the higher mental functions originate as actual relations between human individuals. (1978: 57 [1931a: 145])

Hence, for Vygotsky, neither particular higher mental functions nor the system of higher mental functions conceived as a whole (i.e., consciousness) develop through their own immanent logic. Rather, the development of consciousness is constantly mediated and transformed by the evolving relations between the child and the social environment. On Vygotsky's position, the child's interaction with this environment, his or her gradual inauguration into social practices, is conceived not simply as the origin of particular beliefs, desires, hopes, intentions, and so on, but as the source of the child's very *capacity* to believe, to desire, and so on. In Leontiev's words:

> Consciousness is not given from the beginning and is not produced by nature: consciousness is a product of society: it is *produced* . . . Thus the process of internalization is not the *trans-*

ferral of an external activity to a pre-existing, internal "plane of consciousness": it is the process in which this internal plane is *formed.* (Leontiev 1981: 56–7)

Thus, for a Vygotskian, the process in which the child is forced to appropriate the practices of the community is not one that limits or constrains individuality. On the contrary, it is the process in which the child becomes a self-determining, thinking subject. For Vygotsky, socialization represents the process of the *social genesis of the individual.*

Vygotsky's theory of internalization raises many important questions. For example, what is it for an "external," social activity to "occur internally"? When Vygotsky says that the child in his example "internalizes" the action of pointing, does he mean only that the child has learned the meaning of his gesture, that he has acquired the concept of pointing, or does Vygotsky also mean that the child is now able to conduct a kind of "inner pointing," to, as it were, point in thought? In the light of the crucial role of internalization in Vygotsky's theory, it is surprising that such questions have been little explored by his followers. I shall restrict myself here to defending Vygotsky from one inviting objection to his position.

The objection is as follows: In his example about pointing, Vygotsky seems to imply that, at some stage in the process he describes, the child realizes that his (or her) grasping movement represents his wants to the adults around him. It is this "realization" that constitutes the acquisition of the concept of pointing: The child has internalized a primitive language rule (e.g., "When you want *x*, point to *x*"). However, something important is missing in this account. We lack an explanation of how the child is able to "link his unsuccessful grasping movement to the objective situation as a whole" (Vygotsky 1978: 56). That is, Vygotsky does not explain how a purely material movement suddenly becomes endowed with significance for the child. This inadequacy in Vygotsky's theory derives from the fact that he offers an entirely external, or third-person, account of internalization. Such an account, the objection continues, inevitably neglects the real issue, for how the child is able to see his own actions as meaningful must surely be expressed in the relation between the child and the contents of his mind. It must be some event in the child's mental world that constitutes the genesis of meaning, and such an event cannot be described from Vygotsky's third-person perspective.

This objection makes two related, misguided assumptions. First, it implies that any satisfactory account of internalization must make sense of what the process is like from the point of view of the child. However, although we can certainly tell a first-person story about "what it is like" for a subject who already possesses a language to acquire new concepts, such a first-person account could never be appropriate in a theory of the child's acquisition of his or her first concepts. We have no idea how to imagine what it is like to develop the ability to imagine, to think about what it is like to come to be able to think, to hope, to want, to believe. And we have no such idea not through lack of imagination, but because there is no idea to have. There is no first-person perspective on the acquisition of those abilities for, prior to their acquisition, the child has no perspective. Thus, the qualitative leap from a stage of primitive problem-solving activity to fully developed consciousness mediated by language cannot be retrospectively bridged by an act of imagination.[11]

The objection's second faulty assumption is that meaning must be analyzed as a special relation between the subject (the child) and the contents of his or her mental world. On this view, some fact about the subject's mind determines what he or she means. Therefore, facts about meaning are distinctively subjective facts, to be grasped only from a subjective point of view. Accordingly, if we seek to explain the inauguration of this relation, we are required to capture the relevant subjective facts; we must "look into the child's mind" where the difference made by successful internalization will be decisively

11 Vygotsky explicitly denies that psychology must always seek a "first-person" understanding of psychological facts. In an interesting discussion of the vision of ants, he denies that when we seek to explain the nature of a form of experience, we must capture *what it is like* to undergo such experience: "[W]e can study how the ant sees, and even how it sees things which are invisible to us, without knowing how these things seem to the ant, i.e., we can establish psychological facts without in any way proceeding from internal experience or, in other words, from the subjective. Even Engels, it seems, does not consider this fact significant for science: he who worries about this, he says, is beyond help" (Vygotsky 1927a: 314n; cf. Engels 1873–83: 239–40).

marked. A good example of such a position is classical empiricism, which holds that words or signs have meaning as the names of *ideas*. Ideas are conceived as private mental entities, which are like pictures of objects. They represent the world to the subject, who refers to objects in the world *via* ideas. On this picture, concept acquisition occurs when the child comes to associate a certain sign with a certain idea: The child comes to name his or her sensations. But, as Wittgenstein (1953) has shown, such a conception is fraught with difficulties. If an idea is treated as a mental "picture," it will require *interpretation* if the child is to set up the correct association between sign and idea. Such interpretation, however, requires powers of abstraction and memory, conceptions of relevance and similarity, that cannot rightly be assigned to a child learning a *first* language. These are powers, both Vygotsky and Wittgenstein would argue, possessed only by creatures that already have a language. It will not help the empiricist to argue that some *other* idea in the child's mind determines how the first is to be interpreted, for this starts a vicious regress: The interpreting idea will itself require interpretation. It thus seems that the empiricist's only option is to hold that the ideas before the child's mind require no interpretation because they are *intrinsically representational* mental objects. But this is a council of despair, for at best the invocation of such objects is just a metaphysically laden way of saying that interpretation must end *somewhere*, and at worst it is the incantation of the very philosophical prejudice Vygotsky is challenging: that meaning can only be understood as a special property of mental objects.

Internalization and the critique of Piaget

So far, we have defended internalization as a theory of concept acquisition following Vygotsky's claim that "the most important type of internalization" is where children "master the rules in accordance with which external signs must be used" (1931a: 184–5). However, there is a second, related way in which internalization figures in his work, and it emerges in his critique of Piaget's notion of "egocentric speech" (1934: 23–79 [1986: 12–57]).

Egocentric speech is the chatter with which children between the ages of about 3 and 7 accompany their actions. According to Piaget, such speech is a manifestation of the child's "autistic thought"; that is, the child inhabits a dreamlike reality of its own construction that he or she describes in a constant babble of self-directed discourse, intelligible ultimately only to the child. Piaget argues that, as the child engages in increasingly more social forms of communication, egocentric speech diminishes and eventually disappears, "driven out" by the dominant social modes of discourse.

Against Piaget, Vygotsky contends that the origin of egocentric speech lies not in autistic thought but in social speech itself. For Vygotsky, egocentric speech represents a stage in the child's assimilation of social speech. This claim, he argues, is supported by two considerations. First, Vygotsky shows experimentally that egocentric speech lessens when the child is alone, suggesting that egocentric speech is social in form: It is, at least in part, directed toward an audience. Second, the fact that children accomplish tasks less successfully when forced to do them silently reveals that egocentric speech fulfills the same function Vygotsky attributes to the early forms of social speech proper: It facilitates problem-solving activity. Egocentric speech, however, does not contribute to problem solving in the same way as developed social speech. In egocentric speech the child does not seek to communicate anything specific to an audience (like, say, an appeal for help). Neither is the child "talking to himself" or "reasoning with herself" about the problem to be solved. Rather, in egocentric speech children "talk themselves through" their actions, their speech figuring as part of the object or the activity in question. However, despite this difference in role, Vygotsky maintains that egocentric speech remains an embryonic form of social speech.

Vygotsky also contests Piaget's conception of the fate of egocentric speech. While Piaget holds that egocentric speech is eventually annihilated by social forms of discourse, Vygotsky argues that its disappearance is only a disappearance from view. Egocentric speech, Vygotsky maintains, is in fact the "genetic root" of *inner speech,* the subject's capacity to conduct a silent dialogue with him- or herself. Thus, for Vygotsky, egocentric speech is not simply destroyed. Rather, it is internalized and transformed into a new psychological function: inner speech. Thus, where for Piaget the explanation

proceeds from the individual to the social (autistic thought →
egocentric speech → social speech), for Vygotsky it proceeds
from the social to the individual (social speech → egocentric
speech → inner speech).

Vygotsky's discussion of the origins of inner speech thus
introduces a second conception of internalization. Here internalization is represented not as the assimilation of specific linguistic rules but of overt speech patterns. The defence of this
conception of internalization will depend on the success of experiments exploring the supposed transition from egocentric
to inner speech.[12] It will also rest on the intelligibility of Vygotsky's conception of inner speech itself.

12 Vygotsky's inventive use of experiment is an important aspect of his
work neglected in my presentation. Vygotsky rarely employs the
kinds of tools associated with orthodox experimental psychology:
control groups, standardized testing procedures, explicit "coding
schemes" for the interpretation of data, and so on. His empirical research might therefore strike the modern reader as wanting in
rigour and objectivity. It would be a mistake, however, to assume that
Vygotsky's efforts represent a failed attempt to do experimental psychology as it is now understood. On the contrary, his research strategies were quite deliberately created for the analysis of psychological
phenomena as he conceived them. As we saw above, Vygotsky holds
that psychological capacities can be understood only through an
analysis of their *development*. This development is argued to proceed
through the internalization of activities that are first realized in
public interaction with others. This led Vygotsky to the idea that
psychological development can sometimes best be studied if the anal-
ist actively intervenes in that development by, for example, offering
subjects new psychological tools with which to undertake operations
under investigation (see the memory experiments described in Vygotsky [1929]; Bakhurst [1990]), or engaging subjects in activities
thought to precipitate internalization, so as to observe the relationship among (a) what subjects can achieve unaided, (b) what they can
achieve when assisted by others, and (c) the trajectory of their subsequent development (see Vygotsky [1978: chap. 6] and the literature
on the "zone of proximal development," e.g., Rogoff and Wertsch
[1984]). Furthermore, Vygotsky believed that the insights gained by
employing such interventive techniques are often best presented by
describing particular cases in detail, rather than giving statistical
data for a large sample of subjects. Finally, his sensitivity to the
theory-ladenness of all experimental inquiry led him to make no
formal distinction in his writings between theoretical and empirical research. His manuscripts therefore read as sustained arguments
for a particular theory of mind illustrated to a greater or lesser extent by reference to experimental research. In this, however, he frequently spins the web of theory and experiment so tightly that readers must remind themselves that he is not referring to compelling

Inner speech and thought

Vygotsky's discussion of inner speech in the final chapter of *Thought and Speech,* dictated on his deathbed, is one of the most interesting, though least conclusive, aspects of his contribution (1934: 295–361 [1986: 210–56]). Vygotsky insists that inner speech cannot be conceived wholly on the model of vocal speech. Inner speech represents a mental function with its own specific nature.

> Inner speech is not the interior aspect of external speech – it is a function in itself. It still remains speech, i.e., thought connected with words. But while external thought is embodied in words, in inner speech words die as they bring forth thought. Inner speech is to a large extent thinking in pure meanings ["senses" would be a more consistent translation – D. B.]. It is a dynamic, shifting, unstable thing, fluttering between word and thought, the two more or less stable, more or less firmly delineated components of verbal thought. (1986: 249; slightly abbreviated in [1934: 353] translation)

However, Vygotsky argues that although inner speech is irreducible to external speech, it should by no means be seen as irretrievably buried in the private cognitive world of the subject, accessible to the psychologist only through introspection. On the contrary, Vygotsky holds that inner speech is not an essentially private phenomenon. First, inner speech has its origins in a public form of speech – egocentric speech. Second, as a transformed and reconstructed form of social speech, inner speech is itself capable of public expression. Vygotsky contends that inner speech is made manifest in certain forms of discourse, especially in art and poetry. The psychologist is thus able to analyze the specific structure of inner speech by attention to both its public source and its public expression.

Vygotsky's account of the structure of inner speech is confined to some remarks about its special syntactic and semantic features. Drawing on the work of the Soviet formalist Yakubinsky (1923), Vygotsky argues that the *syntactic* peculiarity of

Footnote 12 (*cont.*)
> *thought*-experiments, but to actual empirical findings. (For more detail of the experimental grounds for Vygotsky's rejection of Piaget, see Wertsch [1985a: 116–21].)

inner speech is its "predicalization" (*predikativnost'*); that is, since the "speaker" supposedly knows what he (or she) is "talking" about, he "tends to leave out the subject and all words connected with it, condensing his speech more and more until only predicates are left." Thus Vygotsky concludes that "predication is the natural form of inner speech; psychologically, it consists of predicates only" (1986: 243 [1934: 344]). The *semantic* peculiarity of inner speech is that it is thought "in pure senses." To clarify this idea he draws on Paulhan's distinction between sense and meaning (see Vygotsky 1934: 346ff.[1986: 244ff.]). This distinction treats the "meaning" of a word as its dictionary-style definition, whereas its "sense" is the sum of psychological events aroused in consciousness by the word (see Wertsch 1985a: 95). While the former is said always to remain relatively constant, the latter is in continual flux. This shifting sphere of sense is invoked to account, first, for the richness of the "sentences" of inner speech, which are said to be formed from the juxtaposition and amalgamation of "images," and second, for the unique, subjective character of the inner speech of each individual, a subjectivity that makes expressions of the inner speech of others so difficult to understand.

Vygotsky's remarks on the structure of inner speech are no more than suggestions for a theory he did not live to develop. However, his concern that such a theory should be constructed is itself revealing. Vygotsky, who was much influenced by Russian literary theory, never lost his early interest in the language of art (see Vygotsky 1925b [1971]). In his account of the semantics of inner speech we see him struggling to develop a theoretical framework that would explain the capacity of the artist (and particularly the poet) to convey a rich semantic content with few linguistic components. While analytic philosophers may deride the primitive distinction between sense and meaning on which his account rests, Vygotsky, in turn, would have scorned the analytic philosopher's propensity to tie the primary meaning of expressions to rigid "assertibility" or "truth" conditions and to consign issues of "imagery" and "metaphor" to the outer regions of the theory of meaning. For Vygotsky, such issues are central to our understanding of the nature and possibility of the most basic utterances of inner speech.

Behind the plane of verbal thought lies a level further inward than inner speech: the realm of pure thought itself. According to Vygotsky, "the flow of thought is not accompanied by the simultaneous unfolding of speech" (1934: 354 [1986: 249]). Such pure thought is not identical to any particular form of its expression; indeed, it may strongly resist verbal formulation. Thought plays the role of the shifting background of the subject's mental world against which any particular component – belief, desire, intention – is given sense, and against which alone the subject's utterances can have meaning. This background must be seen not so much as a passive representation of reality, a way of *seeing* the world, but as a motivational structure, a way of *being* in the world. Vygotsky writes that

> Every sentence that we say in real life has some kind of subtext, a thought hidden behind it ... Every thought creates a connection, fulfils a function, solves a problem ... Thought is not begotten by thought; it is engendered by motivation, i.e., by our desires and needs, our interests and emotions. [Therefore] behind every thought there is an affective-volitional tendency, which holds the answer to the last "why" in the analysis of thinking. (1986: 250–2 [constructed from 1934: 353–4, 355, 357])

Conclusion

With this last "why," we come to the end of our exposition of Vygotsky's position. We have followed his thought from his critique of the prevailing climate to his recommendations for a theory of consciousness based on the idea that the higher mental functions stand in interfunctional relations of mutual determination. On the way, we have met several important ideas: unit analysis, genetic explanation, internalization, and inner speech. I have tried to show how these notions are related in a unifying theoretical vision.

To conclude, I want to pick out two aspects of Vygotsky's thought that made a special contribution to Soviet intellectual culture, helping to create the universe of discourse in which Ilyenkov and his contemporaries worked. The first is Vygotsky's use of Marxism. While it is now widely recognized that Vygotsky's expressed commitment to creating a "Marxist psychology" was genuine, we still await an adequate analysis of Vygotsky's debt to Marx. Commentators are usually content merely to draw parallels between the two thinkers. Benjamin Lee, for example, argues that "Vygotsky's solution at the psychological level was like Marx's at the social level" (Lee 1985: 68). He points out that both Marx and Vygotsky held "an interactionist viewpoint of the relation between consciousness and activity" (67); both explored the interfunctional relations within their respective objects of inquiry (68–70); and both held that the principles that govern the development of those objects are irreducible to natural (i.e., biological) laws (74). However, while such parallels are many and incontrovertible, their existence does not so much solve the problem as pose it more sharply. To understand the relation between Vygotsky and Marx we need to do more than state the parallels between them: We must explain them.

As Lee suggests in a later article, a plausible conjecture is that the similarities between Marx's and Vygotsky's theories derive from the latter's conscious attempt to apply to the problems of psychology the dialectical method Marx had developed for the study of capitalism (Lee 1987: 88, 95–6). Vygotsky writes:

> I want to find out how science has to be built, to approach the study of the mind having learned the whole of Marx's method . . . In order to create such an enabling theory-method in the generally accepted scientific manner, it is necessary to discover the essence of the given area of phenomena, the laws according to which they change, their qualitative and quantitative characteristics, their causes. It is necessary to formulate the categories and concepts that are specifically relevant to them – in other words to create one's own *Capital*. (Vygotsky 1978: 8)

Vygotsky's debt to Marx's method is most conspicuous in his ideas about explanation. For example, not only is his attempt to give a genetic explanation of the mind modelled on Marx's historical account of the development of capitalism, but his very suggestion that genetic explanation must proceed via the investigation of an appropriate "unit" of analysis is based di-

rectly on Marx's identification of the commodity as the starting point of his theoretical reconstruction of capitalism (see
Chapter 5). It thus seems plausible that the parallels between
Marx and Vygotsky are to be explained by their use of the
same method.

However, if such an explanation is to succeed, we need to
understand both the nature of Marx's dialectical method, and
why it was appropriate for Vygotsky to apply that method,
forged for the analysis of political economy, to the problems
of *psychology*. The discussion of dialectics in Chapter 2 suggests that, at the time Vygotsky was writing, Soviet thinkers
would have been divided on such issues. The Deborinites, for
example, would have argued that, since all phenomena are
ultimately governed by the same universal, dialectical laws
of development, Marx's successful analysis of the development of capitalism reveals principles of explanation that can
be generalized and applied in any domain. On this view, Vygotsky can be seen as abstracting such general principles
from Marx's work and applying them directly to psychology.
The parallels between the two thinkers' results would then be
said to follow from the fact that all phenomena, natural, social, and psychological, are ultimately governed by these
same principles. However, some Mechanists, like Lyubov Akselrod, argued against the Deborinites that dialectical method
cannot be formulated as a set of universal principles, but must
be seen as a technique for following the specific nature, or
"logic," of the object of inquiry. As such, the dialectical method is said to be "indissolubly tied to concrete content," its application guided wholly by the particular contours of the object of inquiry (Akselrod 1927b: 149). On such a view, what
Vygotsky learned from Marx cannot be reduced to a codifiable procedure, but must be seen as something analogous to a
skill or craft. On this understanding of dialectical method, as
on the first, parallels between results obtained from the method's application in different domains are explained in terms
of the similar structure of the different objects of investigation.
However, on the second view, this structural similarity is not,
as the Deborinites supposed, something intelligible independently of the method's application; it is something the dialectical method *reveals*.

Vygotsky's idea that the search for method is intrinsically linked with the analysis of the object itself and involves formulating concepts "specifically relevant" to the nature of that object, suggests that he would have endorsed Akselrod's conception of dialectical method rather than the "objective dialectics" of the Deborinites (Vygotsky 1978: 8). Indeed, Vygotsky's shrewd diagnosis of the vacuousness that besets conceptual frameworks when they aspire to global explanatory power is reason to believe that he would have held the Deborinites use of dialectics in contempt (see Vygotsky 1927a, and the opening of this chapter). It thus seems that what Vygotsky appropriated from Marx is best represented as a method, conceived on the model of a skill or technique for following the specific nature of the object of inquiry.

This conclusion is, however, only as intelligible as the conception of dialectical method it invokes. At first sight, this conception seems obscure. Is it really possible to represent a method, which Soviet philosophers claim to be *scientific*, as a skill that resists codification and cannot be understood independently of its application to some specific domain? This is a question that subsequent developments in Soviet philosophy have helped to answer. In Chapter 5, we shall explore Ilyenkov's attempt to give real theoretical content to dialectical method, construed as a means to follow the particular logic of any object.

A second feature of Vygotsky's contribution that raises issues of direct concern to contemporary Soviet philosophers is his view that a Marxist psychology must conceive of consciousness as a "social product," created in each individual through his or her socialization into the practices of the community. Interestingly, James Wertsch (echoing complaints made by some of Vygotsky's Soviet contemporaries) has recently claimed to discern a tension between this conception and some of Vygotsky's remarks on the relation of "natural" and "social" lines of development. According to Wertsch, Vygotsky's "theoretical statements" commit him to an "emergent interactionism" where development is a "fusion" of natural and social forces that "coincide and mingle with one another" (see Wertsch 1985a: 43–7; cf. Vygotsky 1960: 47). However, despite this supposed commitment, Vygotsky offers no analysis of the natural influences on mental development, focusing

> almost exclusively on the way in which cultural forces trans-
> form the natural line of development. That is, he tended to
> view the natural line as providing "raw materials" that are
> then transformed by cultural forces. He said virtually nothing
> about how changes in the natural line of development might
> affect cultural forces ... [The result is] an explanatory system
> in which principles from the natural line in reality play no
> role. (Wertsch 1985a: 43, 46)

In contrast to Wertsch, Ilyenkov would have argued that Vygotsky's "extreme emphasis on social development" was the great strength of his theory rather than its weakness (Wertsch 1985a: 46). Ilyenkov believed that, although the proper development of the "natural line" is a necessary condition for socialization to take place, we cannot think of the mental life of the child as a product of the interaction of two "equal" factors, the natural and the social. Socialization represents the transformation of the natural by the social, its "negation," the outcome of which is a social being, a *person* (*lichnost'*), who inhabits a qualitatively different environment and is subject to qualitatively different influences than the infant or the animal.

Not all Soviet philosophers and psychologists share Ilyenkov's optimism that Vygotsky's theory, thus understood, is the best way to construe Marx's famous thesis that the essence of man "is the ensemble of social relations" (Marx 1845: 29). Indeed, many hold that so radical an understanding of the social origins of consciousness is counterintuitive, entailing absurdly that the mind is created by social forces as if "out of nothing," or that physical factors have no influence on mental development. In Chapter 7, we shall examine how Ilyenkov defends his very strong interpretation of Vygotsky's idea of "the social genesis of the individual" against such criticisms.

Our discussion of Ilyenkov thus promises to illuminate both Vygotsky's Marxist method and his social theory of the mind. However, before we turn to Ilyenkov himself, we must consider the third, and perhaps most formative, influence on his work: Lenin's contribution to philosophy.

4

LENIN AND THE LENINIST STAGE
IN SOVIET PHILOSOPHY

No account of what Ilyenkov inherited from the history of Soviet philosophy would be complete without a discussion of Lenin. Ilyenkov revered Lenin's work as a model of philosophical excellence, admiring especially his conviction that certain philosophical disputes were of such political significance that revolutionaries could not help but enter the philosophical arena. Indeed, Ilyenkov believed that the disputes in which Lenin himself had participated were by no means dead, but remained of considerable relevance to both philosophy and politics, and he thought of himself as taking up Lenin's cause (see Ilyenkov 1980: esp. 6–22).

In this chapter, I aim to appraise Lenin's approach to philosophy critically and to explore its place in Soviet philosophical culture, examining in particular its significance for Ilyenkov. Although Lenin's major philosophical works, *Materialism and Empiriocriticism* and the *Philosophical Notebooks,* were written before the 1917 Revolution, an important part of Lenin's role in the Soviet philosophical tradition was not formed until the 1930s, when the Bolshevizers – Stalin's new philosophical leadership – introduced the notion of a "Leninist stage in Soviet philosophy." The idea that Marxist philosophy had entered this new stage remained a prominent theme throughout the

Stalin era. As Ilyenkov was educated in this period, it is inviting to contrast the idea of the Leninist stage with Lenin's actual contribution, especially since Ilyenkov himself rebelled
against the Stalinist orthodoxy by championing a position he
thought authentically Leninist. I therefore begin this chapter
by examining Lenin's place in the philosophy of the 1930s.
I then turn to Lenin's philosophy itself to see what Ilyenkov
might have found there. I hope to show that Lenin's legacy is
double-edged: Although Lenin's philosophy helped Ilyenkov
to define his project, it contributed in like measure to the formation of Ilyenkov's opponents.

The Leninist stage in Soviet philosophy

The suggestion that Lenin's work had precipitated a new stage
in Soviet philosophy is present as early as the Bolshevizers'
first manifesto, the *stat'ya trëkh*. Here Mitin, Ral'tsevich, and
Yudin cite Lenin's contribution to materialist dialectics as her-
alding a new era in Marxist thought:

> It was precisely Lenin who offered the richest and most com-
> plete understanding of the Marxist dialectic. Lenin's work on
> the theory of dialectic is an exceptionally vivid page in the de-
> velopment of Marxist philosophy. The theory of dialectic is
> elevated to unprecedented heights and, at the same time, the
> problem of how to understand it *concretely* unfolds. Lenin's
> work contains the very richest material for the criticism of
> mechanistic revisions of the dialectic and, at the same time, is
> an excellent model of merciless criticism of the scholastic,
> formalistic ruination of the dialectic, which transforms it into
> a collection of empty phrases and statements conjuring them-
> selves up out of thin air. (1930: 4)

The Bolshevizers' call for Soviet philosophers to recognize this
new stage was a central theme in their case against the Deborinites, who were said to have so "undervalued Lenin as a philosopher" that they had failed to recognize the new epoch in
Marxist philosophy he had initiated (see Chapter 2). Notwithstanding the weakness of this argument, the Central Committee itself endorsed the Bolshevizers' stance in its resolution of
25 January 1931 and demanded a thorough "working out (*razrabotka*) of the Leninist stage in the development of dialectical

materialism" (O zhurnale "Pod znamenem marksizma" 1930: 1–2). This "*razrabotka*" soon became the obsession of the new philosophical leadership.

Yet, despite the excitement about the new era he had supposedly introduced, insightful analyses of Lenin's philosophy are rare in the literature of this period. Rather, the level of discussion is typified by Mitin's schematic account in his "Results of a Philosophical Discussion" (1930). Here, Lenin's achievement in philosophy, as in political theory, is said to consist in the extension of Marxist methods to circumstances unencountered by Marx and Engels. Just as Lenin's theory of imperialism accounts for the crises in a new era of capitalism, so his theory of knowledge generalizes the results achieved by the natural sciences since Engels's time, explaining the "deep crisis" of the new physics from the standpoint of materialist dialectics. In addition, Lenin's contribution is deemed novel for its criticisms of recent revisionist and anti-Marxist philosophy, for introducing the notion of *partiĭnost'* into Marxist philosophy, and for deepening our understanding of the Marxist theory of cognition as materialist dialectics, enabling a better grasp on the relation between Marx and Hegel.[1]

Given his grand claims about the brilliance of Lenin's philosophy, the poverty of Mitin's analysis is puzzling. For example, he gives no reason why Lenin's materialism is as innovative as, say, his theory of imperialism. Yet such reasons are needed, for the mere extension of Marxist theory to cover a period that Marx and Engels themselves did not see is, in itself, scarcely enough to justify talk of a new stage in Marxist thought. Odder still, Mitin does not succeed in isolating aspects of Lenin's contribution neglected by the Deborinites. For them, Mitin's "analysis" would be a collection of truisms (see Yakhot 1981: 210–17).

The Bolshevizers' failure to substantiate their claims suggests that their preoccupation with the Leninist stage was mo-

---

1 Paradoxically, the Bolshevizers rarely appealed to the familiar argument that Lenin's great contribution was the transformation of Marxist theory into revolutionary practice (a contribution worthy, in an obvious sense, of talk of a "new stage"). Since this argument was popular among the Deborinites, the Bolshevizers were forced to dispute it, implausibly claiming that it cast Lenin purely as a practician and undervalued his contribution to theory.

tivated by reasons other than scholarship. A clue lies in the quotation that introduced this section. This passage is more than a simple eulogy: It contains a direct appeal to Lenin to justify the party's current ideological line, "the battle on two fronts in philosophy" (see Chapter 2). It could be suggested that the real motivation for talk of a "Leninist stage" was to establish Lenin as a special authority to which the party could appeal to justify its policies. The message was that, since only Lenin had been able to develop Marxism in Russia creatively, only those who followed the "Leninist path" could lead the Soviet Union to a successful future, and only the party was taking that path. This suggestion has been persuasively developed by Yakhot, who offers a yet more elaborate account of the Bolshevizers' motivation (1981: 196–220). For him, the true focus of the Leninist stage was not Lenin, but Stalin. Yakhot argues that the strategy of presenting Lenin as the ultimate authority was camouflage for the rapidly developing cult of personality. With the Leninist stage came the idea that Stalin, "Lenin's best pupil," "the greatest Leninist of our epoch," was uniquely able to interpret and employ Lenin's wisdom (Mitin 1931: 51, 1932: 14). The greater Lenin's authority, the more fortunate it was that Stalin was "Lenin today":

> We will fulfil our tasks more successfully the better we learn the uniquely correct interpretation of Leninism which Comrade Stalin has given us and which he develops as a living, many-sided, and creative teaching, in unbreakable connection with the tasks of the proletariat in our especially revolutionary age. (Kammari and Yudin 1932: 117)

Indeed, the Bolshevizers soon lost even a formal interest in the analysis of Lenin's contribution in favour of hysterical testimonies to Stalin's genius:

> There is no doubt that our party, smashing counterrevolutionary Trotskyism, smashing right opportunism, breaking the Mechanists and Menshevizing Idealists, will be able to guarantee the further development of theoretical work so that it can be equal to those great tasks that stand before the proletariat. This is guaranteed because at the head of our party stands an outstanding dialectician, the leader of our party, Comrade Stalin. (Yudin 1932: 127)

And precisely because Stalin gives us an example of such an effective understanding and application of Marxism, he also gives us an example of the further theoretical elaboration of the questions of materialist dialectics. In fact, one only has to remember Stalin's work on the question of agricultural teams, on the subjective and the objective factors in historical development, on the categories of possibility and actuality, his criticism of the theory of equilibrium . . . , for it to become clear just what kind of theoretical development of materialist dialectics he gives us. (Mitin 1931: 51)

Thus the rhetoric of the "Leninist stage" is interesting not only for what it reveals about Lenin, but also for the light it casts on Soviet philosophy under Stalin. The philosophy of the Leninist stage is, in fact, the philosophy of the Stalin era.[2]

What, apart from its infatuation with Stalin, characterizes Soviet philosophy under the banner of the Leninist stage? The most striking feature is its codification in a primitive and stylized form. The Bolshevizers had long lamented the absence of a textbook on Marxism–Leninism suitable for mass consumption. In 1938, their pleas were answered by the publication of the *History of the Communist Party of the Soviet Union (Short Course)*, which contained in its fourth chapter an account of Marxist philosophy supposedly composed by Stalin himself

2 Yakhot argues that, despite the apparent focus on Lenin, it was Stalin that commanded the philosophy syllabuses: "Lenin hardly figures in the prospectus for dialectical materialism published in 1937 [see Proekt (1937)]. Stalin dominates. In the recommended literature for a number of themes there is not one of Lenin's works; students are recommended only Stalin . . . and Beria [the then–Minister of State Security]. A joint collection of Lenin's and Stalin's works figures in two places, but not Lenin alone. The mask is finally thrown aside. The destruction of Lenin is demonstrated. The philosophical programme published in *Bolshevik* concludes with a separate theme: 'Comrade Stalin's development of materialist dialectics.' But no Lenin." (Yakhot 1981: 208). This is certainly an overstatement. If we consider the fuller prospectus published in *Pod znamenem marksizma*, we see that of the 182 hours of the projected course, only 30 are devoted to the "Leninist–Stalinist stage in the development of Marxist philosophy," and of those, only 12 include reference to Stalin (including the conclusion Yakhot mentions). Lenin is the focus of the other 18. It is true that Beria is cited, but only once. Nevertheless, although Stalin may not have dominated the official curriculum, interviews with philosophers who studied in Moscow during this period suggest that philosophy students were indeed frequently required to expound and interpret Stalin's works.

(*History* 1938: 105–31). This article was immediately treated not as a schematic and popularized introduction to a complex and problematic discipline, but as the definitive work on the subject, the pinnacle of human reasoning. As such, it came to define the parameters of all Soviet philosophical discussion.

The "Fourth Chapter" begins with a characterization of dialectical materialism as "the world-outlook of the Marxist–Leninist party" (*History* 1938: 105). *Dialectics* is contrasted with *metaphysics*. While the latter is said to represent reality as an accidental agglomeration of immobile entities that change only gradually and quantitatively, dialectics treats the world as a system of interconnected phenomena in constant motion and development. This development occurs through internal contradictions within phenomena and, after periods of gradual change, issues in their abrupt qualitative transformation. *Materialism* is contrasted with *idealism*. Where the latter asserts that only our ideas really exist, that reality is the embodiment of some "absolute idea," and that a mind-independent world is unknowable, materialism holds that the world is matter in motion in accordance with natural laws, that the world is an objective reality existing independently of our minds, that matter is primary to consciousness, and that the world is fully cognizable.

Historical materialism is presented as the principles of dialectical materialism applied to social life. The "Fourth Chapter" argues that from dialectics it follows that:

(a) every social system must be evaluated, not from some "timeless" perspective, but from the standpoint of the real conditions that gave rise to that system;
(b) there are no immutable social systems;
(c) revolutions and the class struggle are "natural" phenomena.

From materialism it is said to follow that the development of society is governed by laws with the status of objective truths; therefore, an exact science of society is possible. Materialism further entails that material life is primary, and spiritual (*dukhovnoĭ*) life secondary. (Though it does not follow that ideas are inert: They can facilitate or retard social development.) According to Stalin, to say that the "conditions of material life of society" are primary means that the determining influence on historical development is the mode of production. The mode of production can be distilled into, on the one hand, the *forces of production* and, on the other, the *relations of production*. Stalin offers a basic functionalist account of their relation: Changes in the forces of production require changes in the relations of production. He concludes that the historical development of productive forces has so far issued in five types of society: primitive communal, slave, feudal, capitalist, and socialist.

A salient feature of the "Fourth Chapter" is its crude picture of the relation between dialectical and historical materialism (114–16). The dialectical relationships supposedly discerned in nature are, without argument, carried over to social life in an attempt to give cosmic legitimation to the Marxist theory of social development. For example:

> If the connection between the phenomena of nature and their interdependence are laws of the development of nature, it follows, too, that the connection and interdependence of the phenomena of social life are laws of the development of society, and not something accidental. (114)

This indifference to argument on so controversial an issue distinguishes the "Fourth Chapter" from Soviet philosophical writing both before and after Stalin. One must not, for instance, underestimate the degree to which it represents a departure from Lenin's approach, which, though dogmatic, sustains its polemical energy through openness to argument. Lenin strove to provide a rational foundation for science and to oppose wild metaphysical conclusions drawn in the wake of a scientific revolution; Stalin, in contrast, was simply "stating the facts."

With talk of the Leninist stage at its height, works of philosophy were composed not so much of arguments as of illustrations of "dialectical thinking" drawn from Stalin's writings and speeches. It is this, above all, which lends "bolshevized" Soviet philosophy its terrifying unreality. An excellent example is Mitin's argument that Stalin's analysis of different kinds of "internal contradictions" has deepened materialist dialectics. The basis for Mitin's claim is Stalin's distinction between

(a) class struggle before the formation of the collective farms
    (between kulaks who own the means of production and
    the agricultural workers who produce), and
(b) class struggle within the collective farms (between those
    who, still dogged by individualist and kulak mentality,
    seek to use inequalities to their own advantage, and those
    who wish to eliminate these inequalities).

For Mitin, this mundane distinction shows

> how Comrade Stalin reveals a *qualitative* difference between
> class struggle in the countryside before the collective farms
> and elements of the class struggle within the collective farms.
> Only by perfectly possessing the method of materialist dialec-
> tics, the method of genuinely concrete analysis of complex,
> concrete reality, only with the ability to apply the most im-
> portant laws of materialist dialectics in a Leninist way – the
> laws of quality, quantity, measure, the law of the unity of op-
> posites – can he give such a clear analysis of the special na-
> ture of the collective farms . . .
>   All Comrade Stalin's works contain an inexhaustible sum
> of such examples of materialist dialectics. (1931: 52)

The institutionalization of this kind of discourse, together with
the schematization of Marxism–Leninism on the model of the
"Fourth Chapter," are central features of the "official" philosophy of the Stalin era. It was the philosophy of this period
which prompted the exiled Berdyaev to argue that

> Soviet philosophy is not truly philosophy at all [but] . . . a the-
> ology: It has its revelation, its holy books, its ecclesiastical au-
> thority, its official teachers; it presupposes the existence of one
> orthodoxy and innumerable heresies. Marxism–Leninism
> has been transformed into a scholasticism *sui generis*, . . . The
> distinguishing of heresies has attained a degree of refine-
> ment difficult for the uninitiated to imagine. . . . The direc-
> tions of the Communist Party are the basis of philosophical
> work, and this work is carried on in an atmosphere of contin-
> ual nervousness of falling into heresy.
>   . . . Creative philosophical thought cannot flourish in such
> an environment, and it amply accounts for the shuffling, the
> endless repetition, the monotony, the limitedness of Soviet
> philosophy, its petty sophistries, the reciprocal accusations and
> denunciations, the fundamental necessity of lying; neither

talent nor genius can make headway ... It must be added with sadness that all this is a horrid caricature of Christianity. (1933: 211–12, 215–16)

For Ilyenkov, the perversity of the Leninist stage made a return to Lenin's actual contribution inevitable. We turn now to consider what he found there.

Lenin's critique of Empiriocriticism

I shall assess Lenin's contribution through an analysis of *Materialism and Empiriocriticism,* the work argued to have inaugurated the new stage in Marxist philosophy (see, e.g., Kedrov 1961: 5). This is not an uncontroversial choice. While Ilyenkov speaks for the majority of his philosophical contemporaries when he describes *Materialism and Empiriocriticism* as "a classic of dialectical materialism, which elucidated in general form all the major contours and problems of this science" and "completely exposed every kind of idealism," many Western commentators would agree with Alain Besançan that the work does not belong to the history of philosophy at all (Ilyenkov 1980: 4). Rather, it is seen as an amalgamation of elements plundered from the classics of Marxism and "stuck together into a particular ideology" (Besançan 1981: 206), "a work which smells of its author's mainly pragmatic and polemical intentions" (Liebmann 1975: 442). Even those sympathetic to Lenin commonly concede the primitiveness of *Materialism and Empiriocriticism,* arguing that in the later *Philosophical Notebooks* he rejected the vulgar materialism of his earlier work for a more sophisticated position, influenced by what he called the "clever idealism" of Hegel.[3] *Materialism and Empiriocriticism* is certainly polemical. It is also not wholly original, drawing heavily on Engels and Plekhanov. Nevertheless, I intend to take its philosophical content seriously to show that a more sympathetic reading of the work better ex-

3   It is sometimes argued that Lenin meant to include himself among those who had failed to understand Marx when he wrote in his *Philosophical Notebooks:* "It is impossible completely to understand Marx's *Capital,* and especially its first chapter, without having thoroughly studied and understood the *whole* of Hegel's *Logic.* Consequently, half a century later none of the Marxists understood Marx!!" (Lenin 1895–1916: 180).

plains the nature of its influence on subsequent developments in Soviet philosophy. We may note that this reading invites us to see a continuity between *Materialism and Empiriocriticism* and the *Notebooks,* the early Lenin introducing issues that he subsequently came to see as benefiting from a more Hegelian treatment. On this view, which is faithful to Ilyenkov's own interpretation, there is no "break" between the works, since the later is an attempt to extend the resources available to deal with the issues discussed in the earlier (see Ilyenkov 1980: esp. 8–9).

Materialism and Empiriocriticism defends a form of dialectical materialism against philosophical idealism. In particular, Lenin's target is "Empiriocriticism" – the positivist philosophy, developed in the late nineteenth century by Ernst Mach and Richard Avenarius, that was highly influential among sections of the radical Russian intelligentsia. Although the Russian Empiriocritics included Mensheviks like P. S. Yushkevich and N. Valentinov, the best known were the Bolshevik luminaries A. A. Bogdanov and A. V. Lunacharsky. In consequence, Empiriocriticism was thought of as a Bolshevik philosophy. Lenin sought to reinstate a more orthodox position as the theoretical credo of the Bolsheviks.[4]

Following Engels, Lenin holds that all philosophical positions are ultimately either materialist or idealist (Lenin 1909a: 25 [32–3], 359 [338]).[5] The two camps are divided on their accounts of the reality of the external world, its independence from thinking subjects, and the degree to which knowledge of it is possible. There is no third option: "Agnosticism," the view that, since knowledge of reality is impossible, the issue between materialism and idealism is void, is said to collapse into idealism.[6] Thus, Lenin's tactics are to demonstrate Empi-

---

4   The Bolshevik interest in Empiriocriticism allowed the Mensheviks to portray their rivals as revisionists. Plekhanov taunted the Bolsheviks on this score as early as the Third Party Congress in April 1905, and he repeated the charge at the Fifth Congress two years later. Lenin must have feared that the entire Bolshevik faction would be seen as a group of "revisionists" who had renounced Marxist orthodoxy.

5   References in square brackets are to the English edition (Lenin 1909b).

6   The Soviet line is usually that agnosticism is a form of idealism (Marx and Engels 1968: 730n297), though it is sometimes admitted,

riocriticism's commitment to idealism and to commend the materialist case against it.

However, as the Russian Empiriocritics thought their doctrine a complement to Marxism, they naturally denied that they were idealists. We must therefore be clear about the nature of the idealism Lenin attributes to them. The idealist Lenin attacks is committed to three principal tenets:

1. The idealist holds that knowledge is ineradicably subjective; that is, we cannot be said to have access to, or to come to an understanding of, reality as it is *in itself,* independent of human forms of understanding.
2. Lenin assumes the idealist is led to this conclusion by his methodological solipsism, that is, the view that philosophical investigation must begin from experience, conceived as the logically private experience of the individual subject. Lenin holds that the methodological solipsist is forced to the skeptical conclusion that, as we are directly acquainted only with experience, we can never attain knowledge of an external world "behind" or "beyond" experience. Confronted only by reality as it is "for us," we are trapped in a world of appearances, cut off from the world we take to cause our experiences and to be represented by them. Thus we must conclude that we have no grounds to believe our experiences resemble the actually existing objects they seem to represent. The choice is either

   (a) to conclude that reality in itself is unknowable, or
   (b) to jettison the external world as an incomprehensible metaphysical abstraction and to construct reality out of appearances.

   Contemptuous of the agnosticism of (a), Lenin is concerned with the full-blooded idealism of the latter course.
3. Lenin holds the idealist to be an antirealist about necessity. Our experiences exhibit familiar regularities: We think of them as standing in various law-governed relations (e.g., of cause and effect, spatiotemporal relations) that science formulates as "laws of nature." These laws underwrite our

following Engels himself, that it can appear as a veiled form of materialism (see *Fundamentals* 1982: 21n1).

confidence in the regularites of experience by representing them as, in some sense, necessary. Lenin's idealist denies that we can think of this necessity as a property of nature itself. We cannot appeal to the structure of reality "in
itself" to explain the structure of experience. Rather, the
idealist argues that experience is organized as it is, not because reality itself has that organization, but because our
minds impose structure on experience. As Karl Pearson put
it, "the laws of science are products of the human mind
rather than factors of the external world ..." (quoted from
Pearson 1900, in Lenin 1909a: 165 [160]).

To what degree is Russian Empiriocriticism a form of idealism as Lenin understands it? Lenin thinks that textual evidence settles this question. However, since the Empiriocritics
renounced Lenin's very framework and dismissed the materialist–idealist dichotomy as a pseudoproblem, Lenin risks
begging the question by treating their opposition to certain
materialist tenets as a positive allegiance to idealism. Empiriocriticism is a difficult philosophy that cuts across familiar
categories. For instance, Russian Empiriocritics might have
agreed that knowledge is ineradicably subjective, but have denied that we are therefore in any sense "cut off" from reality.
It takes philosophical work to show this position incoherent, or
that the reality with which we are said to remain in contact
can only be understood on idealist lines. Lenin, however, too
quickly rests his case on quotations with an idealist ring to
them.

Short of a detailed analysis of Empiriocriticism, we must be
content with the modest conclusion that there are reasonable,
though perhaps not conclusive, grounds to associate Empiriocriticism with the doctrines of Lenin's idealist. Let us begin
with the conception of experience offered by Mach himself.
The opening sections of his *Knowledge and Error* present his
idea of the worldview, given to every subject, from which all
inquiry must begin:

No thinker can do more than start from this view, extend and
correct it, use his forebears' experience and avoid their mistakes as best he may, in short: carefully to tread the same path
again on his own. What, then, is this world-view? I find myself surrounded by moveable bodies in space, some inanimate,

others plants, animals and men. My body, likewise moveable in space, is for me a visible and touchable object of sense perception occupying a part of sensible space alongside and outside other bodies, just as they do ... In general my body appears to me under a perspective quite different from that of all others ... Besides, I find memories, hopes, fears, drives, desires, a will and so on, of whose development I am as innocent as of the existence of the bodies in my surroundings. The foregoing considerations and the movement of the one definite body issuing from that will mark that body as mine. When I observe the behaviour of other human bodies, not only practical needs but also a close analogy force me, even against my will, to hold that memories, hopes, fears, motives, wishes and will similar to those associated with my body are bound up with other human and animal bodies ... (Mach 1976: 4–5)

The Cartesian style of such passages – the model of the individual building up a picture of the world by reflection on the contents of his or her mind, and the idea that we are acquainted with the mental life of others by an inference based on analogy from our own case – strongly suggests that Mach was committed to methodological solipsism (see Pannekoek 1938: 53). In addition, Mach openly embraces the conclusion that, Lenin argues, inevitably follows from the attempt to construct the world out of experience: "[I]t is true," Mach admits, "that the world consists of our sensations" (Mach 1900: 8 [1914: 12]; see also 1900: 20 [1914: 29]).

If it is probable that Mach endorsed methodological solipsism, it is certain that he was an antirealist about necessity. Following Pearson, he holds that we should not think of the laws of nature as descriptions of reality as it is in itself, but as devices to read order into experience, "restrictions that under the guidance of our experience we prescribe to our expectations" (Mach 1976: 351). He offers a kind of Darwinist account of their origin, in which cognition is a process of the adaptation of individual to environment: "[T]he laws of nature are a product of our mental need to find our way about in nature, so that we do not stand estranged and baffled in front of natural processes" (1976: 354).

Mach's conception of experience thus seems to lead inexorably to idealism. It is therefore significant that it was precisely his conception of experience that his Russian followers found attractive. The Soviet Machists shared the Russian intelligentsia's long-standing preoccupation with the creation of an integral worldview combining rational, scientific explanation in history with a conception of human agents that accords them ethical integrity (see Kelly 1981: 89–90). To this end they sought an epistemological and ethical complement to Marxism. But unlike the other principal revisionist strain in Russia, the "Legal Marxism" of Struve and Berdyaev, which turned to Kant to provide a philosophical foundation for Marxism, the Machists scorned any recourse to transcendental philosophy and the timeless dictates of the categorical imperative, claiming that Marxism and positive science must be the foundation for philosophy and not vice versa (Bogdanov 1905–6: bk. 3, xxii–xxiii). Seeking to be in tune with the sciences, the Russian Empiriocritics rejected the old-fashioned realism of Plekhanov's orthodoxy as quickly as the mysticism of the Legal Marxists, turning to Mach's conception of experience for a nontranscendent foundation for scientific investigation.

The Russian Machists were captivated by the image of science, not as describing some realm beyond experience, but as producing progressively more adequate ways of organizing experience. First, they felt Mach's naturalistic, neo-Darwinist picture of cognition was in harmony with a Marxist conception of science as a historically developing form of ideology. Second, the idea of cognition as "systematizing the content of experience" seemed to answer Marx's call to conceive of "the thing ... as *human sensuous activity, practice*" (Marx 1845: 28). But more than this, it was the idea that "the world of experience has been crystallized and continues to be crystallized out of chaos" that most captured their imagination (Bogdanov 1905–6: bk. 3, xxxiii; 1921: 1). History could be seen as the drama of humanity conquering brute nature (which Bogdanov identified with primitive, chaotic forms of organization) through a series of transformations in the organization of experience. Thus Bogdanov came to see questions of political revolution as *technical* questions about the nature and possibility of such transformations of experience. From his futuristic interest in issues of planning and technology, *tektology*, or "universal organizational science," was born (see the discussion of Bogdanov as a Mechanist in Chapter 2).

Much of the theoretical weight of Bogdanov's notion of *organization* derived from his adoption of Mach's antirealism:

> Laws do not belong at all to the sphere of immediate experience; laws are the result of a conscious reworking of experience; they are not given in experience, but are created by thought, as a means of organizing experience, of harmoniously bringing it into agreement as an ordered unity. (Bogdanov 1905–6: bk. 1, 40)

And from this antirealism, Bogdanov was led to the view that objectivity itself is a product of human organization:

> The objectivity of the physical bodies that we encounter in experience is established in the last analysis on the basis of mutual verification and agreement in judgments [*vyskazivanie*] of different people. In general, the physical world is socially agreed, socially harmonised, in a word, *socially organized experience*. . . (Bogdanov 1905–6: bk. 1, 36)

Thus, after establishing a commitment to idealism in Mach's view of experience, we have followed the development of that view in the hands of his Russian disciples to arrive at what seems like an expression of pure idealism: Reality is "socially organized experience."

Bogdanov would have attempted to rebut this charge of idealism. For him, "materialism" and "idealism" were terms of art of the old-fashioned dualism of mental and physical that Empiriocriticism overcomes. Idealists were supposed to believe that reality was, in some sense, fundamentally mental or ideal. However, on Mach's monistic stance, the basic constituents of reality are the "elements" we are presented in experience. We refer to some of these elements as "physical" and some as "mental"; but this simply marks a distinction between those elements given to all subjects and those given to only one. In Bogdanov's terms, the distinction between mental and physical is the distinction between individually and socially organized experience. Thus the mental and the physical are not two basic realms of being, but just elements under different descriptions (see Mach 1900: 14 [1976: 13]). Since the mental–physical distinction is drawn *within* experience, it makes no sense to think of the elements of experience themselves as mental or physical. Thus to say that the world is constructed out of experience is not to say that it is nonmaterial.

Bogdanov's denial that experience is either mental or physical obliges him to say *something* about its ontological status (even if only that nothing can be said). Sometimes he calls the elements of experience "sensations," which seems to make them mental occurrences in individual minds (or, possibly, physical occurrences in brains) after all. More often, though, he claims that Empiriocriticism treats experience primarily as something supraindividual, a claim more faithful to the spirit of the above defence. (For an assertion of both positions in the same breath, see Bogdanov 1905–6: bk. 3, xviii–xix.) For if Bogdanov takes experience to be "collective" or "socially organized," then surely he cannot be a methodological solipsist, conceiving of all experience on the model of individual experience. And once it is denied that all experiences are happenings in individual minds, then it is perhaps possible to argue that experience is not a mental phenomenon.

Disappointingly, however, Bogdanov's talk about "collective experience" seems to be consistent with methodological solipsism. For him, to say that experience of an object is "socially organized" is to say that the data relevant to determining whether the object is "objective" or "real" necessarily include considerations about the behaviour of other people. To know whether an object is real I need to know what others take it to be. But the data on which I make judgments about the beliefs of others are just the data of *individual* experience. Thus, for Bogdanov, collective experience is not a rival to individual experience, but a type of individual experience: It is just shared individual experience. His view is therefore compatible with the idea that all experience is the private experience of individual subjects, and that we build up our picture of the world on the basis of that experience. Indeed, it is not only compatible with methodological solipsism, it *is* methodological solipsism; for the very point of Bogdanov's appeal to socially organized experience is to explain how, on the basis of individual experience alone, the subject acquires the concept of objectivity. The answer is that each subject determines the objectivity of judgments by appeal to his or her experiences of the behaviour of others, an answer that many methodological solipsists have endorsed (e.g., Russell 1948).

Lenin thus had reasonable grounds to suspect that Bogdanov, like Berkeley, cannot give sense to the idea of a world existing outside all experience (see esp. Bogdanov 1905–6: bk. 3, xix).

Although Lenin often writes as if a position is conclusively refuted merely by showing it to be idealist, he does venture some account of why Empiriocriticism's idealism is a bad thing. For instance, he holds that Empiriocriticism cannot give an adequate account of how nature existed prior to humankind and of the role of the brain in the possession of psychological states (Lenin 1909a: 71–84 [75–86], 84–92 [86–94]). Further, he argues that Empiriocriticism has two disastrous philosophical consequences. First, as we noted above, Lenin argues that Empiriocriticism collapses into solipsism:

> If bodies are "complexes of sensations," as Mach says, or "combinations of sensations," as Berkeley said, it inevitably follows that the whole world is but my idea. Starting from such a premise it is impossible to arrive at the existence of other people besides oneself: It is the purest solipsism. Much as Mach, Avenarius, Petzoldt and Co. may abjure solipsism, they cannot in fact escape it without falling into howling logical absurdities. (35–6 [42]; cf. 41 [47], 92–6 [94–7]) [7]

Second, Lenin argues that Empiriocriticism leads to conceptual relativism. If we deny that truth consists in a relation between our beliefs and an independently existing reality, then truth must somehow be a function of the organization of our beliefs. For example, the Empiriocritics argued that belief sets disturbed by the input of new information tend to equilibrium, and that we call "true" those beliefs that lend our belief set a greater stability, coherence, and economy. But, says Lenin, it is possible for some subset of beliefs to lend an individual's total belief set greater coherence than it would otherwise possess (and greater than it would possess by the inclusion of any other available subset), yet for the beliefs in this subset nonetheless to be (mostly) false. In fact, Marx's theory of ideology requires that this be so (Lenin 1909a: 125 [124]).

These arguments may not be conclusive, but it is doubtful

7 Bogdanov frequently tried to rebut this charge (see, e.g., 1905–6: bk. 3, xix–xx).

whether Lenin believed that there could be knockdown arguments against idealism, and, despite his uncompromising style, he might have settled for the weathering effect of incessant criticism in lieu of one solid blow (Lenin 1909a: 28 [35]). In fact, the critique of idealism was a subsidiary part of Lenin's strategy. He attached far greater importance to proclaiming the positive Marxist materialism he described as "cast from a single piece of steel" (346 [326]). In the light of this, I propose to turn directly to his positive account.

Lenin's materialism

Lenin's materialism is a form of philosophical realism, that is, the belief in the existence of an "external," material, world as an objective reality existing prior to and independently of thinking subjects (1909a: 125–6 [124]).[8] The material world is the only objective reality. Since the external world is independent of human beings, we can think of it as a "thing-in-itself" or as a reality of "things-in-themselves," the "being" of which does not depend on us. However, Lenin, unlike the Kantian, does not hold that things-in-themselves are in principle beyond our cognitive grasp. On the contrary, the material world is a knowable reality; as we acquire knowledge of the world so we transform it from a thing-in-itself into a thing-for-us (97–123 [98–122]). Thus, for Lenin, the principal contrast in epistemology is not that between the knowable and the unknowable, but simply the contrast between the known and the unknown (the not-yet-known).

Lenin holds that human beings come to know reality through sense perception: "[T]he first premise of the theory of knowledge undoubtedly is that the sole source of our knowledge is sensation" (126 [127]). On the basis of the senses, the thinking subject builds up a conception of the world. This conception stands to reality itself as a portrait to its model, or a photograph to its subject. That is, the adequacy of the picture depends on the degree to which it resembles, reflects, or corresponds to (*sovpadat' s*) how things are. When our conception

8 Note that Lenin himself rejects the term "realism" because it "has been bedraggled by the positivists and other muddleheads who oscillate between materialism and idealism" (1909a: 56 [60]). I prefer, however, to keep the term in play.

corresponds to the world it is true. Thus we can think of our theories of the world as attempts to *copy* reality (281 [265]).

It is fundamental to Lenin's position that human beings are capable of constructing theories that adequately reflect the way things are: Objective truth is possible (123–33 [122–31]). Although truth consists in correspondence, the criterion of truth is practice: We test the truth of our conception of the world by acting upon it, for the explanation of why it is possible to live by a theory includes the fact that the theory is an adequate representation of how reality is (140–6 [138–43]). Of course, at any particular point in history the theories we actually hold are only *relatively* true: approximate copies of reality, capturing the truth only partially. But as history progresses and our theories improve, so they tend toward *absolute* truth (133–40 [131–8]).

Our theories represent the objects of the material world as standing in various relations with each other, their movement governed by certain natural laws. For Lenin, the laws of nature reflect the nature of reality: The necessities they encode are real necessities in nature (157–95 [153–87]): "[T]he world is matter moving in conformity to law (*zakonomernyi*), and our knowledge, being the highest product of nature, is in a position only to reflect this conformity to law" (174 [169]).

Lenin is adamant that his materialism is not committed to any substantive account of the nature of matter. The ever-developing story of the structure of matter is the province of the natural sciences and not philosophy. Philosophical materialism is said to keep an open mind about all the properties of matter except one: "[T]he sole 'property' of matter which philosophical materialism is committed to recognizing is the property of being an objective reality, of existing outside our mind" (275 [260–1]). In fact, Lenin's materialism, following Engels, is committed to the further, stronger thesis that matter is "primary" with respect to consciousness (39-40 [46]). This is the view that

1. consciousness is a property of highly developed matter, a function of the living brain (see 39–40 [46], 84–92 [86–94], and the discussion beginning on 226ff. [237ff.]);
2. the content of consciousness is determined by the influence of the external world upon the subject.

This, in a nutshell, is Lenin's materialism. Lenin is convinced that, whatever scientists may think they believe, the theory he describes – with its picture of science gradually uncovering how things are "out there," its bold epistemological optimism, and its faith in the evidence of the senses – is the philosophical position intuitively adopted by all scientists. He thinks this theory obvious and commonsensical, an expression of "the 'naïve realism' of any healthy person who has not been an inmate of a lunatic asylum or a pupil of idealist philosophers ..." (54 [69]). Lenin sums up his position's strengths in the following passage:

The Machians love to declaim that they are philosophers who completely trust the evidence of our sense-organs, who regard the world as actually being what it seems to us to be, full of sounds, colours etc., whereas to the materialists, they say, the world is dead, devoid of sound and colour, and in its reality different from what it seems to be, and so forth . . . But, in fact, the Machians are subjectivists and agnostics, for they *do not sufficiently* trust the evidence of our sense-organs and are inconsistent in their sensationalism. They do not recognise objective reality, independent of man, as the source of our sensations. They do not regard sensations as a true picture of this objective reality, thereby directly conflicting with natural science and throwing the door open for fideism. On the contrary, for the materialist the world is richer, livelier, more varied than it actually seems, for with each step in the development of science new aspects are discovered. For the materialist, sensations are images of the sole and ultimate objective reality, ultimate not in the sense that it has already been explored to the end, but in the sense that there is not and cannot be any other. This view irrevocably closes the door not only to every species of fideism, but also to that professorial scholasticism which, while not recognizing objective reality as the source of our sensations, "deduces" the concept of the objective by means of such artificial verbal constructions as the universally significant [*obshcheznachimii*], the socially-organized, and so on and so forth, and which is unable, and frequently unwilling, to separate objective truth from belief in sprites and hobgoblins. (130 [128–9]; see also Lenin's "Supplement to Chapter 4, Section 1," 381–4 [359–61])

Ambiguity in Lenin's materialism

Lenin's materialism is usually taken to be clear and unequivocal. I shall argue, however, that is not so: Lenin's position is ambiguous between two different forms of realism. To see this ambiguity, however, we must first consider the general framework within which Lenin poses the central issues discussed in *Materialism and Empiriocriticism.* Much of the debate is framed within a distinctive "methodological model," which we may call "two-worlds epistemology." The first world in question is the mental world of the subject: the world of occurrent thoughts, sensations, emotions, beliefs, intentions, desires, and so on, of which the individual subject is thought to be the centre. The subject has "direct" access only to the contents of this world. The second is the object world of material things, existing independently of thought and somehow represented to the subject in thought. On this dualistic model, the principal philosophical task is to provide a picture of how the two worlds can meet, and epistemology, in particular, concerns itself with how there can be cognitive contact between subject and object. However, within the terms of the dualism, this task is not easy, for the logical distinctness of the two realms gives rise to a number of familiar skeptical problems. For example, the subject's privileged access to the contents of his or her own mind is obtained at a price: The subject is left with only an indirect access to the object world, with which he or she is acquainted only via ideas. However, do we not need independent access to both ideas and objects if we are to satisfy ourselves that our ideas are adequate representations of objects as they really are? Indeed, without such dual access, how can we know there is really an object world at all? Such issues form the philosophical idiom of *Materialism and Empiriocriticism.*

This subject–object, or "two-worlds," dualism is owed, in its modern form, to Descartes. However, many later philosophical positions are framed within its logic. One such is Locke's empiricism. For Locke, the senses, the sole source of knowledge, present the subject with "ideas." These ideas are the primary objects of acquaintance. The subject is aware of things beyond the mind only in virtue of his or her more immediate awareness of ideas: "[T]he Mind, in all its Thoughts and Reasonings, hath no other immediate Object but its own Ideas, which it alone does or can contemplate" (Locke 1689: IV.i.1). Locke's theory is often accused of allowing our representations of the world to come between us and the world itself. As Bennett puts it, "Locke puts the objective world, the world of 'real things,' beyond our reach on the other side of the veil of perception" (Bennett 1971: 69). And Berkeley, of course, chose Locke's theory of experience as his target.[9]

Another version of the dualism lies in many nineteenth- and early twentieth-century readings of Kant.[10] Locke offers

9   I am aware that this simple exposition risks being unfair to Locke himself. The charge that his theory of experience puts the real world beyond our cognitive reach sometimes rests on the idea that Locke held that we are never aware of objects themselves, but only of ideas. In fact, he is better seen as offering a theory of perception as a double awareness of both sensation (directly) and object (indirectly).

10 The "Kantian" who figures in this chapter (and who later re-emerges as a foil to Ilyenkov in Chapter 6) is a familiar figure in nineteenth- and twentieth-century epistemology and in many Soviet philosophical debates. It is a live issue, however, how this Kantian position relates to the views of the real Kant. Although Kant writes as if we may have knowledge only of "appearances" and not of "things as they are in themselves," it is misleading to read him as portraying the subject–object relation as one between two worlds, the first a subjective world of "mere" appearances, the second a "real" world of unknowable things-in-themselves that somehow "underlie" appearances. When Kant writes "appearance," he means not a mental entity representing some thing that remains hidden from us, but the-thing-that-appears-to-us, that is, the real, independent object of our thought. Indeed, his project is to understand what it is to know such real things and not simply *mere* appearances, and he thinks his philosophy shows that we can have knowledge of the objects that comprise our world, not just knowledge of appearances-of-objects. Kant argues, of course, that this project can be conducted only from the possible perspective of a subject. Therefore, our thoughts of things as they are independent of the possible perspective of an observer – i.e., our thoughts of "things-in-themselves" – lack content. They are consistent but empty thoughts. Thus, for the historical Kant, the contrast between "appearance" and "thing-in-itself" is not the contrast between a world of "seemings" and a world of real but transcendent things, but a contrast between the world characterized from the perspective of possible experience (experience that may reveal how that world truly is) and the empty thought of a perspectiveless conception of that (same) world. In fact, as Raymond Geuss has suggested to me, this more refined reading of Kant may be not unlike the position

us a view of perception as passive reception: "[I]n the reception of simple ideas, the understanding is most of all passive" (Locke 1689: II.i.25). The mind receives ideas rather in the way wax receives the imprint of a seal. But this view, combined with Locke's extreme empiricism, is open to serious objections. For example, reflection on the ideas we passively receive from the senses alone cannot account for the origin of many ideas that lend essential structure to our conception of reality – like the ideas of necessity and of the self. While Hume was content to accommodate this fact *within* empiricism, the Kantian proposes a different solution. He argues that experience, as empiricism conceives it, is too poor a medium to form the basis of all our knowledge. Rather, we should admit that the senses yield no more than a chaotic "manifold" of impressions, a mass of unorganized, preconceptualized "input." To explain how our experience issues in a conception of the world, the Kantian solution is to reject the passive model. It is the subject's active contribution to cognition that makes this conception possible. Thus, the Kantian treats cognition as the necessary amalgam of, on the one hand, raw "data," "the given," pure content, contributed by the object world and, on the other, a conceptual scheme provided by the subject through which the data are filtered. Our conception of the world issues from the imposition of this scheme upon the brute deliverances of sense. It is the indissoluable unity of two elements. As Kant himself puts it, "thoughts without content are empty, intuitions without concepts are blind" (Kant 1788: A51 = B75).

This rationalist version of subject–object dualism, "the dualism of scheme and content," also breeds skeptical worries. Again, we seem to deny ourselves cognitive access to reality in itself. Our minds can only reach reality once the content it offers us has been processed through a conceptual grid. But this is to reach only as far as things-as-they-are-for-us; the world prior to the operation of our concepts, the world of things-in-themselves, remains unknown to us. Another apparent danger is relativism. The nature of our conceptual scheme is, no doubt, tied to our nature. Perhaps creatures sufficiently

that Ilyenkov defends in his "theory of the ideal." However, it is the cruder, "two-worlds Kant" who is the target here.

unlike us would possess a different scheme. What, then, is to say that our conceptual scheme is the only valid way of synthesizing the data of sense?

In *Materialism and Empiriocriticism,* Lenin seems to assume that his opponents are committed to scheme–content dualism. On this basis, he argues that their views are prey to skepticism and relativism. However, Empiriocriticism is better seen as aiming to overcome dualism, rather than to advocate it. The Russian Empiriocritics believed that the intelligentsia's preoccupation with classical philosophical topics, like "skepticism," "the mind–body problem," and "other minds," was a symptom of its fragmentation and estrangement. These were problems, they argued, that subject–object dualism had created, and that would remain insoluble so long as the dualism was maintained. The Empiriocritics therefore urged the rejection of dualism in all its forms, proclaiming monism a necessary condition of an integral worldview. (Hence Bogdanov named his theory "Empiriomonism.")

How, then, did the Empiriocritics attempt to overcome the dualism? Essentially, their strategy was to erase one half of it: the external world of things-in-themselves. Rather than posit a material reality existing somehow beyond experience, the Empiriocritics represented reality as a construction out of experience itself. This way there could be no room for, say, skeptical doubts about our access to reality. If Empiriocriticism is an idealist philosophy, this move is the root of its idealism, the source of the idea that "reality is socially organized experience."

In this broad framework, a materialist realist can make two contrasting responses to Empiriocriticism. I want to suggest that Lenin's position is ambiguous between the two. The first, "conservative," option is to try to reinstate the external world within the terms of subject–object dualism. The conservative realist insists that "behind" or "beyond" our ideas exists a material world that provides the content on which our minds go to work. As a conservative realist faithful to Lenin could not question the knowability of things-in-themselves, he or she would have to maintain that, although we have immediate access only to the contents of our own minds, we are in no sense prisoners of our own conceptions. Rather, we are capable of forming a picture of the nature of reality in itself. To do this involves distinguishing those elements in our conception of the world that accurately reflect reality as it is from those which we ourselves have contributed to the conception. This is not simply a recommendation to distinguish truth from error. We are capable of forming a picture of the world only because we have certain perceptual and cognitive capacities. This picture will obviously be affected by the kind of capacities we have. Our capacities constitute the *perspective* from which we view the world. To take a familiar example, we see the world as coloured in virtue of the kind of visual organs we have. While it would be eccentric to hold that, therefore, our attributions of colour to objects are literally false, we cannot think of the world as it exists independently of us as having colour: Colour is a property that gets into the world in virtue of the presence of observers with the right kind of visual equipment. Thus our conservative realist holds that we are capable of forming a kind of perspectiveless conception of the world by disentangling from our picture of reality those anthropocentric features we contribute in virtue of the peculiarites of our psychological makeup. This perspectiveless picture of reality has been called "the absolute conception of the world" (see Williams 1978: 240–9).[11]

This first option may be seen as a defence of Locke, insisting against the skeptic that not only can we make sense of an independently existing reality, but we can also, on the basis of the ideas it causes in us, form a conception of its nature. Alternatively, in more Kantian terms, the conservative expresses confidence that the contribution of anthropocentric features of our conceptual scheme can be disentangled to leave a picture of reality as it is independent of the operation of the scheme.

The second possible response to Empiriocriticism is more radical. This response proposes that we reject outright the "two-worlds epistemology" in which the debate has so far been posed. On this "radical" realism, there are not two worlds that must somehow be shown to be connected by the ingenuity of philosophers, but *one:* The subject is located in

11   Note that the conservative realist's distinction between "anthropocentric" and "absolute" conceptions of the world is analogous to the distinction between "scientific" and "everyday" conceptions attributed to the Mechanists in Chapter 2. It is also part of the empiricist picture introduced in the penultimate section of Chapter 1.

objective reality. Our place within the material world may be special, but we are nonetheless a part of it. The radical holds that we need to overcome the idea that the contents of our minds somehow come between us and reality, either in the form of a "veil of perception" or a conceptual scheme. For instance, we should think of perception not as a filtering process resulting in the apprehension of a special kind of inner object (an "idea"), but as an openness to reality itself. The subject must be seen as having immediate or direct access to reality. None of this is to say, of course, that we have instant access to the truth. Our conception of the world can be, and often is, riddled with error. But we are only able to be wrong about reality because our minds are capable of reaching right out to it.

If the conservative response is in the spirit of eighteenth-century, or "classical," empiricism, the radical expresses an antagonism to subject–object dualism reminiscent of Hegel:

> Of a metaphysics prevalent today which maintains that we cannot know things because they are absolutely shut to us, it might be said that not even the animals are as stupid as these metaphysicians; for they go after things, seize them and consume them. (Hegel 1830b: sec. 246, *zusatz*)

For the radical, the materialist rewriting of Hegel urged by Marx is motivated in part by the desire to make good sense of the unity of subject and object. The project is to find a materialist reading of the thesis of the identity of thinking and being in the idea that, when we get the world aright, thought and reality stand in a relation of identity, not correspondence.

Both Empiriocriticism and radical realism, then, are hostile to the two-worlds dualism. The difference between the two strategies is that where Empiriocriticism tries to locate reality in the subject's experience, the radical realist's solution is to locate the experiencing subject in reality. For the realist, the Empiriocritic's error is to be hostile to dualism too late. Overly impressed by the opposition of subject and object, the Empiriocritic follows the dualist's arguments to the point where the only remaining monist option is to jettison the object world altogether. But this throws the baby out with the bathwater.

As Danny Goldstick has noted, Lenin has usually been seen as adopting the first, conservative, option (Goldstick 1980:

1–2). This may be because the radical realist has rarely been taken seriously; talk of a materialist version of the identity of thinking and being is, after all, obscure. We shall return to radical realism later in this work. For now, however, it is enough to grasp the basic distinction between the two options: One works within the dualism of subject and object, the other rejects it wholesale. Let us turn to examine how some of Lenin's remarks point toward a conservative, others toward a radical, response.

It is Lenin's "reflection theory" that suggests that he endorses the conservative form of realism. Some form of Lockean "representative" realism, on which we are directly acquainted with mental entities alone, seems implied by his claims that "sensations" (*oshchushchenie*) are "images" (*obraz*) or "reflections" (*otobrazhenie*) of objects; that to perceive an object is to have a mental image caused by the object and that resembles it; and that truth consists in thought "copying" reality. On this interpretation, it is natural to read Lenin as simply dismissing skeptical worries generated by classical empiricism: We can be sure that our conception of reality is a (relatively) accurate one.

Lenin not only advocates reflection theory, he explicitly contrasts it with the thesis of the identity of thinking and being. For instance, he is critical of Bazarov's formulation that "sense-perception is the reality outside us," affirming that when Engels holds that "perceptions of the object and of its properties coincide with the reality existing outside us," the term "coincide with" should be read as "correspond to," and not as "are identical with":

> Are you trying to make capital of the ambiguous Russian word *sovpadat'*? Are you trying to lead the unsophisticated reader to believe that *sovpadat'* here means "to be identical" and not "to correspond"? (1909a: 114 [114])

However, Lenin's opposition to the identity thesis does not show that he rejected radical realism, for he reads Bazarov's remark that "sense-perception is the reality outside us" as an expression of Berkeleian idealism: To identify thinking and being is to hold that reality is thought and thus to deny the existence of anything independent of the mind. As such, Lenin is clearly not opposing an interpretation of the "identity of thinking and being" congenial to radical realism.

While Lenin's suspicion of the identity thesis does not prove he rejected radical realism, it could be thought to show that he did not fully grasp the possibility of such a theory; for had he done so, he might have read Bazarov more sympathetically, taking the identification of sense perception and reality to mean that in sense perception we perceive reality itself rather than any intermediary. Nevertheless, there is no evidence that Lenin clearly saw the possibility of an antidualist materialism yet consciously opted for representative realism.

While reflection theory suggests conservative realism, there is equally plenty of evidence that Lenin was hostile to subject–object dualism. First, Lenin shares the radical realist's insistence that the world we experience and inhabit is the external world itself. Objective reality is not a transcendent realm. Although Lenin boldly states that materialism is committed to acknowledging reality "beyond the realm of perception" he makes it clear how this must be understood. The relevant contrast is not between reality that is perceivable and reality that is in principle not accessible to us, but between the part of reality that is currently within our "sphere of observation" and that which is, at the given time, contingently beyond it:

> Engels is speaking of being *beyond* the point where our sphere of observation ends, for instance, the existence of men on Mars. Obviously, such being is an open question. And Bazarov, as though deliberately refraining from giving the full quotation, paraphrases Engels as saying that "being beyond the realm of perception" is an open question!! ... Had Engels ever said anything like this, it would be a shame and disgrace to call oneself a Marxist. (1909a: 117 [117])

Moreover, the very purpose of Lenin's account of "things-in-themselves" is to deny that the material world is a transcendent reality:

> But the whole point is that the very idea of "transcendence," i.e., of a boundary in principle between the appearance and the thing-in-itself, is a nonsensical idea of the agnostics (Humeans and Kantians included) and the idealists. (116–17 [116])

Things-in-themselves are knowable. Lenin concurs with Bazarov's ridicule of Plekhanov's view that the "belief" in the external world "is an inevitable *salto vitale* of philosophy" (144 [141]). For Lenin, our knowledge of the external world is in no sense a leap from sense experience to something beyond which we know only by inference. We are in direct contact with the external world.

Furthermore, Lenin is critical of the propensity to construe sensation as a barrier between subject and world:

> The sophism of idealist philosophy consists in the fact that it regards sensation as being not only the connection between consciousness and the external world, but as a fence, a wall, separating consciousness from the external world – not an image of the external phenomenon corresponding to the sensation, but as the "sole entity" [*edinstvenno sushchee*]. (46 [51])

If we deny that sensation comes between us and the world, we leave room for the view that the world is manifest to us in sensations, that we have direct access to reality itself. To develop this view would involve dissolving the "myth of the given," the idea that we are immediately acquainted only with sensation, in favour of the view that what we are "given" in sensation is the material world itself. This is precisely Lenin's strategy:

> Don't you understand that such expressions as the "immediately given" and the "factually given" are part of the rigmarole of the Machians, the immanentists, and the other reactionaries in philosophy, a masquerade, whereby the agnostic (and sometimes, as in Mach's case, the idealist too) disguises himself in the cloak of the materialist? For the materialist the "factually given" is the outer world, the image of which is our sensations.
>
> For the idealist the "factually given" is sensation, and the outer world is declared to be a "complex of sensations." (111–12 [111–12]; see also 36–7 [43], 237–8 [226–7])

Here, ironically, we find Lenin arguing for precisely the view we attributed to Bazarov when we mooted a radical reading of his view that "sense-perception is the reality existing

outside us": In perception, we are presented with reality itself.[12]

Earlier, we tried and failed to force the issue in favour of the
conservative interpretation of Lenin's materialism. Now that
we have seen evidence of his hostility to subject–object dualism, might we not attempt to resolve the issue the other way?
All that stands between Lenin and radical realism is reflection theory. Surely, there must be some reading of the view
that minds "reflect" reality that does not entail representative
realism. However, to force such a reading on Lenin would be
artificial. Lenin is no more a consistent antidualist than he is
a consistent dualist. As we have seen, he is quite unmoved by
Empiriocriticism's thirst for monism. A radical realist ought

12   Lenin also attacks the picture of sensation as an interface between
      subject and world on the grounds that it makes solipsism inevita-
      ble: "If the 'sensible content' of our sensations is not the external
      world, then nothing exists save this naked I ..." (1909a: 36–7 [43]).
      From this, Goldstick concludes that Lenin is a direct realist, hold-
      ing that sense perception affords consciousness a "direct connec-
      tion" to the external world (Goldstick 1980: 3). Goldstick makes
      this point as part of a sustained attempt to show that Lenin was un-
      ambiguously a direct realist, holding that "all sensuous experience
      is experience to the effect that something is concretely the case"
      (1980: 17). Goldstick's account of direct realism is based on Arm-
      strong's construal of perception as a form of belief-acquisition
      (Armstrong 1961: 80–135, 1968: 208–90). However, while Goldstick
      is correct to argue that the English translation of the Russian
      "obraz" (what gets caused in us in perception) as "image" is mis-
      leading, making it too easy to read Lenin as a representationalist,
      it would be equally misleading to hold that when Lenin wrote
      "obraz" he meant "belief." Russian has no word that corresponds
      to the analytic philosopher's notion of belief. ("Vera" and "verovan-
      ie" have strong connotations of having faith in, and "ubezhdenie"
      [lit. "conviction"], though closest to the analytic philosopher's us-
      age of "belief," is rarely used in Soviet philosophical parlance.)
      Moreover, the fact that the language of "propositional attitudes"
      is difficult to construe in Russian makes it very implausible that
      Lenin could have believed that mental states are attitudes to propo-
      sitions, and thus that perception should be analyzed as the acqui-
      sition of certain propositional attitudes (Goldstick 1980: 10–11).
      This view has not been popular among Russian philosophers be-
      fore or since Lenin's time (indeed, it was in its infancy in the
      West when Lenin was writing). It is more likely that Lenin, like
      many contemporary Soviet philosophers, drew no clear distinction
      between propositional and nonpropositional mental states. It is
      therefore dubious to read him as endorsing a form of realism that
      gets its sense from that distinction.

to appreciate that the Empiriocritics are coming at the right problem, albeit from a different, and mistaken, direction. Yet Lenin does not seem to recognize this at all. While this failure is not enough to prove him a conservative realist, it frustrates attempts to paint him as a thoroughgoing radical.

Let us take a brief illustration. Philosophical work is needed to give content to radical realism; so far, we have only succeeded in stating the possibility of such a position. One sound intuition is that radical realism depends on rethinking the notion of thought itself, for the conservative option seems compelling so long as we treat thought as occurrences in some "inner" realm. Lenin, however, is not only not interested in challenging this conception, he savagely attacks Avenarius for doing so. Avenarius argues that the idea of the "thinking brain" is a "fetish of natural science." This fetishism is a consequence of a systematic philosophical error: the propensity to "introject," that is, to reify thought as something inside the subject (see Pannekoek 1938: 57–65). Lenin, quoting Avenarius, scornfully describes his position:

> Introjection deviates "in principle" from the "natural conception of the world" (natürlicher Weltbegriff) by substituting "in me" for "before me" (vor mir) "by turning a component part of the (real) environment into a component part of (ideal) thought." "Out of the amechanical [a new word for 'mental'] which manifests itself freely and clearly in the given [or, in what we find – im Vorgefundenen], introjection makes something which hides itself [latitierendes, says Avenarius "originally"] mysteriously in the central nervous system. (1909a: 86 [88]; Lenin's parentheses and brackets)

Bogdanov is quick to see the significance of Avenarius's insight (Bogdanov 1904a: 119; see Lenin 1909a: 87 [89]). To reify thought is to think of it as a modification of a substance; but that substance has to be, in some sense, hidden from view. This inevitably opens the door to skeptical worries, for instance, about other minds. Further, introjection issues in the duplication at the heart of subject–object dualism. Once we have made thought thinglike, it becomes natural to treat its veracity in terms of correspondence between the-thing-that-is-thought (belief) and the-thing-that-is-thought-of (object). Lenin, sadly, does not begin to appreciate the potential in Avenarius's idea, flatly rejecting it as "idealistic rubbish" (88 [90]). In doing so he betrays a narrow conception of the possibilities open to philosophy of mind, assuming that to deny that thought is a function of the brain is to cut it loose from matter altogether, to believe that thought can exist independently of matter. We might expect a radical realist to be more sympathetic to Avenarius and prepared to be more flexible in his or her conception of the mind.

We have arrived, then, at the unorthodox conclusion that Lenin's materialism is ambiguous between two distinct forms of realism. The significance of this for Soviet philosophy emerges if we consider Lenin's influence on Ilyenkov. It was the radical aspect of Lenin's materialism that so impressed him. For Ilyenkov, Lenin's great contribution lay in his rejection of empiricism and positivism, a rejection that, Ilyenkov believed, requires materialism to eschew the dualisms of subject and object, scheme and content, thought and being. Thus Ilyenkov saw Lenin as bequeathing the task of dissolving these dualisms – a task that came to be the focus of Ilyenkov's career.

However, if the radical realism in *Materialism and Empiriocriticism* inspired Ilyenkov, the conservative thread in Lenin's thought influenced philosophers of a different persuasion. For them, reflection theory offered an attractive modern version of Lockean empiricism. With Lenin's attempt to provide a philosophical basis for science, it seemed that the spirit of the Enlightenment had finally arrived in Russia. On this view, the strength of Lenin's position is that it does not attempt to place a priori constraints on scientific explanation, but sees philosophy (as the Mechanists had done) as generalizing the achievements of the sciences. While science alone determines what counts as an explanation, philosophy paints an engaging picture of science's evergoing ascent toward absolute truth in the form of the "absolute conception of the world." Such empiricism finds various expressions in Soviet philosophy. It is evident, for example, in Meliukhin's ontological materialism (1966), in Tiukhtin's cybernetics (1972), and in Dubrovsky's philosophy of mind and ideality (1980). All presuppose that philosophy's business is to provide an account, within the Cartesian framework of conservative realism, of science's attempt to reach absolute knowledge.

Thus the ambiguity in Lenin's materialism has given rise to two opposing schools of thought within contemporary Soviet philosophy. Sometimes when antagonistic schools of Soviet philosophers appeal to the same authorities, commentators conclude that they are either unable to perceive the conflict, or too cynical to care about it. Neither is true in this case: Both sides may legitimately appeal to Lenin; however, because of the special nature of Lenin's authority within Soviet culture, Soviet thinkers have not been well placed openly to discuss ambiguities in his thought. Consequently, both camps have proceeded as if the other side of Lenin's materialism does not exist. For instance, Ilyenkov defends a version of the thesis of the identity of thinking and being without mentioning Lenin's remark that it is an "outrageous theoretical distortion of Marxism" (Lenin 1909a: 345 [324]; cf. Ilyenkov 1964a).

To sum up: While the germ of radical realism in Lenin's philosophy exercised a formative influence on Ilyenkov's philosophical concerns, Lenin also inspired the very school of scientific empiricism that Ilyenkov came to see as his principal opponent.

Lenin's philosophy as politics

Materialism and Empiriocriticism was not just a contribution to a philosophical discussion; it was also a political intervention. In 1908 Lenin and Bogdanov were rivals for the leadership of the Bolshevik faction. They were divided not only on questions of high theory, but also on questions of revolutionary strategy. For instance, at this time Lenin believed that the Russian Social-Democratic Party should continue to exploit legal channels of political participation, sending deputies to the State Duma, the fragile representative assembly established by Nicholas II. In contrast, Bogdanov and his supporters considered the Duma a farce. They argued either that the party should recall its deputies, or that they be allowed to remain only so long as they obeyed the Central Committee's instructions. Moreover, it seems that by late 1908, Bogdanov, unlike Lenin, was prepared to forsake legal political activity altogether and proceed directly to armed insurrection (see Service 1985: 178).

Bogdanov and Lenin deemed these to be issues on which

the fate óf their movement depended, and as their disagreements intensified, Lenin moved to oust his rival. He chose to focus his attack on Bogdanov's philosophy. Bogdanov was highly regarded for his theoretical acumen; to show that Bogdanov and his supporters' position was not only false, but a betrayal of Marxism, would do irrevocable damage to their credibility. Lenin's strategy was successful: *Materialism and Empiriocriticism* was published in April 1909; two months later Bogdanov had been driven out of the Bolshevik faction.

In light of this, the production of *Materialism and Empiriocriticism* has often been perceived as a piece of pure political opportunism. This interpretation, to which Bogdanov himself subscribed (1910: 221), is supported by the fact that, in 1904, Lenin had entered a long-standing agreement with Bogdanov not to allow the philosophical differences between their groups to erupt into a public dispute. This agreement facilitated an unprecedented alliance, or "bloc," within the "Bolshevik Centre" that allowed the Bolsheviks to maintain their strength within the Social-Democratic Party.[13] Yet in 1908, after the Russian Empiriocritics published a number of overtly revisionist writings, Lenin wrote to Maxim Gorky that he was now "absolutely convinced" that Empiriocriticism was "ridiculous, harmful, philistine and obscurantist from beginning to end" and felt himself "duty bound to speak out against it" (Lenin 1958–69: vol. 47, 151). As Aileen Kelly points out, however, nothing of substance had changed in the Empiriocritics' philosophical views (Kelly 1981: 111–12). She therefore concludes that the motive for Lenin's change of heart was purely political. He produced *Materialism and Empiriocriticism* not because he suddenly recognized that philosophy was crucially important to politics, but because he saw his chance to crush a rival with whom compromise was no longer necessary.

Few Soviet philosophers, however, have subscribed to such an interpretation. On the contrary, even the most progressive of Soviet Marxists have usually championed *Materialism and Empiriocriticism* as exemplifying the relevance of philosophical theory to political debate. For example, in his 1980 *Leninist Dia-*

13   The Bolshevik Centre, formed in 1906, was the autonomous central apparatus of the faction working within the formally reunited Social-Democratic Party. An interesting account is given in Volodin (1982: 37–45).

lectics and the Metaphysics of Positivism, Ilyenkov does not dispute that Lenin sought to gain strategic advantage by attacking Bogdanov's philosophy. But far from concluding that Lenin was an unscrupulous opportunist, Ilyenkov defends the political integrity of *Materialism and Empiriocriticism,* arguing that Lenin shrewdly diagnosed the disastrous political implications of Empiriocriticism and that Lenin's philosophical materialism, properly understood, was essential to the Bolshevik cause.

Ilyenkov's essay is disappointing; produced posthumously from a censored version of an unpublished manuscript, the text is repetitious and dogmatic. Nevertheless, the work represents an interesting testimony to Lenin's enduring significance for Soviet philosophical culture. Moreover, the case Ilyenkov makes on Lenin's behalf is not without interest. In what follows, I attempt to bring out the substance of Ilyenkov's argument.

Ilyenkov seeks to show how Empiriocriticism generated poor political theory. Following Lenin, he accuses the Empiriocritics of recasting Marxist explanations in scientistic jargon in order to represent all social issues as technical questions about the organization of self-developing systems (Ilyenkov 1980: 95, 125–6; cf. Lenin 1909a: 348–9 [328]). Bogdanov, for example, treats class divisions as a function of the different organizational roles that emerge with the division of labour (Bogdanov 1905–6: 85–142, esp. 139–42). Accordingly, the struggle between the bourgeoisie (or "organizer" class) and the proletariat (or "executant" class) is portrayed as a struggle for organizational supremacy. The bourgeosie must ultimately lose because, as organizers and not producers, they become increasingly estranged from "the technical-production process" and can no longer sustain an ideology that serves to "organize the experience" of the proletariat. Empowered by their technical expertise, the proletariat succeeds the bourgeoisie as the organizing function of the production process, and establishes new and distinctively proletarian ways of organizing experience.

It is significant that certain key economic and political categories of Marxist theory are marginalized in Bogdanov's account. For example, the concept of ownership, which Marx invokes to explain the division of labour itself, plays only a minor role in Bogdanov's reading. Moreover, where Marx sees conflict over property relations as the driving force of history, Bogdanov portrays social change as the outcome of a dialectic of modes of organization, from the technical, to the administrative, to the ideological. Bogdanov's redrafting of Marx is concerned to represent social relations as governed by general principles of organization, themselves instances of laws governing the development of all complex systems. He thus conceives of society as part of a complex self-organizing machine or organism, ultimately governed by general laws like the law of the conservation of energy, or the "principle of equilibrium." Bogdanov is therefore led to translate Marx's economic and political categories into terms to which such general laws may apply. His "organizational" rhetoric allows him to portray class conflict as a disturbance or discoordination within the system that is ultimately resolved by the system's general tendency to establish equilibrium.

Ilyenkov, again following Lenin, is scathingly critical of Bogdanov's strategy (see, e.g., 1980: 77–8). At best, he argues, Bogdanov contributes nothing to Marxist theory because his theories are ultimately parasitic upon those of Marx's. For example, we cannot interpret the metaphors of organization and equilibrium, let alone make predictions on their basis, without retranslating them into Marx's terms. At worst, however, Bogdanov's translation of Marx makes it impossible to see the "real contradictions" that drive the social process (Ilyenkov 1980: 52, 101–2). For Ilyenkov, such contradictions may be expressed only in irreducibly political and economic terms (in terms relating the "forces" and "relations" of production). To represent these contradictions in terms of a "general systems theory" not only elevates the discussion to a debilitating level of abstraction, it also robs us of a conception of historical agency. For Bogdanov, it seems, classes and individuals are no longer the makers of history; instead, both are seen as facets of a complex self-organizing machine, their actions subsumed by quite general laws of its regulation. In turn, the development of society is portrayed as a technical process in which this machine attains ever more "rational" forms of organization, that is, forms of organization that minimize conflict and maximize equilibrium.

Ilyenkov argues that the ways in which Bogdanov's philosophy influenced his politics are especially evident in his science fiction novels, *Red Star* (1908) and its sequel *Engineer Menni* (1913). Consider the former, a book that imaginatively anticipates many later works of the genre. It tells the story of a Russian Revolutionary, Leonid N., who is transported to Mars. There he finds a perfect communist society: a world of superb technology and harmonious social life in which private property has been abolished together with the state and all forms of repression. Lenni, however, a hypersensitive intellectual, is overwhelmed by Martian life and falls ill. During his malaise, he discovers that Mars is a dying planet and that the Martians have a plan to colonize Earth that requires the extermination of the human race. Lenni murders the plan's principal advocate. Humanity is saved, however, by Netti, the Martian doctor who has become Lenni's lover. In an eloquent speech, she convinces the Martians that they should not judge earthlings by their present contradictions; Mars must sacrifice future Martian generations to Earth's "stormy, but beautiful ocean of life" (Bogdanov 1908: 119). Lenni's crime is excused by his illness and he is transported back to Earth, later to return to Mars to further an alliance between the two planets.

Ilyenkov objects to the scientism of Bogdanov's fiction (see 1980: chap. 2, esp. 64–9). Throughout *Red Star,* for example, Bogdanov appeals to "physical" or "natural" considerations to explain social phenomena. Martians are said to be more rational than humans in virtue of the effect on the Martian climate on the intellectual development of their species. The geography of Mars is invoked to account for the homogeneity of the Martian race, the absence of national boundaries and different languages, and the low incidence of war in Martian history. Furthermore, the plot is made to turn on Lenni's "psychophysiological" incompatibility with his Martian hosts. While such pseudoscientific explanations are common in science fiction, Ilyenkov finds their like incongruous in a putatively Marxist work.

Also curious is the image of technology in Bogdanov's science fiction. Though Bogdanov spoke out vehemently against Bolshevik flirtations with Taylorism, his own vision of communist production itself threatens to reduce workers to appendages of the technical process. The chapter in which Lenni vis-

its a Martian factory is revealing (Bogdanov 1908: 62–8). The
Martian economy is presented as a vast, finely tuned machine in which human labour seems largely to have been
reduced to the supervision of a mechanized production process. Workers are free to choose their posts in light of the
economy's needs as revealed by the Institute of Statistics, but
their mobility is possible only because most work is un-
skilled. Workers seem to derive fulfilment from the labour
process in virtue of their admiration for their tools. Indeed, for
Bogdanov, the only danger posed by technology is that Martian workers become so mesmerized by the marvellous machines they supervise that they may, in an act of involuntary
suicide, express their wonder by casting themselves into the
mechanism (Bogdanov 1908: 67–8). Ilyenkov remarks:

> Bogdanov's philosophy is thus, like no other, in harmony
> with the specific illusions of our age we call "technocratic."
> The secret of these illusions is the deification of technology
> ... And with this, the engineering–technical intelligentsia
> begins to look – to all eyes including their own – like a special
> cast of sacred-servants of this new god. (1980: 87–8)

Hence, in *Red Star*, Bogdanov describes a society where the
state has "withered away" and the "administration of things"
is apparently left to an élite of technical experts. However, as
Ilyenkov points out, these experts do not simply give voice to
the conclusions of science or the dictums of bureaucratic imperatives: Their status is somehow taken to empower them to
make momentous moral and political decisions about the fate
of whole civilizations (Ilyenkov 1980: 69–72). For Ilyenkov,
this is a chilling vision of the politics of communism.

   However, it is neither Bogdanov's perversion of Marx nor
his utopian fiction that provokes Ilyenkov's most insistent criticism, but the political consequences of Bogdanov's antirealism. Ilyenkov reminds us that, by viewing reality as a construction of our ways of organizing experience, Bogdanov
cannot represent science as discovering "how things are":
Science is simply one among the modes of experiential organization. Accordingly, for Bogdanov, philosophy's task cannot be to appraise critically the relation between our scientific
forms of understanding and the independent reality they pu-

tatively characterize. Philosophy is rather a nonrevisionary discipline: Its task is not to challenge science but to generalize its results. Thus, for Bogdanov, traditional philosophical inquiry is to be replaced by a "universal organizational science" concerned to formulate general principles of organization, under which the modes of explanation employed in the special sciences may be subsumed. Ilyenkov objects that Bogdanov's position robs us of a rational account of scientific progress. For Ilyenkov, scientific research, in both the natural and social sciences, must be seen as producing increasingly more adequate conceptions of an independently existing world. Moreover, part of the explanation of why our conceptions change is that they are driven to do so in confrontation with this recalcitrant reality. Echoing the Deborinites case against the Mechanists, Ilyenkov insists that the process in which science struggles to capture reality – a process he calls the "materialist dialectic" – is itself a legitimate object of critical philosophical inquiry. The philosopher may help the scientist comprehend the nature and possibility of science itself; without philosophy, science remains unreflexive and uncritical (Ilyenkov 1980: passim, esp. 130).

Ilyenkov applauds Lenin for grasping the political significance of this seemingly abstract controversy. Lenin and Bogdanov's respective epistemologies, he suggests, underlie their contrasting views of revolutionary strategy (1980: 168–70). For Bogdanov, while the radical intelligentsia may be deeply involved in the staging of revolution and in the nurturing of proletarian culture, it cannot see itself as having arrived at some "objectively true" theory of the world, which it may simply impose on the masses to precipitate revolution and in the name of which the new society must be built. The thirst for such objective truth is, for Bogdanov, a typical symptom of the alienated intelligentsia's quest to overcome its partial and fragmented conception of the world with a universalizing theory that provides a foundation for all knowledge and a justification for political action (see Bogdanov 1904b: esp. 254). On Bogdanov's view, political revolution is ultimately a revolution in the social organization of experience. Revolution must therefore involve the emergence of a new, intrinsically proletarian culture. Such a culture will issue, not from the totalizing theories of the intelligentsia, but from the self-development of the

proletarian movement itself. Such a position stands in dramatic contrast to Lenin's idea of a revolutionary party. Since the
publication of *What Is to Be Done?* in 1902, Lenin had maintained that the success of the revolution depended on the party's hierarchical organization under the leadership of a small,
highly disciplined group of professional revolutionaries. This
élite, drawn largely from the intelligentsia, derived its unity
from its commitment to Marxist theory, "correctly" understood. Moreover, for Lenin, the truth of this theory lent these
revolutionaries the insight and authority to lead the revolution: The party must take this Marxist truth to the masses who,
left to themselves, would not develop socialist ideas. Ilyenkov
therefore reads *Materialism and Empiriocriticism* as the philosophical counterpart of *What Is to Be Done?* In his vehement
defence of the possibility of objective knowledge, Lenin seeks
to establish an epistemology compatible with his idea of a vanguard party armed with the truth that will enable them to lead
the proletariat to victory (Ilyenkov 1980: 45).[14]

It can be argued that Ilyenkov's *Leninist Dialectics* is unfair to
Bogdanov. For example, for all its technocratic foibles, Bogdanov's science fiction abounds with creativity; one need only
consider the portrayal of gender in *Red Star,* which, in its
treatment of Lenni's sexual encounters with the androgenous
Netti, casts interesting light on the growing sexual revolution
within the Russian intelligentsia in this period. Ilyenkov,
however, ignores this and other virtues of the novel to dismiss
it as "boring and pretentious" (1980: 62). Moreover, Ilyenkov
makes no attempt to *argue* that Lenin's conception of revolutionary strategy was superior to Bogdanov's. As one might expect of Soviet writing of this period, the correctness of Lenin's
political vision is simply a presumption of Ilyenkov's discussion. Nevertheless, for all its weaknesses, Ilyenkov's essay
does show how Lenin and Bogdanov's philosophical positions
were intimately related to their respective politics. Thus, contrary to the usual Western reading, *Materialism and Empiriocriticism* cannot be portrayed simply as a polemic of only tangen-
tial relevance to issues of political substance.

It is ironic that, in his defence of the political integrity of

---

14   Ilyenkov anticipates the excellent discussion in Service (1985: 178–
     83).

Materialism and Empiriocriticism, Ilyenkov finds himself uncritically defending the notion of the vanguard party. For it was the idea of the disciplined party, leading the proletariat to a glorious future in virtue of its mastery of the "correct line," that found such graphic expression under Stalin. Indeed, on "the philosophical front," the Bolshevizers, possessed of the revealed truth (soon to be codified in the *Short Course*) and sweeping aside all those who did not share it, can be seen as an embodiment, albeit a perverse one, of Lenin's doctrine. For this reason, the "Leninist stage" is aptly named. Thus, while Ilyenkov was right to link the philosophy of *Materialism and Empiriocriticism* to the politics of the vanguard party, it is sad that he did not, or could not, assess this politics more critically. For it was Lenin's conception of revolutionary activism that helped create the very philosophical climate that he and other members of his generation sought to rebel against.

Ilyenkov also ignores the fact that the manner in which Lenin makes his case in *Materialism and Empiriocriticism* had damaging effects on the subsequent character of Soviet philosophy. The work is not just polemical, it is abusive. For example, Lenin writes:

> The infinite stupidity of the philistine, smugly retailing the most hackneyed rubbish under cover of a new "Empiriocritical" systematization and terminology – that is what the sociological excursions of Blei, Petzholdt and Mach amount to. A pretentious cloak of verbal artifice, clumsy devices in syllogistic, subtle scholasticism, in a word, as in epistemology, so in sociology, the same reactionary content under the same flamboyant billboard. (Lenin 1909a: 341–2 [322])

As one of *Materialism and Empiriocriticism*'s first reviewers, I. A. Il'in, commented:

> It is impossible not to be struck by the extraordinary tone in which the whole essay is written . . . the literary impertinence and impoliteness goes as far as a direct insult to the most basic standards of decency. (Il'in 1909)

It was not just the rudeness of *Materialism and Empiriocriticism* that disturbed Lenin's contemporaries. They also deplored his method of argumentation: the constant appeals to authority,

the crude ad hominem arguments (taken to the point of trying to discredit philosophers by merely associating them
with the "camp" of "idealists"), the obstinate denial that there
is no "third way" between materialism and idealism, and so
on. As Akselrod and M. Bulgakov remarked in their reviews:

> The unpleasant side of [Lenin's] book, apart from the incalcu-
> lable amount of abuse, is the way in which issues are evaluat-
> ed, not so much in their essence, as from the point of view of,
> as it were, their loyalty to social-democracy. (Bulgakov 1909)

> In the author's argumentation we see neither the pliability of
> philosophical thought, nor the exactness of philosophical defi-
> nition, nor a deep understanding of philosophical problems.
> (Akselrod 1909)

Lenin's idiom had a catastrophic effect on Soviet philosophical discourse. *Materialism and Empiriocriticism* was aimed primarily at a small, intelligentsia audience that was hard to in-
timidate intellectually. However, after the Revolution, with
the intelligentsia rapidly diminishing, the work became the
central philosophical text for a mass readership. Lenin's book
was inherited by a new generation that, though it had only
recently become literate, set itself the task of leading Soviet
culture. This generation, typified by the Bolshevizers, drew its
very conception of the purpose and method of philosophy
from *Materialism and Empiriocriticism*. It is ironic that Lenin, for
all his passion for argument, should have facilitated the intellectual atrocities of the Leninist stage precisely by the way he
argued. Berdyaev comments:

> Lenin himself wrote: "We do not want anything to be accept-
> ed with the eyes shut, to be an article of faith. Everyone should
> keep his head tight on his own shoulders, and think out and
> verify everything for himself." Lenin himself thought as an
> individual and not as part of the "collectivity" which he creat-
> ed, but these words have not taken root ... [A] large part of
> Russia has adopted the coarseness of his language, as when
> he said that "dialectical materialism throws the idealist swine
> who defend God on to the dung heap." He professed a deep re-
> spect for Hegel and read his *Logic* assiduously ... [Yet] when
> Hegel defends the idea of God, Lenin writes, "You felt pity for
> this poor little godlet, you idealist swine." That is [now] the

style of nearly all anti-religious propagandist writing. (Berdyaev 1933: 213–14)

The influence of Lenin's style of philosophizing far outlived the Stalin period to affect even the best of modern Soviet philosophers. Even Ilyenkov, whose best writings are free of unthinking dogmatism, cannot resist mimicking Lenin's idiom when he writes about Lenin himself. This is especially so in *Leninist Dialectics* where, for example, Ilyenkov sometimes writes as if the intelligentsia's interest in Empiriocriticism were a kind of conspiracy, dubs priests "professional enemies of materialism and the revolution," and asserts that "mother history" has proved Lenin right (see 1980: 136–9, 128, 57).

It might be argued that we should not judge Ilyenkov by *Leninist Dialectics*, which, as we noted above, was assembled posthumously from a censored manuscript. Moreover, it could be suggested that Ilyenkov's real purpose in this work was not to discuss the dispute between Lenin and Bogdanov as such, but to project his own controversy with modern Soviet positivists onto that historical debate. On such an interpretation, Ilyenkov can be seen as quite deliberately appropriating Lenin's philosophical idiom in the course of "ventriloquating" his own position through Lenin's.

This reading may make for a more subtle approach to Ilyenkov's essay. It only confirms, however, our assessment of Lenin's influence on Soviet philosophy. That Ilyenkov should choose to conduct a contemporary debate surreptitiously by using an historical authority as the mouthpiece of his own position, that he should have to present that authority as wholly above criticism, that the work should end up being censored so that it appears as a eulogy to the very conception of philosophy that necessitated the initial subterfuge – all these are symptoms of a philosophical culture in which Lenin's legacy is deeply implicated. And by participating in that culture, Ilyenkov inevitably reproduces some of its worst aspects. In this case, for example, whether or not Ilyenkov's target was historical Empiriocritics or contemporary positivists, his book serves to perpetuate the suppression of Alexander Bogdanov, one of the most interesting of the Bolshevik intellectuals. This is another irony, for, notwithstanding their dramatic differences, Bogdanov's resolute monism and his interest in the world-creating power of human agency have much in common with Ilyenkov's own philosophical project. Such ironies, so familiar in the Soviet philosophical tradition, may not have been lost on Ilyenkov himself.

Conclusion

The principal aim of this chapter has been to investigate Lenin's contribution to Soviet philosophy and to explore its influence on Ilyenkov. We discovered that a deep ambiguity in Lenin's materialism rendered his work able to inspire not only Ilyenkov's Hegelian quest to establish a form of direct realism, a conception of the unity of subject and object in knowledge, but also the scientific empiricism influential among Ilyenkov's opponents. Furthermore, the conception of philosophy presented by *Materialism and Empiriocriticism* has exercised an analogous dual influence. While Ilyenkov discerned political integrity in Lenin's philosophical assault on Bogdanov, championing *Materialism and Empiriocriticism* as an example of a new, politically charged and distinctively Soviet philosophy, the work also inspired the philosophy of the Stalin period, legitimating the Bolshevizers' philosophical vanguard and helping to create the perverse character of Soviet philosophical discourse. Thus, if Lenin created Ilyenkov, he also made possible Ilyenkov's opponents: the philistines of the Leninist stage and the scientific empiricists of the modern era. We turn now to examine Ilyenkov's philosophy itself.

ILYENKOV AND DIALECTICAL
METHOD

Our analysis of Ilyenkov's work begins with his treatment of
Marx's dialectical method, the topic of his highly regarded
first book, *The Dialectics of the Abstract and the Concrete in Marx's
"Capital,"* and of many other of his early writings. In Marx's
"method of ascent from the abstract to the concrete," Ilyenkov
chose a subject as controversial as it is obscure. Why did this
aspect of Marx's legacy so capture his imagination?

First, Ilyenkov held that Marx's command of dialectical
method had made possible the creation of *Capital,* the culmination of Marx's research and the highest expression of his
thought. Thus, part of Ilyenkov's aim was to cast light on the
composition of that work and the evaluation of its arguments.
Ilyenkov would have thought that this in itself was an essential project, agreeing with Lucio Colletti that the class consciousness of the proletariat "cannot be derived from any-
where but *Capital*" (Colletti 1969: 236).

Second, Ilyenkov was convinced that the potential applications of Marx's method were not confined to the theory and
practice of political economy. On the contrary, he held that
Marx had developed a method of universal significance, a
necessary condition of successful inquiry in any domain (Ilyenkov 1967a: 186). What Lenin called the "logic of *Capital*"

contained "the only possible and correct procedure for the solution of the specific task of the theoretical cognition of the
world" (Ilyenkov 1960a: 135; cf. Lenin 1895-1916: 319). Hence,
not only was the method itself of enormous scientific significance, but the question of how a method of such explanatory
power could be possible was of great philosophical concern.
Answering this question would define a Marxist position in
philosophy, and would do so, Ilyenkov believed, in a way that
would give sense to the dialectical identity of thinking and
being (Ilyenkov 1971a: 237).

Third, Marx's method appealed to Ilyenkov as an ideal subject to rejuvenate Soviet philosophical debate after two difficult
decades of arid orthodoxy. Such a topic demanded the reintro-
duction of high standards of scholarship. Apart from Marx's
1857 *Introduction,* the classics of Marxism offered only occasional paragraphs devoted directly to method. Ilyenkov was
therefore forced to turn to *Capital* itself, and to the recently published *Grundrisse,* to excavate the method from its application
there. The imaginative way he set about this had a stimulating effect on his contemporaries. His courage in grappling
with difficult issues and problematic conclusions was much
admired, even among those, of both older and younger generations, who were skeptical about his interpretation (e.g., Rosental 1960; Batishchev and Davydov 1961). Here was a philosopher who could make Marxism exciting again, who saw its
classical texts not as weapons to turn on one's enemies, but as
contributions to an evolving philosophical culture. Ilyenkov's
expertise in the history of philosophy recalled the quality and
energy of Soviet debate in the 1920s and early 1930s, when
lively discussions of Marx's method had been conducted by
representatives of many fields, including (apart from the philosophers discussed in Chapter 2) the economist Rubin, the
lawyer Pashukanis, and, of course, Vygotsky (see Pashukanis
1924; Rubin 1928). Mikhaïl Lifshits, the distinguished Soviet
philosopher and pupil of Lukács's, recalls the refreshing effect
of Ilyenkov's arrival on the intellectual scene:

> After the war much changed, and times were not easy . . .
> When Ilyenkov turned up at my place of refuge with his He-
> gelian problems of "alienation" and "reification" times were
> such that philosophical subtlety was prone to raise a smile . . .

[Yet] I remember that when I read his early manuscript about dialectics in Marx's *Capital* I understood that the years of the war and the postwar events had not completely eliminated the best of the previous decades, and that by some miracle, the seed that had been thrown then onto the grateful earth, though thoroughly trodden underfoot, had sprouted nonetheless, but in a different and unrecognizable form . . .

By this I don't mean to diminish Ilyenkov's originality. He was travelling in the same direction, but at a different time and by a different route. I only want to say that his appearance in my lair was proof, as it were, of *the law of the preservation of thought,* of the way that thought is reproduced in new conditions, if it somehow serves them. In him I unexpectedly found an ally just at the time when the élan of the educated and thinking Marxist youth of the 'thirties remained only a happy memory . . . (Lifshits 1984: 6-7; cf. Kozulin 1984: 29-30)

Not all Ilyenkov's contemporaries would remember him so warmly. His passion to retrieve Marx's method, and the intellectual tradition that had sought to develop it, was further motivated by the conviction that they both had been betrayed. His work, therefore, presented a political as well as a philosophical challenge. This was not welcomed by everyone. Lifshits describes how for "the fierce enthusiasts of orthodoxy of those years Ilyenkov was an 'outsider,' even though his originality consisted precisely in his return to the classics of Marxism," and how his relations "were strained to the limit" with those "ideologues" and "careerists" who sought to construct "cults of their own personality" (1984: 7). Ilyenkov's unpopularity in such circles persisted throughout his career.

However, though estranged from certain quarters of the Soviet philosophical world, Ilyenkov was far from the only Marxist of the period fascinated with Marx's method. Many Eastern European Marxists felt its relevance as they struggled to extricate their theory from Stalinism and to remake contact with the intellectual ethos of the first two decades of the century. Ilyenkov's early work thus represents one among a number of notable contributions, including those by the Ukrainian émigré Roman Rosdolsky (1968; see Anderson 1976: 98–9; Mepham 1979) and the Czech Jindřich Zelený (1962).

What may we expect to learn from Ilyenkov's work on dialectical method? Earlier in this book, we encountered the topic in our discussions of Akselrod's criticisms of Deborin (Chapter 2) and of Vygotsky's debt to Marx (Chapter 3). Ilyenkov's work helps us attain a better understanding of the issues involved in those discussions. Interestingly, he does so by offering more than a purely metatheoretical elucidation and defence of the method. Ilyenkov sought in Marx a method he could himself apply to a range of philosophical issues, notably to the nature of the "ideal" (i.e., the nonmaterial) and the human "essence" (Ilyenkov 1974a: 3–6). Indeed, it is Ilyenkov's application of the method, rather than his theoretical commentary upon it, that proves the better test of its plausibility. Thus, while Ilyenkov's commentary is interesting and important in itself, the full significance of his concern with Marxist method will emerge only later, when we consider his "philosophy of activity" in Chapters 6 and 7.

The method of ascent from the abstract to the concrete: A synopsis

Marx's dialectical method represents cognition (*poznanie:* the process of coming-to-know) as a movement from "abstract" to "concrete." What does this mean? First, we must be clear about the general aspirations of "dialectical" method. Allen Wood offers sound advice:

> Neither in Hegel nor in Marx is dialectical thinking really a set of procedures for inquiry, still less a set of rules for generating or justifying results ... Dialectical method is best viewed as a general conception of the sort of intelligible structure the world has to offer, and consequently a programme for the sort of theoretical structure which would best capture it. (Wood 1981: 190)

"Concreteness," according to Ilyenkov, is a property of that "intelligible structure," a property of the object of knowledge as it exists in reality:

> A concrete object is an "integral object," multivariously divided within itself, rich in determinations, and historically formed. It is like, not a separate isolated atom, but a living organism, a socioeconomic structure, or similar formation. (Ilyenkov 1968c: 77)

Thus the object of knowledge is a "system," "totality," or "whole" composed of individual phenomena integrally related to each other; that is, the parts are pictured as essentially related to one another, their natures constituted by their position and role within the whole. (In Chapter 3, following Vygotsky, we called such relations "internal relations.") Concreteness may be seen as a function of the strength of the relations between components: The tighter the bonds of mutual determination between its parts, the more concrete the whole.

Following Hegel, a concrete totality is often referred to as a "unity in diversity," or "unity of opposites" (see Ilyenkov 1960a: 88–100; cf Hegel 1830a: sec. 33). This signifies not only that the parts of the whole possess different properties, but that their differences form the basis of their reciprocal determination: "[O]ne individual thing is as it is, and not another thing, exactly because the other is diametrically opposed to it" (Ilyenkov 1960a: 91). Thus, the structure of the whole is founded upon the diversity of its parts. This diversity is also taken to explain the *dynamic* nature of the concrete whole. The differences between parts put them in tension, as a result of which they undergo changes issuing in the development of the whole.

Concreteness is, then, a property of the object of cognition. Moreover, it would seem to follow from the purported universality of Marx's method that concreteness is a property of *all* objects: All objects of knowledge are concrete wholes.[1] Thus, the task of cognition is to "reproduce" the concrete totality in thought. To understand the nature of any particular component we must grasp both

1 Ilyenkov (1962a: 197–8) endorses the view that all objects of knowledge are concrete totalities. Elsewhere, however, he distinguishes between two sorts of object encountered in reality: (1) "organic wholes [that] develop their own parts from out of themselves" and (2) "mechanistic wholes" in which the parts can exist independently of the whole (1967a: 193). On the most consistent interpretation, Ilyenkov holds that reality "as such" is an organic whole containing both organic and mechanistic wholes as subsystems. Mechanistic wholes are themselves components of organic wholes, and their parts, although "externally" related to each other qua parts of the whole, nonetheless occupy internal relations with other phenomena. Accommodating mechanistic wholes in reality would permit Ilyenkov to hold (sensibly) that not all relations are internal relations.

1. its role within the concrete whole through an account of the internal relations it bears to other components, and
2. the history of its origin and development:

> To *comprehend* a phenomenon means to establish its place and role in the concrete system of interacting phenomena in which it is necessarily realized, and to find out precisely those traits which make it possible for the phenomenon to play this role in the whole. To *comprehend* a phenomenon means to discover the mode of its origin, the rule according to which the phenomenon emerges with necessity rooted in the concrete totality of conditions, it means to analyze the very conditions of the origin of phenomena. (Ilyenkov 1960a: 177)

However, for Ilyenkov (1) and (2) are not separable tasks, for analysis is to reveal how the matrix of relations of mutual determination is possible through an account of the evolution of the whole they constitute. Analysis is, therefore, simultaneously structural and genetic (cf. Zelený 1962: 9, 113–14).

How does cognition begin? A concrete whole is an *organized* entity. The task, therefore, is to establish its "principle of composition." In his analysis of capitalist society as a concrete totality, Marx claims that

> There is in every social formation a particular branch of production which determines the position and importance of all the others, and the relations obtaining in this branch accordingly determine the relations of all the other branches as well. It is as though light of a particular hue were cast upon everything, tinging all other colours and modifying their specific features: or as if a special ether determined the specific gravity of everything found in it. (1857: 146)

Ilyenkov's generalizes this thought: For any object O that is a concrete whole, there will be some particular component C that determines the position of all the other components. C is thought of as an elementary form of the whole. Like O itself, C is an internally contradictory formation. As it develops through these contradictions, C gives rise to, or evolves into, O. Thus to trace the development of C is to reconstruct O in a way that presents its evolution as a necessary consequence of the unfolding of contradictions within C. C, therefore, is

... the kind of particular which simultaneously is a universal condition of the existence of the other particulars recorded in other categories.[2] That is, a particular entity whose whole specificity lies in being the universal and the abstract, that is, the undeveloped, elementary, "cellular" formation, developing through contradictions immanently inherent in it into other more complex and well-developed formations. (Ilyenkov 1960a: 59)

C is a "universal" because it constitutes "the law of the existence, change and development of particular and individual phenomena in their connection, interaction and unity" (Ilyenkov 1960b: 301). The universal of O represents the *essence* of O; it is that which makes O the O that it is. For Ilyenkov, to have a *concept* of an object is to grasp this universal, to know its essence.

In what way, then, is cognition an "ascent from abstract to concrete"? By "abstract," Ilyenkov understands anything

picked out, isolated, existing "on its own," in relative independence from everything else, – any "side," aspect or part of a real whole, any determinate fragment of reality or of its reflection in consciousness. (Ilyenkov 1967a: 192)

There are three senses of "abstract" here:

1. A conception of some object is said to be abstract$_1$ if it is partial or one-sided.
2. An entity is an abstraction$_2$ if it is considered in isolation from the whole of which it is an essential part.
3. An entity is an abstraction$_3$ if it exists in relative autonomy from that whole (as a so-called real abstraction).

All three senses figure in Ilyenkov's account of cognition as an ascent from abstract to concrete. Cognition is pictured as proceeding from a partial, one-sided (abstraction$_1$) conception of O, through the isolation (abstraction$_2$) of C (a real abstrac-

2 By "category," Ilyenkov means the fundamental concepts of a science or, more generally, of a conception of the world. In this he follows normal Soviet usage (see Spirkin and Yaroshevskii 1983). Categories describe (or aspire to describe) reality as it is. Thus, categories are necessary forms of thought only in the sense that the correct description of the world requires us to employ them.

tions, existing prior to the whole to which its gives rise), to the reconstruction of O as a concrete totality.[3]

Ilyenkov, after Hegel, calls C a *concrete universal* in contrast to the notion of universals dominant in nondialectical philosophy. This nondialectical conception represents the universal of O in terms of properties shared by all instances of O. Universals are thus construed as

> sameness, as a property abstracted, isolated from particular and individual phenomena, as the abstract identity of all or many things or phenomena with one another in one or other respect, as features possessed by all on the basis of which they are mentally united into a class, set, type, or kind. (Ilyenkov 1960b: 301)

Such "abstract universals" are taken to be entities qualitatively distinct from the particulars subsumed under them. The classical empiricist tradition, for example, treats the universal as a special kind of idea, general in form, embodying the common characteristics of the diverse particulars subsumed under it. On this view, the universal stands to the particular as species to individual. For Ilyenkov, however, the universal, understood concretely, can itself be a particular, existing alongside the other particular components of the whole of which it is the "cell":

> The universal, which reveals itself in the particularities (*oso-bennost'*), of the individual characteristics of all the components of the whole without exception, exists itself as a particular individual alongside the others that are derived from it. There is absolutely nothing mystical in this: Fathers often live long among their sons ... The universal, understood genetically, exists, obviously, not only in the ether of abstraction, not only in the realm of word and thought, and its existence neither annuls nor diminishes the reality of its modifications, of the particular individuals derived from and dependent upon it. (Ilyenkov 1974a: 256–7)

This, in schematic form, is Ilyenkov's rendition of the method of ascent from abstract to concrete. Even within Soviet

---

3 The "priority" in question may be logical rather than temporal; see the discussion of Ilyenkov's historicism below for his account of the relation between the "logical" and the "historical."

philosophical circles, his claims on behalf of dialectical method are highly controversial. For example, notwithstanding Lenin's enthusiasm for the concrete universal, few Soviet philosophers would agree with Ilyenkov that there was anything "obvious" about its status (Lenin: 1895–1916: 99). To make Ilyenkov's position plausible, or even intelligible, we must look hard at the arguments he produces in its defence.

Ilyenkov develops his position through a critique of the contrary views of his opponents. Of these, he takes a form of scientific empiricism (which he sometimes calls "positivism") most seriously. This empiricism, which finds its classical statement in the British empiricists,

1. holds that all knowledge is derived from experience, and
2. endorses a form of methodological solipsism on which each individual subject is represented as constructing a picture of the world out of sense experience given in perception (see the discussion of Lenin's critique of Empiriocriticism in Chapter 4).

Ilyenkov's interest in this position was motivated by two factors. First, he took it to be the highest historical expression of the nondialectical conception of cognition he sought to undermine. Second, he was concerned about the growing influence of empiricism within Soviet philosophy itself. As we have seen, there is a history of empiricism (both "scientific" and "idealist") within Soviet philosophy among groups, such as the Empiriocritics and the Mechanists, that champion the universal explanatory prowess of natural science and the liberating potential of technology. As the USSR emerged from the tragic absurdities of "proletarian science," the thaw of the early 1960s saw a resurgence of scientific and technological optimism. This found its reflection in Soviet philosophy as a renewed concern to uphold the objectivity and autonomy of science. Thus, many of Ilyenkov's contemporaries were attracted to the scientific empiricist's conception of objective reality: the idea of the "absolute conception of the world." As we observed in Chapter 4, empiricism, the philosophy of the Enlightenment par excellence, was appealing to those who sought a philosophical basis for science that would explain its objectivity without challenging its autonomy.

Ilyenkov aimed to dispel the attractions of empiricism and to establish his dialectical method as the only possible framework for Marxist science and philosophy. However, to do so, he had to prove not only the falsehood of empiricism, but also the compatibility of his proposed alternative with philosophical materialism. Ilyenkov's idiom is thoroughly Hegelian (for Hegel on abstract and concrete, see Inwood 1983: 366–80). He needed to show that these ideas can be removed from Hegel's elaborate idealist system without losing their sense. Thus, after Ilyenkov's critique of empiricism – an important component of his legacy in its own right – we will turn to the compatibility of dialectical method with materialism.

Ilyenkov versus the empiricist

Ilyenkov argues that the empiricist, in contradistinction to Hegel and Marx, represents cognition as a movement from concrete to abstract. In so doing, however, the empiricist is said to operate with a different understanding of the terms "abstract" and "concrete," according to which the concrete is "particular, sensually perceived things or their perceptual images" (1960a: 14–15), "uninterrupted, indefinite 'sensual givenness'" (1960a: 36), whereas the abstract is "everything not given in individual experience (31), ... the general forms of things, their identically repeated qualities and lawlike relations, expressed in terms, names, and numbers" (15).

Clearly, by presenting the subject as processing the brute particularity of "sensual givenness" into a conception of the world employing general concepts and relations, the empiricist does portray cognition as a movement from concrete to abstract in the senses defined above. So general a characterization is, however, of minimal philosophical interest. The meat of Ilyenkov's case emerges only as he probes into the details of his opponent's position. His writings succeed in identifying a number of specific aspects of the empiricist picture that each construe some aspect of cognition as a movement from concrete to abstract. I shall consider two: the empiricist's theory of concept acquisition and his conception of objective reality.

The empiricist's theory of concept acquisition

For the empiricist, human knowledge has a hierarchical structure. At its foundation is "the boundless sea" of sense particulars, "the concrete as such," while at its summit stand our most general concepts and beliefs, "the abstract as such" (Ilyenkov 1971a: 240). Ilyenkov savagely attacks the empiricist's account of the first step of this hierarchy: the formation of concepts from the data of perception. By so doing, he aims to show that his opponent's theory cannot explain how knowledge can even begin.

The empiricist construes concept formation itself as a movement from concrete to abstract, holding that we acquire concepts by a process of abstraction from the (concrete) data of sense. For example, we are said to attain the concept of whiteness by abstracting the common feature from samples of white things and naming it "white." Mackie, commenting on Locke, describes this process:

> I see a white piece of paper at a particular time and place, and notice that it resembles in colour other pieces of paper, cups of milk, fields covered with snow, and so on; I pay attention to the feature in which it resembles these other things and pay no attention to the shape or size of the piece of paper or its surroundings or even to the time at which I see it; I remember this feature and associate the word "whiteness" with it ... and I am thus ready to use the same word "whiteness" with respect to that same feature in any other things at any other places and times ... (Mackie 1976: 110; cf. Locke 1689: II.xi.9)

Such a concept is, of course, an "abstract universal," a "verbally fixed abstraction of the similarity possessed by all or many sensually contemplated things" (Ilyenkov 1960b: 302). The abstract universal embodies the necessary conditions for something to be an X in the form of the shared characteristics of X's. It represents the *criterion* of X-hood: Once we have the concept of X, we can employ it to test whether some particular is an X. The universal is also the *meaning* of the word that names it: The concept of X is the meaning of "X." To know what "X" means is to know the criterion of X, what it takes for something to be (an) X.

Ilyenkov's critique of this conception is powerful but confusing. For example, at first sight it may appear that he and the empiricist are simply addressing different questions. It might be argued that whereas the empiricist is trying to explain how we form basic concepts, Ilyenkov's favoured "method of ascent from the abstract to the concrete" is really best seen as a technique for constructing theories out of such concepts. The two positions are not, therefore, obviously incompatible. On the contrary, since we cannot begin to build theories until we have general concepts, it may even seem that the empiricist's picture is a natural complement to Ilyenkov's (cf. Ilyenkov 1960a: 101–6, 136). Can we not see the empiricist as describing the origin of the "abstract" material on which Ilyenkov's method goes to work; that is, as describing what Ilyenkov calls "the reduction of the concrete fullness of reality to its abridged (abstract) expression in consciousness ... without which no special theoretical research can proceed or even begin" (Ilyenkov 1960a: 137)?

Although Ilyenkov did toy with the idea of an alliance with empiricism in his very first article (1955), all his subsequent works on the subject categorically reject the empiricist's account.[4] Ilyenkov is adamant that the empiricist's theory of the material from which we build our picture of reality is inadequate. Confusion is nonetheless perpetuated by the poor quality of some of Ilyenkov's arguments. For example, he sometimes ridicules his opponent for treating all analysis as classification of objects according to common features. This is, however, a gross misrepresentation. No empiricist would, as Ilyenkov claims, hold that how radio receivers work can be discovered by listing their shared features, or that philosophy, as the most general science, searches for properties common to all phenomena, for "what a crocodile has in common with Jupiter and the solar system with value" (1960a: 171; 1968c: 71). Such jokes rebound on Ilyenkov, for they obscure the substance of his case. We need therefore to separate the grain

4 In that early article Ilyenkov writes, "The formula that the only correct method for theoretical thinking is 'the ascent from the abstract to the concrete,' of course, does not in the least distort the fact that each step of this ascent involves the formation of new abstractions from the sensually given manifold and that *this abstraction takes place approximately in the way that Locke described*" (1955: 52; my emphasis).

from the chaff. I believe Ilyenkov's writings can be shown to contain a two-pronged argument designed to prove

1. that even if abstraction as the empiricist imagines it were possible, its results would not be able to fulfil the functions he attributes to them, and
2. that such abstraction is anyway not possible.

I shall take each in turn.

(1) Ilyenkov claims that, even if we could abstract common features from the data of sense, such abstraction would not yield true *concepts*. He argues that "a concept is something more than simply an abstract universal fixed by a word, the meaning of a general term" (1971a: 258–9). To say that some subject S possesses a concept of X is to say more than S knows how to pick out and refer to X. Possession of the concept enables S to determine whether something is an X *in hard cases*. Abstract universals, however, will not do this. For example, it will not necessarily be possible to settle whether some animal should be counted as "human" by appeal to the common properties of human beings, determined independently of that case (Ilyenkov 1960a: 62–77; illustrated by appeal to Vercors 1952). The concept of X must express not simply *what* properties X's share, but *what accounts for* the similarities and differences of their various manifestations. To know this is to understand the real nature of X. But this understanding may be achieved only by grasping the relations of X to the whole of which it is a part, or, if X is itself a concrete totality, by understanding the matrix of internal relations that compose it.

An important point of philosophical principle is at stake here. Ilyenkov is denying that we can identify

(a) what we know when we know the meaning of the word "X" and
(b) knowledge of the nature of X, what it is for something to be (an) X.

Interestingly, the assimilation of (a) and (b) is the basis of a well-known species of twentieth-century philosophy, "ordinary language philosophy," an approach that Ilyenkov takes to embody many of the confusions he detects in empiricism. This approach distinguishes sharply between *empirical truths*, discovered by looking at the world, and *conceptual truths,* established by analyzing concepts. Analyzing the concept of X is identified with looking at what "X" means, at how we use the word "X." The ordinary language philosopher holds that only such conceptual analysis can reveal what X necessarily is; the essential properties of X are embodied in our language and cannot be discovered empirically. The reason is this: If we learn empirically that X possesses some property p, then possession of p will not be among the criteria for employing the term "X," since we can talk about X in ignorance of p. But if we can use "X" in ignorance of p, then we can imagine that X can exist without p. If this is imaginable, then it is logically possible that X exists independently of p. Therefore p cannot be an essential property of X, since it is logically impossible for something to exist independently of its essential properties. By contrast, Ilyenkov, in denying that (a) and (b) can be assimilated, holds that truths about the natures of things can be established, perhaps can only be established, by analysis of facts obtaining independently of our ways of talking. Thus, science can discover truths about the essential properties of objects, about what they necessarily are. For Ilyenkov, something is a concept only if it embodies such truths.[5]

Ilyenkov pursues his critique by accusing the empiricist of Platonism. The empiricist forgets, he claims, that his abstract universals "belong not to the real existence of things; but are the inventions and creatures of the understanding, made by it for its own use, and concern only signs" (Locke 1689: III.iii.11). Instead, the empiricist attributes to them real existence, "as if alongside the empirical world of particular sensually perceptible individuals there exists a special world acces-

---

5 In the past two decades many representatives of the Anglo–American tradition, notably Kripke and Putnam, have sought to resist the assimilation of (a) and (b) (see Putnam 1962, 1973; Kripke 1980). Interestingly, Locke himself is not guilty of the assimilation. He distinguishes between (1) the "nominal" essence of X – the abstract general idea of X that gives the meaning of "X" – and (2) its "real" essence, the "real, but unknown, constitution of [its] insensible parts; from which flow those sensible qualities which serve us to distinguish them one from another" (1689: III.iii.17). While nominal essences are inventions of the mind, real essences are part of the fabric of the world and are discoverable by science. Ilyenkov, however, does not acknowledge Locke's insight.

sible only to thought" (Ilyenkov 1971a: 345). It then becomes attractive to think of the empirical world we experience as a fleeting manifestation of the abstract universal (1971a: 341–2). This picture has all the disadvantages of Hegelianism with none of the advantages (1968c: 70).

Although these accusations of Platonism may appear fanciful, John McDowell has indeed argued that a form of Platonism is implicit in the empiricist's very idea of how universals may be of "use" to the intellect (McDowell 1981). Following Wittgenstein, McDowell maintains that the empiricist thinks of concepts as marking out "rails" along which our thoughts must run. The rails are "there anyway," independently of our thought processes and language practices (which, according to Ilyenkov [1977b, 1979d: 122–5], the empiricist conflates). They mark out the path that constitutes correctness in those processes and practices. To acquire a concept, then, is to engage one's "mental wheels with these objectively existing rails" (McDowell 1981: 146). Thus, the empiricist's theory of universals provides a model of how thought is able to "lock in" to reality.

While Ilyenkov would welcome the idea that to possess a concept is to engage with reality in a special way, he would deny that the empiricist makes proper sense of this engagement. On the empiricist's model, the content of a concept, or the meaning of a word, determines all its possible applications: The rails "stretch to infinity." Thus, grasping the concept is a guarantee of correctness, a guarantee that our thought and speech will stay "on the rails." The concept, then, is thought to embody *necessity*, the necessity that determines why it must be employed this way and no other. Ilyenkov denies, however, that abstract universals could be capable of embodying such necessity. Inspired by Spinoza, he argues that abstract universals are backward looking: Since their content is determined by empirical generalization from past experience, nothing in that content can guarantee what will constitute correctness in future (cf. Spinoza 1677: 235). Abstract universals are always underdetermined by the data. To possess them would be to live in fear that "any new fact may overturn the abstraction, ... (for) no guarantee can be found in experience that the universal expresses a genuine universal form of things and not simply a subjective fiction" (Ilyenkov

1962a: 182). By contrast "a genuine idea [what Spinoza calls *notiones communes'*], as distinct from a simple abstract universal [*'notiones generalis universalis'*], must contain necessity, following which one can explain all the directly observable properties of the thing" (1960a: 21; see also 22). The fact that to possess a genuine concept is to understand how X *can* present itself in experience is the basis of our confidence that it will not be defeated by future experience.

(2) The arguments in (1) show that abstract universals could not play the role attributed to them by the empiricist. Ilyenkov turns the screw by arguing that the formation of abstract universals is impossible. The empiricist claims that our conceptual scheme is formed by abstraction from sense experience, but, Ilyenkov claims, such abstraction is only possible if the subject already possesses a conceptual scheme. Thus the empiricist is forced to presuppose what he seeks to explain (Ilyenkov 1971a: 258–9). For example, we imagine that the subject forms concepts by identifying objects given in experience and making judgments about the resemblances between them. But *how* does he (or she) identify these objects? And on what basis does he decide that they share the *same* property? (Cf. the "Wittgensteinian" defence of Vygotsky in Chapter 3.)

Ilyenkov believes that these problems derive from the empiricist's methodological solipsism. If we suppose that each individual subject constructs a picture of the world "from scratch," we shall be forced question-beggingly to attribute to him or her conceptual skills in order to account for how cognition gets started. Ilyenkov's answer is to reject the methodological solipsist's "Robinson Crusoe epistemological model" (Ilyenkov 1960a: 41). In its place, he suggests that, for each individual, the starting point of cognition is not unprocessed sense experience but a conception of the world *inherited* "ready made" from the community of which he or she is a member. This conception confronts the human child as a form of "social consciousness," objectified in the environment by the practices (both linguistic and other) of the community. As the child learns to reproduce these activities, so he or she appropriates a conception of the world. This is not a conscious process, but the process of becoming conscious. Thus, perception is never a relation between a pure subject and raw experiential

data, but between a socially formed subject and objects "refracted" through the "prism" of social consciousness. Ilyenkov writes:

> Rising to conscious life within society, the individual finds
> [a] preexisting "spiritual environment," objectively imple-
> mented spiritual culture. The latter is opposed to individual
> consciousness as a specific object which the individual has to
> assimilate taking into account its nature as something quite
> objective. A system of forms of social consciousness (in the
> broadest possible sense, including forms of the political organ-
> ization of society, law, morality, everyday life, and so on, as
> well as forms and norms of actions in the sphere of thought,
> grammatical syntactic rules for the verbal expression of no-
> tions, aesthetic tastes, etc.) structures from the very outset the
> developing consciousness and will of the individual, mould-
> ing him in its own image. As a result, each separate sensual
> impression arising in individual consciousness is always a
> product of the refraction of external stimuli through the ex-
> tremely complex prism of the forms of social consciousness
> the individual has appropriated. This "prism" is a product of
> social human development. Alone, face to face with nature,
> the individual has no such prism, and it [the prism] cannot
> be understood from an analysis of the relation of an isolated
> individual to nature. (1960a: 40–1)

This passage, written before Ilyenkov had read Vygotsky,
strikingly recalls the latter's theory of "the social genesis of
the individual" (discussed in Chapter 3). Gone is the abstract
thinking subject of classical epistemology; instead we have
an individual who "rises to conscious life" only through incorporation into a community. In this way, Vygotsky and Ilyenkov strive to give content to Marx's enigmatic remark that
"man is a *zoon politikon* in the most literal sense: He is not only a social animal, but an animal who can individualize himself only within society" (Marx 1857: 125). If their project can
be made to succeed, empiricism's "epistemological individu-
alism," the basis of its theory of concept acquisition, will be
conclusively refuted.

The empiricist's conception of objective reality

A different respect in which the empiricist represents cognition as a movement from concrete to abstract is his or her ac-

count of the formation of the scientific picture of the world. This account presupposes a particular conception of objective reality, the end of scientific inquiry. This idea, attributed to the conservative realist of Chapter 4, holds that something is objectively real if and only if it exists independently of all observers. Thus, to capture objective reality, science must form a conception of the world as it exists in itself, "independently of any thought or experience" (Williams 1978: 64). As we have seen in previous chapters, the empiricist holds that our "everyday" picture of reality is lent a degree of anthropocentricity by the kind of mind and sensory apparatus human beings possess. For example, we see the world as coloured, yet colours are not properties the world possesses independently of perceivers: They are "projected" onto reality by our minds. Science's task, then, is to form an "absolute" conception of the world from which all those properties visible from our merely "local" perspective have been purged or "abstracted."[6] Ilyenkov comments that, on this view,

> everything "concrete" came to be understood as a product of the activity of the sense organs, as a certain psychophysiological state of the subject, as a subjectively coloured replica of a colourless, abstract geometrical original. The prime task of cognition was conceived thus: To reach the truth it was necessary to erase or sweep away all those colours contributed by the nature of the senses to the sensually given image of things to reveal the abstract geometrical skeleton or schema...
>
> The picture turned out thus: Outside man's consciousness there exist only eternally immutable abstract-geometrical particles combining themselves according to just as eternal and immutable abstract-mathematical schema, while the concrete exists only within the subject, as a form of the sense perception of abstract-geometrical bodies. Hence the formula: The only true path to truth is to soar from the concrete ... to the abstract. (Ilyenkov 1962a: 179–80).

6 The absolute conception of reality represents "knowledge of a reality which exists independently of that knowledge, and indeed (except for the special case where the reality known happens itself to be some psychological item) independently of any thought or experience" (Williams 1978: 64). Strictly, the absolute conception should not simply eschew all local representations of the world, but attempt an explanation of how these different representations are possible (Williams 1978: 245–6).

Since Ilyenkov holds that objective reality is a concrete totality of mutually determining parts evolving through its immanent contradictions, he vehemently denies (1968c: 62–3)
that it can be reduced to a collection of simple, immutable,
and indivisible particles interacting in purely "external" relations.[7] Reality as a concrete totality is irreducible to the sum of
its parts, for the nature of those parts is determined by their
place in the whole.

However, it is not simply the empiricist's particular, atomistic vision of reality that provokes Ilyenkov's scorn. More
significantly, he dismisses the empiricist's very criterion of
objectivity. It is wrong, he claims, to hold that objective reality
contains no properties that somehow get there because of us.
Ilyenkov argues that many nonmaterial, or "ideal," properties
would not be present in a world without conscious agents, yet
they have objective existence. Although these properties may
exist independently of the will and consciousness of individuals, they are not independent of human beings as such, for
they cannot be characterized without essential reference to
consciousness and activity.

Significantly, Ilyenkov's conception of the objectivity of the
ideal is a crucial facet of his rejection of methodological solipsism, for it is precisely the objective ideal that forms "social
consciousness," that "complex and historically shaped sphere
of the material and spiritual culture of humankind," that each
individual must assimilate in order to rise to conscious life (Ilyenkov 1960a: 40). Consequently, Ilyenkov holds that without
appeal to objectively existing ideal properties no acceptable
theory of thought will be possible.

In Ilyenkov's earliest writings these ideas have the status of
confident suggestions. Later, however, as they came to form
the basis of his philosophy of humankind, he began to give
them real substance. We shall consider his arguments later.
For now, we need only observe that his assault on methodo-

7   Relations are "external" if they are not constitutive of their relata.
    Many representatives of the Cartesian and empiricist traditions have
    held that all relations are external relations. For example, Wolff,
    against whom German classical philosophy reacted most strongly,
    asserts that "relation adds no quality to an entity which it does not
    contain itself; for no entity exists in dependence, whether real or
    apparent, of one thing on another" (Wolff 1730: sec. 857).

logical solipsism and his solution to "the problem of the ideal" are bold initiatives. They represent a challenge not just to empiricism but to the entire Cartesian tradition. If Ilyenkov is right, philosophy must undergo a revolution in how it thinks of thought. While the Cartesian tradition has treated thought primarily as a "silent monologue" occurring privately in individual minds, Ilyenkov's Hegelian perspective urges that thought is something necessarily embodied in the interrelations between people and in their intercourse with nature. Only by participation in the social transformation of nature does the individual become a "moment" of the true unit of thought, the community, or culture (Ilyenkov 1973: esp. 136–7). Thus, Ilyenkov's clash with empiricism evolves from a seemingly obscure squabble over the abstract and the concrete into a "clash of two logics" with the very nature of thought at stake.

While Ilyenkov's case against the empiricist introduces the more exciting and original themes of his contribution, his dismissal of the empiricist's atomistic vision of reality returns us to the more sobering topic of concrete totality and the labyrinth of dialectical method. Even if we are persuaded that Ilyenkov has succeeded in removing his principal opponent from the scene, his positive account of Marxist method remains shrouded in mystery, its compatibility with materialism unclear. I turn now to consider this problem directly.

Concrete totality and materialism

The issue of the compatibility of Ilyenkov's dialectical method with materialism is brought into sharp relief when we consider its pedigree. Its roots, of course, lie deep in the German classical tradition. The idea of a concrete whole, or "organic totality," finds its first expression in Kant's analysis of the living organism in the *Critique of Judgement*. Kant describes a living organism as a unity of parts "so combined that they are reciprocally cause and effect of each other's form" (Kant 1790: 219). As the parts "reciprocally *produce* each other," the existence ("presence") and nature ("form") of each depends on its place within the whole. Thus, understanding the whole is the "ground of cognition ... of the systematic unity and combination of all the manifold contained in the given material" (219–20). This understanding is teleological: The organism is a "natural purpose" realized by its parts.

Hegel enthusiastically adopted Kant's conception not just for the nature of living things, but as a model for the self-development of reality as a whole, or "the absolute." The idea that philosophy should be concerned primarily with the absolute, so characteristic of German philosophy after Kant, was inspired by Spinoza, one of Ilyenkov's favourite philosophers. Fichte, Schelling, and Hegel all admired Spinoza's rejection of Cartesian dualism for an idea of reality as one infinite and indivisible divine substance, the true being of the diverse realm of particulars we experience. And all three offered contrasting idealist accounts of how this absolute substance is best conceived. For Hegel, the absolute is spirit or mind, which he understood not as a static, self-identical substance, but as a living, developing *subject*. In an act of pure self-creation, spirit realizes itself by becoming object. The relation between spirit and otherness, subject and object, evolves in and through history until spirit comes to understand the object as its own expression. In this act of ultimate self-consciousness, spirit attains absolute knowledge: "Only this self-*restoring* sameness, or this reflection of otherness within itself – not an *original* or *immediate* unity – is the True" (Hegel 1807: 10).

For Hegel, Kant's idea of organic totality perfectly captures the nature of spirit and "the characteristic form of its self-expression in its objects" (Wood 1981: 192). Spirit represents the self-organizing whole that is the principle, essence, or form of everything that exists. It stands to all things as a living organism to the parts of its body, for while spirit is constituted by that in which it is embodied (as an organism is constituted by its body), it is the substance in which all things have their being and the reason for which everything exists.

Hegel's distinctive "absolute" idealism issues from this vision of spirit as organic totality. First, spirit is not everything that exists, but it is the *end* of everything that exists. Hence, to understand any phenomenon is to see it as a necessary moment of spirit's development, as a part of spirit's self-realization. In this sense, spirit is "primary" over matter. Second, not everything that exists is spirit, but spirit is all that is truly real. For example, although concepts require embodiment in sensible particulars to attain actuality, the concepts themselves represent the true reality embodied in those particulars. Third, since spirit is the foundation of being, and being is the essential embodiment of spirit, thought and being, subject and object, are ultimately identical (though this identity is achieved only through the bifurcation of subject and object), an identity that culminates in absolute knowledge.

On Hegel's picture, the evolution of spirit is dialectical, and our understanding of it is expressed in philosophy by employing dialectical techniques. History is thus conceived as a movement from abstract to concrete: Spirit moves from progressively less abstract conceptions of itself to attain fully concrete knowledge of the world as an organic totality of which it itself is the organizing principle.

Predictably, controversy rages among Marxists as to whether Marx's adoption of the rhetoric of "the ascent from the abstract to the concrete" represents a genuine commitment to dialectical method, and, if it does, whether that commitment involves (in some way) embracing aspects of the Hegelian conception of the world. Some Marxists, seizing on Marx's remark that, in *Capital,* he "coquetted with the mode of expression peculiar to [Hegel]," have argued that, for Marx, dialectics is simply a means of presenting his material, inessential to the substance of his theory (Marx 1873: 103; cf. Suchting 1985: 97–8, in the Althusserian tradition). Ilyenkov, however, vehemently rejects this reading (e.g., Ilyenkov 1960a: 142–4, 163–4; 1971a: 240). According to him, Marx believes that his object, capitalism, is a concrete totality and that only the dialectical method can reveal the essence of such an object. Thus, for Ilyenkov, Marx rejects not Hegel's dialectical method but only his idealist metaphysics. The materialism Marx substitutes, however, preserves the idea of reality as a self-developing organism or concrete totality. Thus, Marx, like Hegel, believes that dialectical method is warranted because reality itself has a dialectical structure. However, whereas for Hegel the dialectical structure of reality follows from the dialectical nature of thought, for Marx it is the other way around. In this way, Marx "stands Hegel on his feet."

Thus, on Ilyenkov's position, the validity of Marx's method hinges on the success of his famous "inversion" of Hegel (Ilyenkov 1967a: 187). Is it plausible, however, that Hegel's dialectics can be wedded to a materialist metaphysic? Notwithstanding the optimism of some commentators, such a marriage is highly problematic (cf. Meikle 1985: 31). As we have seen, Hegel's dialectics and metaphysics are intrinsically related. The idea of organic totality, for example, is a fundamental ingredient of his idealism. For Hegel, the world can have a dialectical structure precisely because it is spirit or thought. We can think of spirit evolving through the resolution of contradictions immanent within it because, since aspects of spirit are thought determinations, it is intelligible that they should stand in *logical* relations like contradiction. Similarly, the bonds of mutual determination between embodiments of spirit may be treated as logical relations between the concepts manifest in them. But in what sense can *material* things be contradictory, or stand in relations of reciprocal determination? Surely, as Berdyaev argued, the imposition of Hegelian categories onto material reality can only result in a grotesque panlogism in which matter, endowed with "all the riches of being ... becomes spiritualised" and "takes on an inner life" as "thought, *logos*" (Berdyaev 1933: 237; the Mechanists expressed similar views, as we saw in Chapter 2). How can a position be "dialectical" *and* "materialist"?

The extent of the problem is clear. It may seem obvious that Ilyenkov's duty is to prove that the material world has a dialectical structure. However, like Marx himself, Ilyenkov advances no general metaphysical arguments to this conclusion. Nor does he follow the Deborinites, and many contemporary *diamatchiki,* and attempt to describe the dialectical structure of matter in dialectical "laws" universally governing material phenomena. However, though this may seem a disappointing omission, Ilyenkov has good grounds for eschewing a general proof of his frequent assertion that dialectical method reflects the dialectical nature of reality itself. To see why, we must turn to his complex and confusing account of how the method is *applied.* I shall focus on one principal aspect: the determination of the concrete universal.

Concrete universals, historicism, and particularism

A concrete universal is the genetic root of a concrete whole, the particular component within it that, in the course of its development, determines the nature and function of all the others. In the theoretical reconstruction of a concrete object, the concrete universal forms the "basic concept" that, by expressing "the real universal form of the self-development of the object under study," allows us to identify "those and only those characteristics that are part of the structure of the given 'self-developing' system of phenomena and that represent the determinants of the given concrete system" (Ilyenkov 1967a: 211). The concrete universal, then, constitutes a privileged perspective from which the object "comes into focus": Its "abstract consideration *coincides directly* with the concrete consideration of the object as a whole" (1960a: 104).

Ilyenkov mentions several examples of concrete universals, but he discusses only one in detail.[8] This is Marx's use of the concept of value as the determining category in his analysis of capitalism. Ilyenkov writes that, on Marx's account,

> The value-form is like a ticket into the realm of capitalist production: Without receiving the stamp of value, neither man nor thing may enter that realm, they cannot begin to function in it as one of its elements, or be seen as an internal ("immanent") moment of this means of production. For the researcher, this fact ... provides a hard and clear criterion for the identification of those specific economic forms that relate to the "pure structure of capitalism," for the identification of such forms from the motley mass of interwoven relations we observe "empirically." (1967a: 211)

For Ilyenkov, Marx's attempt to trace how the value-form develops from its initial, inherently unstable appearance in simple commodity exchange is an attempt to follow the unfolding of capitalism's concrete universal. As the value-form evolves, extending the compass of its determining influence, so the more complex categories of the capitalist economy (money, rent) are derived as forms of its manifestation. The history of capitalism is the history of the value-form.

It is thus clear that the crucial step in any analysis is to discover the concrete universal of the object of investigation. How is this done? A seemingly obvious suggestion is that the

---

8 Ilyenkov cites the protein molecule and the conditional reflex as the concrete universals of the life sciences and the physiology of the nervous system, respectively (1960a: 224–6).

theorist should consult the *history* of the object.[9] After all, we are told that the ascent from the abstract to the concrete is not merely a movement of thought from fragmented to integral understanding; it is supposed to reflect an analogous transition in the object itself as it evolves from a simple agglomeration of dislocated parts into an integrated whole. This evolution is a historical event. Thus, the determining influence of the concrete universal ought to be discernible from an account of the object's history.

Ilyenkov, however, anticipates and rebuts this suggestion. It rests, he claims, on the assumption that the history of the object is simply given to the theorist. However, this assumption is false. When we tell an object's history, we abstract from a mass of historical data just those factors that we take to be the conditions of the object's origin and development. Such abstraction, however, is precisely what the concrete universal is supposed to make possible. Knowledge of the historical conditions of the object's evolution is a *consequence,* and not a precondition, of finding its concrete universal:

> The thing is that the analysis of the facts that concern the emergence and development of the object is impossible without some kind of clear conception of what the object is, the history of which we are trying to analyze. (Ilyenkov 1962c: 314)

Ilyenkov's point is that our theoretical and historical understandings of an object are not independent. There are not two separately intelligible accounts, one a historical story of the object's development and the other a "logical" story in terms of its necessary conditions. A proper historical account, one that *explains* something, presents the development of the object as necessary in the light of certain circumstances. As such, it *is* a logical account: Logical and historical are "identical" (Ilyenkov 1971b: 265):

9   Ilyenkov sometimes suggests that *all* the objects studied by dialectical method are historically developing entities, including even the "laws of nature." He implies that natural laws came into being at the birth of the universe and are capable of changing over time. The time scale of this change is, however, said to be too big to make any difference to physics (see Ilyenkov 1960a: 204–5).

The logical is nothing but the historical correctly understood.
Or rather, the historical, grasped by and expressed in concepts, is the logically correct reflection of reality in thought.
(1971b: 285)

Thus, the concrete universal cannot be simply read off from
the object's history.

Yet while Ilyenkov makes his hostility to this direct "historical approach" clear, a positive alternative is much more
difficult to discern in his writings.[10] Although his very first
article boldly formulates the question of which "methodological considerations and logical requirements" must guide the
theorist's choice of concrete universal (1955: 46), many of his
attempts to answer it directly seem remarkably unexplanatory. For example, he suggests that

> To find out whether a given concept has revealed a universal
> definition of the object or a nonuniversal one . . . one should
> ask oneself whether the particular phenomenon directly ex-
> pressed in it is at the same time the universal genetic basis
> from the development of which all other, just as particular,
> phenomena of the given concrete system may be understood
> in their necessity. (1960a: 76)

This advice is useless, of course, because finding "the universal genetic basis" of an object is the same problem as determining its concrete universal.

Why should Ilyenkov offer us this vacuous advice? I want
to suggest the following charitable interpretation. Ilyenkov
adopts such question-begging formulations because he believes that no general, nontrivial procedure for determining
concrete universals is possible. Instead, all the philosopher can
do is to enjoin the theorist to make the choice on the basis of a
careful analysis of the specific object of investigation. This interpretation provides the best reading not only of Ilyenkov's
reluctance to state a nontrivial formula for establishing concrete universals, but also of his constant injunctions that the
theorist must establish the concrete universal on the basis of a
"complex and meaningful analysis" of *the facts* (1960a: 76).

10 The "historical approach" is an example of what Ilyenkov would
    call "abstract historicism."

These injunctions should be seen not as a strikingly uninformative attempt to give the theorist a procedure to follow, but as a denial that any general procedure is possible. Ilyenkov is warning the theorist not to try to establish the concrete universal by appeal to some rule or law derived from logic, dialectics, or by abstract generalization from the history of science. Rather, the principle of organization of the object of study will only be revealed by a detailed analysis of the particular object itself.

It is tempting to think, of course, that there must be some characteristic that all concrete universals share and that could serve as the acid test of their presence; but this is precisely an instance of the old logic that the dialectical method is supposed to have supplanted! In fact, the idea that there is no nontrivial general decision procedure for determining concrete universals is highly plausible. Since such universals are keys to the cognition of their objects, it would be too good to be true if there was some recipe for deciding what they were.

Nevertheless, whatever its initial plausibility, the "charitable interpretation" is sure to excite the following attack. It will be argued that it is open to the very objection Ilyenkov himself took to the "historical approach." We were told that we could not simply "read off" the concrete universal from the object's history, because a proper account of that history would require knowledge of the concrete universal. It is unclear, however, that we fare better when we try to discover the concrete universal by looking at "the facts." Don't we need the concrete universal to tell what the facts are?

However, the objection is misguided. When Ilyenkov enjoins the theorist to turn to "the facts," he does not mean that we have some access to the object independently of our theoretical conceptions (in the way we were supposed to have access to its history independently of theory). On the contrary, Ilyenkov is suggesting that our judgment of the concrete universal has somehow to be made *within* our existing conceptions of the object. For Ilyenkov, to give a rigorous analysis of the facts is just to subject our existing conceptions to critical assessment:

> The theoretical analysis of the facts and the settling of accounts with previous theory are two insolubly connected sides

of research: One without the other is impossible. Therefore the
question of how we criticize previous theory is just the same
question as how we analyze the empirical facts and how we
develop our theories. (Ilyenkov 1962a: 315)

... A new logical understanding of the facts can emerge only
through the critical assimilation of the results of the previous
development of thought. (Ilyenkov 1971b: 268–9)

The analysis of the facts coincides with an immanent critique of previous theory.

Ilyenkov's rejection of methodological solipsism forms an
important input to this position. From that it follows that the
theorist's starting point is not raw, unprocessed sense experience, or a direct, pretheoretical grasp of the object, but a historically forged conception of it inherited from the tradition in
which he or she is working (1960a: 148). It is thus the object's
presentation in this tradition that must form the basis of the
theorist's judgments about its concrete universal. There is no
suggestion that the theorist simply reads off the concrete universal from the inherited conception. On the contrary, the object is presented to him or her as something problematic, as
something (or as part of something) not fully understood. It is
by exploring the "contradictions" in our present conceptions
that the theorist can come to decide that a certain entity is best
seen as the principle of organization of the whole.

In a sense, the theorist's choice of concrete universal is an
intuition. By this, however, I do not mean that it is a judgment made without specifiable grounds. On the contrary, the
theorist will be able to cite evidence, drawn from the analysis
of previous theory, to support any plausible candidate for concrete universal. The judgment is an intuition in the sense that
it carries no guarantee of success. Ilyenkov's position suggests
that the critique of previous theory will yield various plausible
candidates as the concrete universal of the object of study. The
theorist's task will then be to attempt working theories of the
object on the basis of these candidates. The ultimate choice,
made in the light of the specific subject matter in question,
will be vindicated only to the degree that it yields a theory
rendering that subject more intelligible.

This reading is consistent with the account of Vygotsky's
"unit analysis" of consciousness developed in Chapter 3. Unit

analysis is a prime example of dialectical method as Ilyenkov understands it. Vygotsky treats consciousness as a concrete totality, a whole composed of parts occupying internal, "interfunctional" relations of mutual determination. *Meaning*, which Vygotsky takes as the "unit" of analysis, plays the role of concrete universal, the genetic root of consciousness from which the higher mental functions evolve. Like Ilyenkov, Vygotsky offers no general procedure for establishing the units of psychological analysis. In defending Vygotsky, I argued that his choice of meaning as the unit of consciousness must be treated as a plausible hypothesis formed on the basis of a critique of previous theory. This hypothesis is backed by no logical guarantee and is justified only by the explanatory power of the genetic account in which it figures. This account coincides with the "charitable interpretation" of Ilyenkov's position.

Our discussion has brought out two important features of Ilyenkov's dialectical method. First, the method is *particularist*. That is, it cannot be formulated as a set of general principles neutral with respect to subject. How it must be applied is entirely determined by the specific nature of the object under study. In this, Ilyenkov's position coincides with the view attributed to Akselrod in Chapters 2 and 3. Second, his position is *historicist;* that is, he presents human knowledge as a historical phenomenon, evolving through a relentless process of immanent critique, with each new stage responding to contradictions in the last.[11] New concepts and theories emerge as solutions to these contradictions only to be shown later to suffer contradictions themselves. The significance of each stage lies in the character of its response to the past and the prospects it opens for the future. At all times, the standards by which stages are assessed are drawn from within our developing conceptions themselves; we cannot somehow step outside our theories to compare them with brute reality itself.

---

11   Ilyenkov uses the term "historicism" approvingly in many of his works (e.g., 1960a: 194–222), chiding Althusser for "farming out this excellent term to the representatives of pseudohistoricism, the supporters of one-dimensional-evolutionary understanding of history" (1971b: 285n [this footnote was omitted from the republished version in Ilyenkov 1984a]). Ilyenkov sometimes refers to his own view as "concrete historicism" to distinguish it from the "pseudo-" or "abstract" version that he takes to be Althusser's target.

Ilyenkov's historicism implies a conception of objectivity very different from the empiricist's. For the empiricist,
thought approaches objective reality by liberating itself from
the forms of its embodiment, psychological, physiological, or
historical, to form a conception of reality as it is independent
of all minds. Ilyenkov, however, operates with a different idea,
inspired by Hegel. On this account, our view of the world becomes more objective if we distance ourselves from it to form
a new conception that includes both our initial view and its relation to the world.[12] For example, if our initial conception is
C_n, then we achieve greater objectivity by moving to another
conception, C_{n+1}, which takes the relation between C_n and the
world as its object. The process may continue without end,
C_{n+1} being subsumed within some yet more objective position
C_{n+2}, and so on. This process may be motivated by the realization that our existing conceptions are inadequate. Having
come to see C_n as partial, inconsistent, abstract, we form a new
conception C_{n+1}, which, by giving an account of the relation
between C_n and reality, shows C_n to be mere appearance. Subsequently, C_{n+1} may meet a similar fate. However, the movement to increasingly more objective conceptions need not be
motivated by the judgment that our present conceptions are
flawed. The attraction of the more objective picture may be
that it is broader, not that it exposes weaknesses in the earlier conception. It will show that the earlier conception is a
"perspective" on the world, but not necessarily that the deliverances of that perspective are *mere* appearances. On the
contrary, the more objective picture may demonstrate how insightful and revealing the earlier, "subjective" perspective is.
Thus, for Ilyenkov, contrary to empiricism, the objective view
does not necessarily eschew the subjective, but incorporates
appearance into reality as, in Lenin's words, "*one of the aspects
of the objective world*" (1895–1916: 98). Each successive stage in
knowledge takes us not toward a perspectiveless conception of
reality, but to yet another, more comprehensive, perspective.

The particularism and historicism of Ilyenkov's method
bear heavily on the problem of its defence. In the previous sec-

12   Thomas Nagel discusses this conception of objectivity in his influential *The View from Nowhere* (e.g., Nagel 1986: 4). His treatment is,
however, marred by his failure to distinguish between the two
senses of objectivity under discussion here (see Dancy 1988).

tion we asked how Ilyenkov can show that material reality is the kind of organic totality, or contains the kind of organic totalities, that the dialectical method is supposedly designed to analyze. Ilyenkov's historicism suggests that there will be no general, perspectiveless characterization of reality by reference to which we may assess the claims of any putative truth-delivering method, including his own. Since the method is our means for establishing what the world is like, we cannot compare its deliverances with reality "as such," determined independently of the method. Establishing the intelligible structure the world has to offer and the theoretical structure that would best capture it have to be done simultaneously.

Further, Ilyenkov's particularism denies that there is any substantive general characterization of the method itself that can be assessed independently of its application to some specific subject. If, as Engels suggests, dialectical explanations seek not to subsume particular cases under general laws but to reveal the specific interconnections and tendencies inherent in "the particular nature of each case" (Engels cited in Wood 1981: 199), then, as Wood puts it,

> As far as the philosophical or scientific value of a dialectical system is concerned, everything depends on the details of its execution, on whether the "life of the content" really displays dialectical interconnections and tendencies, and on how well the practitioner of the dialectical method is able to establish each specific connection and transition by good arguments. (Wood 1981: 199)

It thus follows from Ilyenkov's particularism and historicism, first, that the dialectical method stands or falls only by the persuasiveness of its results in the light of the specific nature of the subject under study, and second, that its results can be assessed, not from some Archimedean point, but only in the light of our present conceptions, the history of previous theory and the degree to which we can incorporate them into our practice. The ultimate test of a theory is whether it is livable.

This conclusion explains why Ilyenkov attempts neither formal statements of his method's procedures, nor metaphysical arguments about the dialectical structure of objective reality. Instead, he rightly prefers to develop his position through illustrations of the method in action. The purpose of these il-

lustrations, drawn predominantly from *Capital,* is not to yield
material from which to abstract a codifiable procedure to be
applied in other domains. Rather, they are designed to reveal
what a perfect explanation is like. For Ilyenkov, Marx's explanation of capitalism is perfect because it represents each aspect of its object as *necessary:* It shows how the object could not
but have evolved like this. Ilyenkov seeks to bring out how
this perfect explanation is constructed. He shows that it proceeds by reconstructing the object as a concrete totality, and
that this is achieved by following the object's immanent logic
of development as it evolves through the resolution of tensions,
or contradictions, within it. Thus, while nothing in Marx's
analysis of capitalism determines how the dialectical method
is to be applied elsewhere, it offers us an example of a perfect
explanation, perfection we must seek to emulate in other domains. Although Ilyenkov's illustrations from Marx are seldom wholly convincing, even when he is at his most scholarly and persuasive, their weakness must not obscure the fact
that Ilyenkov's concern with *Capital* is a sustained attempt to
demonstrate the strengths of dialectical method in the only
way he believed legitimate.[13]

It follows from our interpretation that Ilyenkov's conviction
that the intelligible structure of material reality is dialectical
will be ultimately vindicated only by the successful formation of a comprehensive and integral Marxist theory of "nature, thinking, and society." The construction of such a theory is not, of course, the province of philosophy alone, but of
science in the widest sense of the word.[14] It is this theory's
power to transform human life that, Ilyenkov believes, will finally settle the question of its truth. Thus, it appears that the
"proof" of Marx's method lies beyond the scope of Ilyenkov's
contribution. It cannot, as Ilyenkov himself put it, "rest on the
shoulders of one man" (Ilyenkov 1974a: 269).

13 Ilyenkov's best account of Marx's application of dialectical method
    in *Capital* is his elegant encyclopedia article "Logika *Kapitala*"
    (1962c).
14 As we observed in Chapter 2 (n1), the Russian *"nauka"* more readi-
    ly conveys this wide sense than the English "science." *"Nauka"* re-
    fers to any discipline that employs a rational method of inquiry
    designed to reveal the nature of reality. Thus, for Ilyenkov a disci-
    pline is scientific to the extent that it employs his favoured dialec-
    tical method.

Ilyenkov on contradiction

Throughout his career, Ilyenkov held it to be a fundamental assumption of dialectics that

> Objective reality always develops through the emergence within it of concrete contradictions that find their resolution in the birth of new, higher and more complex forms of development. (Ilyenkov 1957: 71)

Ilyenkov claims that the development not only of knowledge but of any object (including concrete universals) is a process of the constant resolution and creation of contradiction. Thus, to reflect objective reality, dialectical method must trace "the mode in which these contradictions are resolved in *the movement of objective reality, the movement and development of the world*" (Ilyenkov 1960a: 244; his italics).[15]

While it is tempting to find some metaphorical reading of Ilyenkov's remarks that renders them innocuous, his writings make it clear that he intends to be taken literally. When Ilyenkov says that there are "objective" or "real" contradictions, he means no less than a statement and its negation can be true of the same (real) object at the same time and in the same respect. In other words, Ilyenkov believes that the law of noncontradiction is false.

Ilyenkov supports his position by invoking the "classical" Marxist argument that the supposition of contradictions in ob-

---

15   It is important to be clear that, although Ilyenkov holds that dialectical method must be alive to objective contradictions, he does not believe that contradictory descriptions of reality are ever the whole story (see, e.g., 1957: 64). Reality does not tolerate the contradictions within it: It strives to eliminate them by evolving into a different form. Thus, thought can be faithful to reality only if it does likewise. A good dialectician is thus not someone who delights in peddling contradictory theories. On the contrary, the dialectician seeks to resolve contradictions in a position as energetically as any metaphysician. Where metaphysician and dialectician are said to differ is that whereas the former treats all contradictions as equally fallacious consequences of subjective error and stops at nothing to banish them from theory, the latter wisely recognizes that some contradictions reflect stages of reality itself and that their correct resolution will trace a path reality has taken (Ilyenkov 1979d: 139, 1979e: 261).

jective reality is essential to account for change.[16] He claims that changing phenomena must be described by means of contradictory formulae (1960a: 251). For example, a moving object must be seen as, at any particular moment in time, "both in one place and in another place, being at one and the same place and also not in it" (Engels 1878: 148). However, this argument fails. When a body moves, it is not in two places at once. Rather, motion is change of place *with* time: At each time in its movement its position is different (albeit minutely different). To explain the possibility of motion we must explain how an object can be in different places at different times. We get no closer to this by the impossible assumption that it can be in different places at the same time.

Ilyenkov might have replied that the Marxist tradition need not attempt to explain *all* change by appeal to objective contradictions. This is unnecessary where change is caused by the influence of external forces. For example, we can often explain how a moving object is in different places at different times by appeal to forces operating on it from without. However, *self*-movement cannot be explained in this way. In such cases, change must be represented as originating from within the nature of the changing entity itself. Here, contradiction is invoked as the motor of self-development: The object is pictured as changing under the influence of the internal conflict of its parts.

The problem with this manoeuvre is that the use of the rhetoric of "internal conflict" to explain self-development does not threaten the law of noncontradiction. Although a self-developing object may trivially be described as a "unity of *A* and not-*A*," nothing forces us to ascribe strictly contradictory properties to it. As Wood comments:

> The principle of [non-]contradiction as formal logicians normally understand it does not deny that things may be composed of different parts or elements with contrasting func-

16   Such a view appears in many classical Marxist treatments of dialectics (e.g., Engels 1878: 32, 147–52; Lenin 1895–1916: 258; Trotsky 1942: 49). It is usually taken to apply to all kinds of change: movement, growth, development, and so on. Note that the law of identity ($A = A$) is often taken to fall alongside the law of noncontradiction on the grounds that an objectively contradictory object is "not identical with itself."

tional values. It does not say that nothing may change its structure, nor even deny that things may have inherent or essential tendencies to such changes. There is nothing "contradictory" – in the formal logical sense – about real conflicts between things, or between the parts or elements of a single thing, or about a thing's having different properties at different times or in different respects. (Wood 1981: 203)

Thus, nothing in the phenomenon of change warrants Ilyenkov's bold conclusion that the law of noncontradiction is false.

Apart from these considerations about change, Ilyenkov appeals to several examples of real contradictions, drawn principally from Marx's analysis in *Capital* (see Ilyenkov 1960a: 237–50). For instance, he argues that Marx's derivation of value turns on the identification of an objective contradiction (Ilyenkov 1957: 67–9, commenting on Marx 1867: 131–55). Value is something a commodity has only relative to some other commodity. When a certain amount of commodity A is taken to be equivalent to (i.e., exchangeable for) a certain amount of commodity B (e.g., $5A = 3B$), then A measures its value relative to B. A is said to be in the "relative form" of value, whereas B, playing the role of A's equivalent, is in the "equivalent form." Now, the relative and equivalent forms of value are mutually exclusive. No commodity may be in both forms simultaneously for, if it were, it could serve as the measure of its own value, and that is impossible. But each commodity *is* simultaneously in both forms because the terms of the equation can be reversed: When A is in the relative form with respect to B it simultaneously plays the role of B's equivalent (and vice versa). Thus the value of the commodity is a consequence of the simultaneous existence of mutually exclusive forms, a living contradiction. Ilyenkov claims that it is by tracing the resolution of this contradiction that Marx derives other crucial economic categories.

However, though in keeping with Marx's own presentation, this argument will not support Ilyenkov's strong conclusions. As Marx himself understands well, value, like length or weight, is a relational property. As his argument rightly assumes, the value of an entity may be measured only in relation to some other entity. Consequently, when the value of A is determined relative to B, the value of B is determined relative to A. But there is nothing paradoxical about this: A is in the relative form *relative to B's* being in the equivalent form and vice versa. *A* is never in the equivalent form relative to itself being in the relative form (i.e., *A* is never its own equivalent).

In fact, Marx's talk of contradiction is designed to draw attention to a paradox that results if one looks for an Archimedean point from which to measure value. How, it may be asked, can commodities determine each other's value unless there is some independent standard against which they can be measured? Marx's point, however, is that this question rests on a mistake. There is no absolute standard of value, just as there is no absolute standard of weight or length. Yet this does not mean that our judgments of length, weight, or value are groundless. Their basis is our practices of measuring, weighing, and, in the case of value, exchanging. The paradox is caused by taking a relational for an absolute property. This is a mistake that Marx is anxious to diagnose, for it is part of what he calls the "fetishism of commodities," the idea (roughly) that commodities possess value independently of our practices. This paradox, though it may reflect some deep contradiction in our thinking about value, can scarcely be said to reflect a contradiction in reality itself.

I conclude that Ilyenkov's account of dialectical contradiction is flawed. He fails to undermine the now orthodox view among commentators sympathetic to Marx that the incompatibility of Marx's method with formal logic is merely superficial (see Wood 1981; Elster 1985: 43–8; Suchting 1985: 81–103).

This failure undoubtedly weakens Ilyenkov's presentation of dialectical method. For instance, it undermines his view that the method can uniquely capture reality because it alone recognizes objective contradictions. Moreover, Ilyenkov unfortunately gives the notion of objective contradiction considerable explanatory work in his theory. For example, it is invoked to explain both the necessity with which phenomena develop and the *necessity* of the inferences by which thought reconstructs that development (which is said to be neither deductive nor inductive, but a dialectical sublation of the two [Ilyenkov 1960a: 162]). Thus, Ilyenkov is left without an account of necessity, either "natural" or "inferential."

Why was Ilyenkov so intent on such a strong interpretation of objective contradiction? Was it blind faith in the "classics"? Or a dogmatic belief in Marxism's superiority to the "old

modes of thinking"? In fact, neither suggestion is wholly correct. To understand the motivation for his views on contradiction, we must turn to Ilyenkov's idea of logic as a discipline.
For him, logic is the "science of thought" (*nauka o myshlenii*).
Its task is to understand how thought proceeds, and how it
ought to proceed, in the analysis of its objects. So understood,
logic is not a purely formal science but a logic of content that,
done properly, represents "the theoretical reflection of scientific thinking" (Ilyenkov 1974a: 5). Moreover, in keeping with
his particularism, Ilyenkov holds that logic's account of how
thought must construct a picture of the world is not characterizable independently of the content of that picture: The logic
of thought coincides with the logic of reality. In Lenin's
words:

> Logic is the science not of external forms of thought, but of the
> laws of development "of all material, natural and spiritual
> things," i.e., of the development of the entire concrete content
> of the world and of its cognition, i.e., the sum-total, the con-
> clusion of the *History* of knowledge of the world. (Lenin 1895–
> 1916: 92–3; quoted approvingly by Ilyenkov [1974a: 225, 1974b:
> 57])

Ilyenkov's work tries to give sense to such a "dialectical Logic" ("with a capital L," as he calls it [1974a: 3], following Lenin [1895–1916: 319]). Success in this project would thus realize
Lenin's much quoted yet ill-understood (Ilyenkov 1974a: 212–
13) idea of the coincidence (*sovpadenie*) of logic, dialectics,
and the theory of cognition (*teoriya poznaniya*).

Ilyenkov was not slow to address the inevitable question of
the relation of dialectical to formal logic. Unfortunately, however, it was to Hegel that he turned for his account. Uncritically adopting Hegel's withering contempt for formal logic,
he argued that its principles embodied implicit metaphysical
commitments to a vision of reality as a collection of static, internally undivided, logically distinct atoms, constituted independently of the relations in which they stand. He therefore
believed that dialectics must renounce the principles of identity and noncontradiction that fostered this bogus vision.

Since the idea that formal logic had been "sublated [*snyat'*,
aufheben] by Hegel's conceptions" (Ilyenkov 1979d: 132) was
associated with the more reactionary representatives of Soviet

philosophy, Ilyenkov's insistence on its truth cost him considerable respect.[17] It seemed that if it were not chauvinism, it could only have been a lamentable ignorance of formal logic's (often extremely fruitful) influence on twentieth-century philosophy that had prompted Ilyenkov's remark that it could play only a "propaedeutic role" (1979d: 132). It is sad that the work of an otherwise scholarly and ingenuous philosopher should contain such a philistine thread.

Conclusion

If the failure of Ilyenkov's views on contradiction undermines his account of necessity, what remains of the idea that cognition is a process of coming to see the object as a concrete "unity in diversity"? After all, it was supposedly by tracing the resolution of its inner contradictions that we were to follow the development of "the logic of the object." It seems now that we know only what this process is *not*. We know that it proceeds neither by strictly deductive nor inductive inference, and that it cannot be characterized independently of some specific subject matter. Yet what is achieving a "concrete understanding" really supposed to be like?

Ilyenkov's particularism suggests that the application of dialectical method is the exercise of a *skill* rather than the operation of any codifiable procedure (cf. Chapter 3). The best way to convey the nature of an unfamiliar skill (short of teaching it) is to appeal to an analogy with one more familiar. What, then, is analogous to the process of coming to see the object as a unity in diversity? Perhaps surprisingly, an appropriate analogy comes from the nature of aesthetic experience. The power to grasp an object as a unity in diversity is, I think, rather like the ability to hear a piece of music as a meaningful whole. To learn to hear the music correctly is to come to hear it as a specifically organized totality in which the relations of necessity

17   Ilyenkov's ignorance may not, of course, be entirely inexcusable. While the influence of formal logic has been greatest on analytic philosophy, Ilyenkov, like many Soviet philosophers expert in the Hegelian tradition, knew German and not English. The insular nature of the Soviet philosophical community at that time would have made it difficult for a philosopher unable to read the original texts to become familiar with ideas at play in the Anglo–American tradition.

obtaining between its particular sounds are evident. Appreciating the music is a kind of reconciliation with this necessity, a realization of why just *this* note is essential here, why that pause must be *just so*, and so on. Several similarities stand out between this picture and Ilyenkov's idea of cognition in general. First, musical understanding of this kind is not achieved by deductive or inductive inference (though it would be false, I think, to deny that it is a process of reasoning at all). Second, such understanding is "particularist" in that it cannot be formulated as a set of general, nontrivial principles that we can take to any piece of music. Third, the understanding demands a "historicist" interpretation. The object of the listener's attention is not unstructured sense data, but a historically presented object. Both the music itself and the listener's ability to hear it as *music* (rather than noise) are historical achievements. The history of music is not just a history of ways of making sound, but also of ways of hearing it. There is no external perspective outside these historical practices from which the process of musical appreciation could be made intelligible, or from which our musical judgments could be assessed. However, though our standards of assessment cannot be grounded independently of our practices of musical appreciation, and though the skills involved cannot be formulated as a set of principles or reduced to an exercise of deduction or induction, debates about musical interpretation can exhibit a high degree of objectivity.

This analogy between musical and theoretical understanding is not meant to be strict. The point is only to suggest that both are areas where the apprehension of necessity is particularist and historicist yet open to rational standards of evaluation.[18] The idea that we can cast light on a method claimed to be scientific by analogy to aesthetic experience will certainly outrage those for whom the aesthetic is the paradigm of the unscientific. Ilyenkov, however, did not share this prejudice, and my aim is to make his position more intelligible, rather than to convert those who are skeptical of its merits.

Differences in time and circumstance may have robbed Ilyenkov's deliberations on dialectical method of some of the

---

18   I have tried to argue (in Bakhurst 1985b) that the same is true of the cognition of moral necessity.

relevance and immediacy that so struck Lifshits. Indeed, the modern reader, particularly in the West, may find them distant and obscure. The same does not apply, however, to Ilyenkov's attempt to put the insights he had gained from his study of Marx's method into action. In contrast to his murky and sometimes inscrutable considerations on method, Ilyenkov's "philosophy of activity" is a theory with far-reaching implications of immediate contemporary relevance. To begin our account, we must return to Ilyenkov's views on "the problem of the ideal," which we introduced in our discussion of his rejection of empiricism. His ingenious solution to this problem forms a central pillar of his philosophy, casting much light on one of the most difficult issues confronting the Marxist in the attempt to "stand Hegel on his feet": the nature and origin of nonmaterial properties in a material world.

6

THE PROBLEM OF THE IDEAL

The "problem of the ideal" is the problem of the status of non-material properties in the material world. The importance Il-yenkov attributes to this issue requires little explanation: A materialist position is defined by its account of the nonmaterial, and stands or falls by the plausibility of that account. Thus, the nature and possibility of dialectical materialism turns on its solution to the problem of the ideal.

Ilyenkov first presented his account of the ideal (*ideal'noe*), or "ideality" (*ideal'nost'*), in a long entry in the Soviet philosophical encyclopedia in 1962, an article that represents his most impressive contribution to the renaissance of Soviet philosophy after Stalin (Ilyenkov 1962b). Ilyenkov never lost faith in the validity of the theory he outlined there, and when he returned to the problem of the ideal in a late article (1979a), he did so not to question his earlier views but to reaffirm them.

Ilyenkov's theory of ideality continues to provoke controversy among Soviet philosophers. While some consider it brilliant, others hold it to be confused and contradictory.[1] This controversy is exacerbated by the abstruse way in which Il-yenkov presents his position. The problems he addresses are

1 Compare the positive remarks in Tolstykh (1981: 29) and Davydov (1986: 31–7) with Dubrovsky's critique (1983: 34–47).

so massive and multidimensional that his answers often seem too quick, condensed to the point of unintelligibility. The primary task of this chapter is therefore simply to explain Ilyenkov's theory. I shall begin with a specific, well-defined issue and gradually extend the discussion to encompass the full scope of his position. Finally, I shall consider how Ilyenkov may be defended from a charge frequently made against him during his life: that his theory of the ideal commits him to idealism.

Ideality, moral properties, and the "ban on anthropocentricity"

At least at first sight, nonmaterial phenomena appear to fall into two classes:

1. mental phenomena (thoughts, beliefs, feelings, sensations, etc.);
2. phenomena that are neither material nor mental in kind (e.g., the various species of value and meaning, and numerous other properties, like hospitability or dangerousness).

While the point of departure of most materialist positions is a theory of the mental, Ilyenkov's materialism begins with an analysis of ideal phenomena of the *second* class. No adequate theory of the mental is possible, he insists, unless we have first understood such phenomena as meaning and value. Such is his emphasis on these phenomena that he usually reserves the term "ideal" for them, contrasting them with the merely mental (*psikhicheskoe*). (I shall follow Ilyenkov's usage; on no account, however, should it be taken to imply that he holds that *only* phenomena of the second class are ideal.)

What philosophical issues surround the status of ideal properties of the second class? Take, for example, the analysis of moral value. Moral theory seems torn between "objectivist" accounts of the status of value, which think of moral properties as constituents of a reality existing independently of thinking subjects, and "subjectivist" accounts, which hold that moral properties originate in us.

Objectivism is motivated by the nature of moral experience (see McDowell 1985: 110). At least sometimes, when we judge that an action is right or wrong it feels as if we are recognizing the presence of a moral property that exists "out there," independently of how we think or feel. This feeling is confirmed by the nature of moral deliberation: When we seek to discover what we are morally required to do, it seems to us as if we must make our thoughts and actions conform to the dictates of an objectively existing moral order.

The admission of objective values has its theoretical attractions. For example, we can explain the compellingness of moral obligation by saying that agents feel they *must* act morally because they recognize an objectively present value, awareness of which in itself constitutes a reason for action. Nonetheless, objectivism seems prone to an obvious objection. Moral values are markedly different properties from those that constitute our paradigm of the objectively existing: the physical properties of the natural world. To hold there are objective values is surely to admit into nature "queer" properties that, while able to influence human action, mysteriously have no place in physical theory.[2] This, it seems, is an insult to the scientific picture of the world.

This "argument from queerness," as Mackie calls it, encourages us to retreat from objectivism into a view that identifies human beings as the source of value (Mackie 1977: 38–42). Values, it is argued, are not part of the world as it exists independently of us. Rather, they originate in our modes of response to the world. One version of such subjectivism, which owes its modern form to Hume, locates moral value in our attitudes of approval and disapproval (Hume 1739: esp. III.i.1). Such a theory, however, must offer some explanation of the moral phenomenology that lent objectivism its attraction. A favoured response is to argue that, although values issue from our natures, our minds "project" them onto reality. Values then appear to be part of "the fabric of the world," even though they are really distinctively subjective properties, "discernible" only by observers with the relevant projective capacity.

Subjectivism's appeal is that it does justice to the intuition that, for all their purported objectivity, moral values are intrin-

---

2 As we noted in Chapter 2, the Mechanists brought analogous arguments against the Deborinites' claim that mental properties, while constituents of objective reality, are irreducible to physical properties.

sically bound up with our natures, so that a world without creatures like us would be a world without moral properties. However, like objectivism, it is beset by problems. First, the idea that we project values onto the world makes it (in some sense) an error to believe that moral requirements derive from the existence of objective values, and this admission may not leave our confidence in the authority of morality intact. Second, projectivism struggles to explain how a brutely objective world, stripped of all purportedly subjective properties, could engage with our minds to warrant the modes of response in which moral properties supposedly originate (McDowell 1985: 119–20).

The choice between objectivism and subjectivism thus appears as a dilemma. Each embodies a plausible intuition, but, as the positions are mutually exclusive, we cannot do justice to both intuitions at once. Such a dilemma is among the things Ilyenkov calls a "contradiction."[3] For him, the appearance of such contradictions is not an obstacle to theoretical development but its very source. He argues that when thought appears trapped between two mutually exclusive and seemingly exhaustive positions, the correct response is not to plump for

3 Ilyenkov's own example of such a contradiction is the opposition between dualism and physicalist monism in the philosophy of mind, a problem closely related to our puzzle about the status of value. Here too it appears that both positions express sound intuitions that are impossible to incorporate in a single theory. We seem compelled to choose either one of the theories, and thereby to sacrifice the insights of the other (Ilyenkov 1960a: 252–4).

We should observe that the opposition between subjectivism and objectivism in contemporary British moral theory is now by no means as stark as my sketch suggests. Recently, representatives of both camps have sought to develop theories that incorporate their opponents' insights. On the one hand, Blackburn has advanced a form of projectivism (the term is his coinage) that, while faithful to the subjectivist tradition, is compatible with a "quasi-realistic" semantics of moral discourse, licensing talk of "moral truth" (Blackburn 1984: chap. 6). On the other, McDowell has argued that a full-blooded moral realism can accommodate the anthropocentricity of moral properties (McDowell 1985). Both Blackburn's subjectivist "quasi-realism" and McDowell's anthropocentric objectivism may therefore be seen as attempts to overcome the dilemma we have identified rather than as instances of its two horns. However, although Ilyenkov's solution to the problem of the ideal anticipates some of the insights of Blackburn's and McDowell's work, his appeal to the concept of activity, as we shall see, represents a radical departure from both.

either, but to strive to uncover the source of the contradiction it-self. Ilyenkov promises that by "tracing out the entire chain of mediating links that connects the mutually exclusive abstract propositions," we shall uncover a third position, the dialectical "sublation" of the two, which incorporates the insights of both while overcoming their weaknesses (Ilyenkov 1960a: 253).

Ilyenkov would find the source of our dilemma about mor-al value in a particular criterion of objectivity. This criterion stipulates that a property is objective if it is *there anyway* inde-pendently of us. We have encountered the criterion before, in the idea of the "absolute conception of the world" endorsed by the Mechanists, the "conservative realist" of Chapter 4, and the empiricist of Chapter 5. The absolute conception operates a "ban on anthropocentricity": Nothing can count as a genuine constituent of objective reality if understanding its nature and origin involves essential reference to us. Ilyenkov's proposal, in harmony with his hostility to the absolute conception, is that we lift the ban on anthropocentricity. By so doing we can preserve the sound intuitions of both objectivism *and* subjectiv-ism. We can say that values get into reality because of us, yet they attain a status in the world of genuine objectivity. Values are real (no complete account of reality could fail to make reference to them), yet we are implicated in their reality. On this view, the objective and the subjective are no longer mutu-ally exclusive categories: Something may be objective (a gen-uine feature of reality) *and* subjective (not characterizable without essential reference to facts about subjects).

This is the structure of Ilyenkov's treatment of all ideal prop-erties. Philosophy that endorses the ban on anthropocentricity will oscillate between objectivist and subjectivist readings not just of moral properties but of all species of value (including the aesthetic and the economic) and other ideal properties, like significance and meaning. In the latter case, for exam-ple, we shall be torn between treating meaning as a property that natural objects can possess independently of observers, and thinking of it as something that individual minds bring to a world that, in its brute physicality, is devoid of signifi-cance. Ilyenkov offers a global response to the problem of the ideal: Renounce the ban on anthropocentricity and attribute to humanity the power to endow the material world with a new class of properties that, though they owe their origin to us, acquire an enduring presence in objective reality, coming to exist independently of human individuals. Ilyenkov locates this power in our status as active beings, as creatures who reproduce the conditions of their existence by labour. It is human activity, he claims, that idealizes nature. By this he means not the projecting activity of individual minds, but "real, sensuous, social, object-oriented" activity (*predmetnaya deyatel'nost'*):

> "Ideality" is like a peculiar stamp impressed on the substance of nature by social human life activity; it is the form of the functioning of a physical thing in the process of social human life activity ... [It is] human social culture embodied (objectified, substantialized, reified) in matter, that is, [a quality] of the historically formed modes of the life activity of social beings, modes of activity which confront individual consciousness and will as a special nonnatural [*sverkhpriroda*] objective reality, as a special object, comparable with material reality, and situated in one and the same space as it (and hence often confused with it). (Ilyenkov 1979a: 148, 139–40)

Ilyenkov's account of the ideal thus opens with two key tenets:

1. ideal phenomena can have an objective existence in the world; *Only when mixed with Matter*
2. they owe this existence to human activity.

Many of Ilyenkov's critics find the first of these claims impossible to accept. Ilyenkov argues that, since ideal properties like value are objective, they cannot be reduced to the phenomena of consciousness or to states of the brain. (In terms of the distinction drawn above, ideal phenomena of the second class are irreducible to those of the first.) The ideal is "not in the head." Thus, he writes that the problem of the ideal cannot be solved

> by rummaging around "inside consciousness," without venturing into the external, sensually perceptible corporeal world, into the world of the tangible, substantial forms and relations of things. (1979a: 149)

> ... The material system of which the ideal is a function and mode of existence ... can only be social beings in unity with the object world through which they realize their specifically human life activity. Under no circumstances can the ideal be reduced to a state of the brain. (1962b: 220–1)

For Soviet philosophers like David Dubrovsky, such a position is manifestly incompatible with materialism. For them, materialism is the view that all and only material phenomena are constituents of objective reality: The world outside our heads is simply matter in motion. Thus, since ideal phenomena are not material, their only possible home is among the phenomena of individual consciousness:

> The ideal cannot be taken beyond the boundaries of the human mind ... [It] is an exclusively subjective reality and is "born and exists" only in the human head, not leaving its confines. (Dubrovsky 1971: 164, 187)

> For us, "the ideal" existing "outside of the head and of consciousness" is either the material, or the Hegelian absolute spirit. (1983: 40)

On this view, Ilyenkov is either talking nonsense or peddling idealism.

Not everyone will share Dubrovsky's hostility to the objectivity of the ideal. Those who do not, however, may yet have difficulties with the claim that ideal phenomena owe their objectivity to human activity. How *could* "sensuous object-oriented activity," a physical operation on a material world, somehow inject into that world a qualitatively different kind of phenomenon?

We need, therefore, to make Ilyenkov's suggestions believable.

The insight about artifacts

The idea that activity is the source of objectively existing ideal properties becomes clearer when we consider Ilyenkov's account of *artifacts* (created objects). For Ilyenkov, artifacts represent a powerful challenge to the ban on anthropocentricity. Notwithstanding the familiar contrast between the natural and the artificial, there is an obvious sense in which an artifact – a table, for example – is a natural entity. A table is clearly a constituent of objective reality, and one that holds no mysteries for the scientist. Yet, an account of a table in purely natural-scientific terms seems to leave something out. Such an account fails to express the difference between being a *table* and being a *lump of wood*. Ilyenkov's suggestion is that this difference can only be marked by appeal to human activity. The relevant species of activity, however, is not mental in kind, for if we treat the properties that make an object an artifact as mental projections, we make too much of the world mind-dependent (cf. Wiggins 1976: 360–4). Rather, for Ilyenkov, it is material activity to which objects owe their status as artifacts.

Ilyenkov gives this appeal to activity content through the idea of "objectification" (*opredmechivanie*) or "reification" [*oveshchestvlenie*]. When an artifact is fashioned, human activity is somehow embodied [*voploshchennyĭ*] in the natural object. In turn, Ilyenkov explains reification in terms of the notion of "form"(*forma*) or "shape" (*obraz*). Human activity gives the object a new form:

> Ideality is a characteristic of things, but not as they are defined by nature, but by labour, the transforming, form-creating activity of social beings, their aim-mediated, sensuously objective activity.
>
> The ideal form is the form of a thing created by social human labour. Or, conversely, it is the form of labour realized [*osushchestvlennyĭ*] in the substance of nature, "embodied" in it, "alienated" in it, "realized" [*realizovannyĭ*] in it, and thereby confronting its very creator as the form of a thing or as a relation between things, which are placed in this relation (which they otherwise would not have entered) by human beings, by their labour. (Ilyenkov 1979a: 157)

Ilyenkov does not just mean that, when an artifact is created, some material object is given a new *physical* form. This is true, but something a natural-scientific account could capture. Rather, in being created as an embodiment of purpose and incorporated into our life activity in a certain way – being manufactured for a *reason* and put to a certain *use* – the natural object acquires *significance*. This significance is the "ideal form" of the object, a form that includes not a single atom of the tangible physical substance that possesses it (Ilyenkov 1979a: 150). It is this significance that must be grasped by anyone seeking to distinguish *tables* from *pieces of wood*.

Ilyenkov sometimes explains this significance by appeal to the concept *representation*. A purely natural object takes on significance when it comes to represent something with which its corporeal form has "nothing in common," a form of human activity:

> It is just here that we find the solution to the riddle of "ideality." Ideality, according to Marx, is nothing but the form of social human activity represented in a thing. Or, conversely, the form of human activity represented as a thing, as an object. (Ilyenkov 1979a: 148)

To sum up, Ilyenkov holds that by acting on natural objects, human beings invest them with a significance or "ideal form" that elevates them to a new "plane of existence." Objects owe their ideality to their incorporation into the aim-oriented life activity of a human community, to their *use*. The notion of significance is glossed in terms of the concept of representation: Artifacts represent the activity to which they owe their existence as artifacts.

Ilyenkov's "insight about artifacts" is designed to show

1. that the ban on anthropocentricity is misconceived, for there is at least one group of ideal properties that have objective existence and that are not characterizable without essential reference to human activity; and
2. that the activity that endows objects with this group of ideal properties is indeed "real object-oriented activity."

The insight is therefore an essential component of Ilyenkov's position. We must be clear, however, about exactly how much it shows. In what way, for example, does it help solve our original dilemma about moral value? It certainly does not follow from the insight about artifacts alone that moral properties have an objective existence that they owe to activity. Rather, the contribution of the insight is that, by lifting the ban on anthropocentricity in one domain, it opens the door to admitting other species of objective, yet anthropocentric, properties. Thus, the insight about artifacts makes it *possible* to argue, as Ilyenkov would, that moral values are part of objective reality.

Ilyenkov would also claim that the insight about artifacts provides a fruitful model for the origin of other ideal properties, including moral values. For Ilyenkov, moral value, like the ideal form of the artifact, should be treated as a species of significance that natural objects (in this case actions and states of affairs) acquire in virtue of their incorporation into human practices.[4] Thus, the insight helps us see that we need appeal to nothing more than human activity to explain the origin of an objective ideal form.

The analogy between artifacts and moral values contributes nothing to our understanding of the specific nature of *moral* properties, for Ilyenkov would offer a similar account of all species of value. Nevertheless, the analogy is thought provoking. For example, Ilyenkov's suggestions undermine the "argument from queerness" against the existence of objective values. Ilyenkov's understanding of the nature of ideality allows us to countenance both the "thorough objectivity" of the ideal while denying that it exists as a mysterious "bodiless substance," cohabiting uneasily with the properties of the physical world (Ilyenkov 1979a: 153). On Ilyenkov's account, there is no inclination to think of moral properties as a realm of peculiar, pseudophysical "ideal atoms" of value distributed across natural properties according to some inexplicable principle (1979a: 153). Indeed, according to Ilyenkov, the ideal cannot be reduced to a "static" property at all, be it either a quasi-natural property, or a property of mental states (1962b: 226). Rather, it exists as a moment of the constant interchange between acting subject and environment:

> The ideal form is the form of a thing, but outside this thing, in human beings as a form of their dynamic life activity, as aims and desires. Or conversely, it is the form of the dynamic life activity of human beings, but outside them, in the form of a created thing. "Ideality" in itself only exists in the constant succession and replacement of these two forms of its "external embodiment" and does not coincide with either of them taken separately. It exists only through the unceasing transformation of a form of activity into the form of a thing and back – the form of a thing into a form of activity (of social beings, of course). (Ilyenkov 1979a: 158)[5]

4 On Ilyenkov's account of ideality, the moral value of an action would be a form of significance lent to a configuration of physical movements in virtue of their incorporation into a system of human practices.

5 In his 1962 encyclopedia article, Ilyenkov gives this thought an evocative Hegelian expression: "Thus, the definition of the ideal is deeply dialectical. It is that which is not, and yet is. It is that which does

Thus, once we see that ideal properties exist, not as paranatural phenomena, but as the form, or shape, taken by natural properties in the course of their transformation by activity, the "argument from queerness" loses its force.

For Ilyenkov, however, it is linguistic meaning, rather than moral value, for which the ideal form of the artifact provides the best model. Words (i.e., word-tokens), be they configurations of sound or marks of paper, are brutely physical entities that have somehow become endowed with significance. How is this possible? Ilyenkov seizes the chance to run the same analysis for words as for artifacts. Indeed, on his account, words *are* artifacts. The meaning of a word is an ideal form acquired by a purely natural object through its incorporation into purposeful human activity. A word owes its significance to its use:

> Thus, the thing does not exist and function as a symbol in virtue of what it is in itself, but because of the system [of activity] in which it takes on its [ideal] properties. Its natural properties therefore bear no relation to its being *as a symbol.* The corporeal, sensually perceptible envelope, the "body" of the symbol (the body of the thing transformed into the symbol) is something completely inessential, transient, temporary; the "functional existence" of such a thing totally absorbs its "material existence," as Marx says . . . A symbol, plucked from the

not exist as an external, sensually perceptible thing, and yet exists as an active capacity of human beings. It is being, which, however, is equal to not-being, or the present being of an external thing in the phase of its becoming in the activity of the subject, in the form of the subject's internal images, desires, motivations, and aims. . . . The ideal exists as a form of the activity of social beings where there occurs, in Hegel's terms, the 'sublation of externality,' that is, the process of the transformation of the body of nature into an object of human activity, an object of labour, and then – into a product of this activity. We can put it this way: The form of the external thing, incorporated into the process of labour, is 'sublated' in the subjective form of object–orientated activity; the latter is objectively [*predmetno*] fixed in the subject in the form of the mechanisms of nerve activity. And then the same metamorphosis occurs in the reverse direction: A representation expressed in words is transformed into a deed, and through the deed, into the form of an external, sensually perceptible thing. These two reciprocal movements actually form a closed circle: thing–deed–word–deed–thing. It is only within this perpetually rejuvenated circular movement that the ideal, the ideal image of a thing, exists" (1962b: 222).

real process of exchange between social beings and nature,
stops being a symbol – the bodily envelope of an ideal image
– at all. Its "soul" vanishes from its body, because that soul was
just the object-oriented activity of human beings, realizing
that exchange between humanized and virgin nature. (Ilyenkov 1974a: 199–200)

This conception of word-meaning is suggestive. First, Ilyenkov reverses a typical direction of explanation. While we
might expect to understand how, if at all, natural objects acquire significance on the model of how words have meaning,
Ilyenkov runs the explanation the other way: For him, words
are just a subclass of idealized natural objects. Second, Ilyenkov offers us a strong reading of the Vygotskian idea that
signs are *tools* (see Vygotsky 1978: 52–7). They are so, not just
in the sense that, as a matter of fact, we use independently
meaningful words as tools (i.e., to get things done), but because the very meaning of a word is constituted by its role in
human activity, by what we use it to do.

To sum up: The insight about artifacts gives us a reason to
reject the ban on anthropocentricity in the case of artifacts, in
favour of the view that the ideal form of the artifact both exists
objectively and owes this existence to object-oriented activity.
Furthermore, the insight provides a fruitful model for the origin of other species of ideal properties, such as moral values
and linguistic meaning.

Agency and the humanization of nature

Although the insight about artifacts is important, it can also
mislead. We must not allow the emphasis on how particular
natural objects become endowed with specific kinds of ideal
property to obscure the general picture of the relation between
human agents and nature that forms the basis of Ilyenkov's
concept of the ideal. Ilyenkov owes this vision to his reading
of the Hegelian tradition, particularly as it finds expression in
the early Marx (esp. 1844, 1845; also Marx and Engels 1845–6;
cf. Hegel 1807: B). The focal point of this picture is human beings' active transformation of nature. As in the insight about
artifacts, the principal theme is that as human beings change
the world to conform to their needs, so their ends and powers
become embodied or "congealed" in natural objects. Through

labour, humankind makes the natural environment "the *objectification* of himself" (Marx 1844: 102). Ilyenkov, however, takes this idea of objectification to have a twofold significance that leads him beyond the scope of the insight on artifacts. First, as nature becomes "humanized," so it serves humanity as a mirror: Man is able to "see himself in a world he has created" (Marx 1844: 74). Thus, objectification is construed as the basis of a form of self-consciousness. Second, the humanization of the world is held to transform nature into a different *kind* of environment. Ilyenkov reads humanization as idealization. The natural world after objectification is a different kind of place because it is now laden with ideal properties, with value and significance. It thus confronts human agents no longer as a purely physical environment, but as a *meaningful* one.

Thus, for Ilyenkov, when Marx and Engels say, "activity, this unceasing sensuous labour and creation" is "the basis of the whole sensuous world as it now exists," they mean that activity, through its objectification, is the source both of the world we inhabit and of the way we inhabit it (Marx and Engels 1845–6: 63). Ilyenkov comments:

> Human beings exist as human beings, as subjects of activity directed both upon the world around them and on themselves, from such time, and for so long, as they actively produce and reproduce their own lives in forms created by themselves, by their own labour. And this labour, this real transformation of their surroundings and of themselves, performed in socially developed and socially sanctioned forms, is just that process … inside which the ideal is born … It is the process in which the idealization of reality, of nature and of social relations takes place, in which the language of symbols is born, as the external body of the ideal form of the external world. In this lies the whole secret of the ideal and its solution. (Ilyenkov 1962b: 223)

Our discussion of artifacts might have created the impression that, for Ilyenkov, the source of ideality lies in the power of activity to daub particular pockets of nature with certain ideal properties, so that objective reality comes to contain two kinds of object, the idealized and the brutely physical. The introduction of Ilyenkov's picture of the relation between human beings and nature shows that such an impression is misleading in two respects. First, Ilyenkov holds that objectification is the source not merely of particular ideal properties but of what he grandly calls "the vast spiritual culture *(dukhovnaya kul'tura)* of the human race" (1979a: 145). The ideal represents the entire edifice of the institutions of social life, born of social activity and "fixed in the substance of reality," where it confronts each individual member of human society as the *total structure of normative demands on his or her activity.* It is only against the backdrop of such spiritual culture, "humanity's inorganic body" (Ilyenkov 1964b: 258) or "objectified social consciousness" (Ilyenkov 1960a: 41), that it makes sense to think of the idealization of particular objects. Thus, for Ilyenkov, the realm of the ideal comprises all:

> the forms of the organization of social (collectively realized) human life activity that exist *before, outside, and completely independently* of the individual mind, in one way or another materially established in language, in ritually legitimized customs and rights and, further, as "the organization of the state"[6] with all its material attributes and organs for the protection of traditional forms of life ... [These forms] stand in opposition to the individual ... as an entity organized "in itself and for itself," as something ideal in which all individual things acquire a different meaning and play a different role from that which they had played "as themselves," that is, outside this entity. For this reason, the "ideal" definition of any thing, or the definition of any thing as a "disappearing" moment in the movement of the "ideal world," coincides ... with the role and meaning of this thing in social human culture, in the context of socially organized human life activity, and not in individual consciousness. (1977c: 81)

Second, Ilyenkov takes objectification to result in the idealization, not of parts of nature, but of nature *as a whole:*

> In human beings, all of nature is idealized, and not only that part that they directly produce and reproduce, or that they use in utilitarian fashion. (Ilyenkov 1962b: 225)

---

6   Ilyenkov uses the term "state" here in the Platonic sense of "the entire totality of social institutions which regulate the life-activity of the individual in its everyday, moral, intellectual, and aesthetic manifestations" (Ilyenkov 1979a: 132).

The emergence of humanity's spiritual culture thus leaves nothing untouched.

Thus, Ilyenkov's vision of the relation between human beings and nature extends the dimensions of the present discussion. We can now add to Ilyenkov's theses

1. that the ideal exists objectively, and
2. that it owes this existence to human activity,

the further theses

3. that ideal properties and relations constitute our "spiritual culture," and
4. that the emergence of this culture represents the idealization of nature as a whole.

The interesting philosophical consequences Ilyenkov seeks to draw from his account depend on taking all four theses seriously.

Alienation and objectification

Ilyenkov believes that his conception of ideality as objectified "spiritual culture" represents what the early Marx appropriated from Hegel.[7] It is well-known that Marx held Hegel's metaphysical system to be not simply false, but a distorted picture of the truth, an "abstract, logical, speculative" expression of real history (Marx 1844: 136). As we saw in Chapter 5, Hegel depicts history as the evolution of the metaphysical absolute, conceived as *spirit*. The development of spirit takes place through a process Hegel calls *"Entäusserung"*: "alienation" or "externalization." Spirit "externalizes itself" by becoming *object*. This "sinking into substance" (Hegel 1807: 490), while in some sense a loss or relinquishment, is the very means of spirit's self-realization, for in the course of history spirit comes to self-consciousness, or absolute knowledge, by recognizing the object world as its own expression.

---

7 Many features of Ilyenkov's account of the ideal are anticipated in Hegel's *Phenomenology of Spirit* [more commonly known as *Phenomenology of Mind*] (1807: esp. B, 104–39). Indeed, in his writings, Ilyenkov presents and develops much of his own position in the course of a sympathetic exposition of Hegel (see, e.g., Ilyenkov 1973, 1979a: 138–40, 145–6).

For Ilyenkov, Marx's insight is to grasp that Hegel's vision of the relation of spirit and world is a mystified expression of the relation between humankind and nature. Hegel's theory of alienation is actually a portrait, refracted through the distorting medium of speculative metaphysics, of human beings' real capacity to objectify themselves in the natural world. What Hegel sees as the activity of spirit is nothing but the activity of real individuals, and the result of this activity is not the positing of the external world *as such*, but rather the transformation of an already existing natural world into an idealized environment. Thus, Ilyenkov argues, in its conception of the ideal, Marxism preserves the Hegelian theses (suitably understood), first, that "the whole colossal body of civilization is 'thought in its otherness,'" and, second, that objectification is the means of the self-realization of the subject (conceived by Marxism as humanity, and not spirit) (Ilyenkov 1973: 130, 1974a: 128). Ilyenkov insists that this, the "rational core" of Hegel's conception of subject and object, not only contains "not one iota of idealism," but constitutes "a serious step in the direction of materialism" (1973: 129–30).

Many of Ilyenkov's opponents would balk at his claim that Marxism's account of the relation of humanity to nature preserves the structure of Hegel's theory of *Entäusserung*. An alternative reading would be that Marx sees Hegel's concept of alienation as a mystified presentation, not of the general relation of humankind to nature, but only of the specific relation of the worker to the object of his or her labour under capitalism. In the *Manuscripts of 1844*, Marx describes how, in the act of production, the workers' creative powers are "embodied" in the objects they produce. Under capitalism, however, workers are able to exercise no control over their products; on the contrary, the world of commodities confronts the workers as an alien power, expressing the economic forces that dictate their activity. In this domination of producer by product, the workers are estranged both from the products of their labour and from the labour process itself, which becomes not a form of self-expression but purely a means of subsistence. Since we are beings who express ourselves in activity, the workers' alienation from their labour represents their alienation from their very selves.

Ilyenkov's opponents might suggest that Marx's debt to the

Hegelian theory of alienation emerges exclusively in this account of the estrangement of labour by capital. On this reading, Marx's genius is to see how Hegel's vision of the alienation of spirit is a speculative, and cosmically legitimized, picture of the alienation of the worker under capitalism; and, accordingly, that alienation is not in fact to be overcome by an act of consciousness, as Hegel believes, but by social revolution that transforms the actual relations between human agents and the objects of their labour. However, the opponents conclude, nothing in Marx's account of alienation implies a grand philosophical theory of the relation of humanity to nature in general.

This interpretation would allow Ilyenkov's critics to argue that, by reading the Hegelian notion of alienation as a general theory of objectification, Ilyenkov, like Hegel himself, turns a specific social relation between worker and product into a universal relation between subject and object. In so doing, not only does he laud in theory that which socialism sets out to destroy in practice, but he commits Marxism to a dubious metaphysic of objectively existing ideal properties. Once we see, however, that all Marx takes from Hegel is a model of capitalist relations of production, it is clear that no such commitment is either necessary or desirable. If Marx is claiming that Hegel's odyssey of spirit is a metaphor for social relations under capitalism, then it is natural to read Marx's talk of "objectification" as merely metaphorical, thereby making no commitment to the objectivity of the ideal (cf. Wood 1981: 38). Thus, the alternative reading of Marx's theory of alienation leaves undisturbed the idea that objective reality is simply matter in motion.

Let us call Ilyenkov's position the "strong reading" of objectification. How would he defend it? Ilyenkov would, of course, in no way wish to diminish the power of Marx's account of the worker's alienation under capitalism. On the contrary, he would have argued that, in order to make proper sense of that account, we need to distinguish clearly between *objectification,* the universal process in which activity is embodied in external form, and *alienation,* a relation, obtaining in only certain conditions, between acting subjects and the objectified results of their activity. In Hegel, this distinction is not drawn, for the objectification of spirit is necessarily its alienation. For Hegel,

the significance of spirit's becoming "burdened with substance" is precisely that spirit loses its spirituality and confronts itself as something other, alien to its true nature (Hegel
1807: 56). It is Marx himself, however, who emphasizes the
distinction between alienation and objectification (*Vergegen-
ständlichung*). By so doing, Marx indicates that Hegel's equation of the two is a mistake. This mistake, however, results not
just in the glorification of alienation by presenting it as an
eternal philosophical truth, but also in the degradation of objectification. For by conceiving of objectification only as "loss
of object," Hegel reduces "the rich, living, sensuous, concrete
activity of self-objectification ... to its mere abstraction" (Marx
1844: 153). Thus, it is clear that Marx distinguishes objectification and alienation in order that the rational core of both notions be preserved. For Ilyenkov, the rational core of the former is preserved by the strong reading.

How does the strong reading help us make proper sense of
Marx's theory of alienation? On Ilyenkov's position, humanity's objectified "spiritual culture" represents a "historically
formed and historically developing system" comprising

> all the universal [*vseobshchee*] moral norms regulating peo-
> ple's daily life activity, legal structures, forms of state-political
> organization of life, the ritually legitimized patterns of activity
> in all spheres, the rules of life that must be obeyed by all ...
> and so on and so forth, right up to and including the gram-
> matical and syntactical structures of speech and language
> and the logical norms of reasoning. (Ilyenkov 1979a: 138)

A crucial feature of Ilyenkov's position is his view of the relation in which the structures of this spiritual culture stand to
the individual. Ilyenkov argues that although these structures
are born of the activity of the community, they confront each
of its individual members as an object. The ideal forms of
reality, and the activities that sustain them, constitute (part of)
the environment into which each human individual is born.
As such, they exercise an objective claim on the actions of the
individual, for each must learn to recognize and reproduce
the activities objectified in these structures if he or she is to
move within the idealized environment. It is as if the practices of the community, through their objectification, mark
out paths each individual must learn to trace:

> All these structural forms and patterns of social consciousness unambiguously confront individual consciousness and will as a particular, internally organized reality, as completely external forms that determine that consciousness and will. From childhood, every individual must reckon far more carefully with such demands and restrictions, and with the traditions that are codified and expressed within them, than with the immediately perceptible appearance of external "things" and situations, or the organic whims, desires, and needs of his individual body. (Ilyenkov 1979a: 138–9)

The fact that ideal forms take shape "behind the back" of consciousness and confront individuals with an absolutely objective claim on their actions explains how it is possible for human beings to see this idealized environment not as an expression of their own creative powers but as an alien authority. Under conditions where these forms rigidly dictate to individuals, the individual will come to see them as autonomous and absolute, either by representing them as manifestations of a divine authority or by attributing to them a quasi-naturalistic status. To attach an autonomous existence to that which is a product of human activity is, for Ilyenkov, what Marx means by *fetishism;* and in fetishizing the ideal, human agents are alienated or estranged both from a product of their activity and from their own creative powers themselves (Marx 1867: 163–7; cf. Ilyenkov 1963: 133).

On Ilyenkov's position, the estrangement of worker from product under capitalism is thus only one instance of alienation: Any facet of our spiritual culture is a possible object of fetishism. This picture has two principal attractions. First, in harmony with Marx's own writings, it extends the explanatory compass of the theory of alienation beyond the relation of worker and product. This enables Ilyenkov to make philosophical sense of, for example, Marx's Feuerbachian hostility to religion as alienated human self-consciousness (Ilyenkov 1968a: 44–56). Second, Ilyenkov's position sheds light on the specific case of the alienation of worker from product. By giving sense to the objective (economic and ideological) relations into which the worker loses the object he or she creates, Ilyenkov helps us see how production, the process of the "appropriation of what exists in nature for the requirements of man" (Marx 1867: 290), can result in the producer standing to his product "as to powers that are alien and hostile to him" (Marx 1844: 76).

For Ilyenkov, however, the attraction of the strong reading is not only that it gives proper sense to Marx's theory of alienation: It also has powerful implications for philosophy. It is an obvious consequence of this reading that, while communism seeks to destroy the conditions in which alienation is possible, it does not do so by destroying objectification. The strong reading makes such a thing unintelligible, for though alienation is not possible without objectification, neither is any norm-governed practice. For Ilyenkov, objectification is an achievement that communism in no way seeks to negate. As Marx himself puts it:

> But atheism and communism are no flight, no abstraction; no loss of the objective world created by man – of man's essential powers born to the realm of objectivity; they are not a returning in poverty to unnatural, primitive simplicity. On the contrary, they are but the first real emergence, the actual realization for man of man's essence and of his essence as something real. (Marx 1844: 151)

For Ilyenkov, by taking this passage seriously we come to see the true significance of the strong reading. Marx suggests that objectification is an achievement because it makes possible the realization of the human essence. The notion of objectification, then, holds the key to what it is for "human beings to exist as human beings" (Ilyenkov 1962b: 223). This is because, Ilyenkov argues, the idea of objectification is the starting place for a materialist theory of *thought*. When Ilyenkov says that the objectified ideal realm that confronts each individual includes our ways of speaking and methods of reasoning, he means not just that how we speak and think is moulded by the practices of the communities we live in, but that the very possibility of thought and language derives from objectification itself. For Ilyenkov, this is true in two ways. First, the structures of humanity's spiritual culture "determine consciousness and will," in the sense that something is only a thinking thing if it is able to reproduce those structures. Second, the objectification of activity is the process through which the world becomes a possible object of thought. He writes:

> It is precisely production (in the broadest sense of the term)
> that transforms the object of nature into an object of contem-
> plation and thought. (Ilyenkov 1974a: 187)

Ilyenkov claims, therefore, that the theory of objectification is
the answer to the questions of how there can be a knowable
world and of how there can be beings capable of knowing it.
Thus, for Ilyenkov, the strong reading forms the basis of dialectical materialism's distinctive solution to the central question of philosophy: the question of the relation of thinking to
being.

Ideality and the possibility of thought and experience

What does Ilyenkov mean when he says that it is in "production," conceived in the broadest sense as the end-oriented
transformation of nature by human activity, that the world is
made an object of thought? To understand the problem to
which activity is supposed to be the answer, consider again
the weakness of Ilyenkov's *bête noire*, classical empiricism.
Empiricism can be seen as a theory about the way in which
reality manifests itself to the mind: The world reveals itself
to us in *sense experience*. For the empiricist, each individual
constructs a conception of the world from concepts entirely
formed by abstraction from the deliverances of his or her
senses. As we saw in Chapter 5, Ilyenkov identifies a serious
flaw in the empiricist's account. The empiricist understands
the experience from which the individual subject acquires *all*
concepts as a panoply of preconceptualized sensory particulars. But if the subject does not already possess an arsenal of
concepts, how can the subject make any sense at all of this experiential imbroglio? Unless the empiricist assumes what he
(or she) is trying to explain, he cannot show how the subject
individuates and identifies events in the "sensuous manifold,"
or how the subject conceives of *this* patch of, say, the visual
field as an experience of such-and-such a kind. In short, experience, as empiricism understands it, possesses insufficient
structure to form the basis of judgment. Thus, we can say that
the empiricist's conception of the relation of subject and object has inadequate resources to explain how the world manifests itself to the mind. Empiricism cannot make sense of the
world as an object of thought.

To explain how experience is possible, it seems we must hold either that the subject possesses prior to experience the conceptual apparatus necessary to organize the chaotic deliverances of the senses, or that those deliverances themselves are organized prior to their presentation to the subject, so that the data of sense already embody, as it were, a conceptual structure that the individual subject simply "absorbs" or appropriates.

The first of these strategies is Kantian.[8] The Kantian holds that, for experience to be possible, the intellect must impose a structure on the brute yieldings of the senses. Stated crudely, he or she argues that the understanding contains the necessary repertoire of concepts, or "categories," as a scheme of a priori forms of thought that prescribe the basic forms of judgment (Ilyenkov 1979a: 140). For the world to impinge upon us in experience, what it presents to us must be filtered through this conceptual scheme. The scheme represents the inevitable geography of the mind, a necessary condition for the very possibility of experience.

While he thinks that the Kantian confronts the right problem, Ilyenkov rejects the Kantian's solution. The Kantian treats cognition as a synthesis of pure, unstructured sensuousness and a priori forms of thought. Yet although this is a unity of scheme and content in which the two components cannot intelligibly be imagined apart, we are still invited to view cognition as an interaction between the deliverances of an independently existing reality and the individual mind. However, since the Kantian holds that nothing can be present to the mind unless it is filtered through our conceptual scheme, he or she is forced to conclude that the world prior to its expression in our concepts is inaccessible to us. Consequently, experience becomes an *interface* between the subject and the reality beyond his or her mind. While we are conscious of how the world is "for us," how it is "in itself" is something our minds cannot determine (Ilyenkov 1964a: 23). Thus, the Kantian explains how experience is possible only at the price of making "things in themselves" in principle unknowable.

Conceived as an attempt to explain how reality can be pres-

---

8 For a discussion of the relation between "the Kantian" who figures in this work and Kant himself, see Chapter 4 (n9).

ent to the mind, this Kantian strategy is strikingly self-defeating. Ilyenkov, however, holds that philosophy need not acquiesce in the Kantian's conclusions. We can adopt the *second* strategy and argue that the data of experience are somehow organized prior to their presentation to the subject. Ilyenkov turns to his theory of the ideal for the basis of this argument. For him, what lends the object of experience structure is not the mind of the individual subject, but the forms of activity of the community:

> All the schemas Kant defined as "transcendentally inborn" forms of the work of particular minds, as the "internal mechanisms" present *a priori* in each mind, in fact represent the forms of self-consciousness of social beings (understood as the historically developing "ensemble of social relations"), assimilated by the individual from without (and confronting him from the very beginning as "external" schemas [patterns] of the movement of culture, independent of his consciousness and will). (Ilyenkov 1979a: 140)

The claim is that, in the idealization of nature, our forms of thought are built into objective reality itself.

Ilyenkov's position begins to take shape when his idea of what the world must be like to be a possible object of thought is complemented by a corresponding conception of what it is to be a thinking thing. To be a creature capable of thought is to be able to relate to the world *as to* an object of thought. Thus, for Ilyenkov, to be a thinking thing is just to have the capacity to inhabit an idealized environment, to be able to orientate oneself in a habitat that contains not just physical pushes and pulls but meanings, values, and reasons. And to have this capacity is, in turn, to be able to reproduce the forms of activity that endow the world with ideality, to mould one's movements to the dictates of the norms that constitute humanity's spiritual culture.[9]

The picture then is this: The idealization of nature by human practice transforms the natural world into an object of thought, and by participating in those practices, the human

9 This is the sense Ilyenkov would give to Marx's seemingly obscure remark that "my relationship to my surroundings is my consciousness" (quoted by Avineri 1968: 71).

individual is brought into contact with reality as an object of thought. Each individual enters the world with the forms of movement that are constitutive of thought embodied in the environment surrounding him or her. It is not that each mind must find the world anew for itself: We are born into a world that history has made cognizable.

On Ilyenkov's account, the capacity to inhabit an idealized environment is not something that the human individual possesses "by nature." Rather, children acquire this capacity as they are "socialized" by the adult members of the community into their practices. As they assimilate, or "internalize," those practices, so they are transformed from epistemically inept masses of brute matter into thinking beings, subjects, persons (*lichnost'*). Inauguration into the community's mode of life is thus the process in which individual minds are born.

Ilyenkov enjoins us, then, to see cognition as a relation not between a structured subject (the Kantian mind) and an unstructured sensory input (preconceptualized sense data), but between a structured object (the historically forged environment, idealized by human activity) and a subject that is initially unformed (the human infant) but that derives its structure as a thinking thing by learning to engage with this object as its structure dictates.

Although Ilyenkov's conception of forms of thought as ideal structures objectified in the "external" world is difficult and strange, his correlative understanding of the origin of individual consciousness is more familiar. It recalls, of course, Vygotsky's theory of "the social genesis of the individual." We shall examine Ilyenkov's defence of this theory in Chapter 7. In the present context, however, we should note the following two considerations.

First, Ilyenkov's account of the individual mind explains his hostility to Dubrovsky's attempt to reduce the ideal to the phenomena of consciousness. For Ilyenkov, the direction of explanation must run the other way. The possibility of individual consciousness is explained by appeal to the ideal, and not vice versa. He writes:

There is certainly a necessary connection between "ideality" and consciousness and will, but it does not take the form imagined by the old, pre-Marxist materialism. It is not that ideali-

ty is an "aspect" or a "form of the manifestation" of the realm
of consciousness and will. Quite the reverse, consciousness
and volition are a form of manifestation, an "aspect" or psychological manifestation of the ideal (i.e., socio-historically
emerging) plan of relations between humanity and nature . . .
The presence of this specifically human object – the world
of things, created by human beings for human beings, the
forms of which [things] are embodied forms of human activity (labour), and not forms naturally inherent in them – is the
condition of consciousness and will and not the other way
around. (1979a: 157, 154)

Second, Ilyenkov's theory of individual consciousness casts
light on his view that the structures of humanity's spiritual
culture exist "objectively." The forms of activity that the child
must appropriate are objective in the sense that they are by no
means arbitrary or conventional. They are neither created by
decision, nor conformed to by choice. Children must adapt
their movements to them if they are to come to think at all.
(Of course, Ilyenkov does not wish to deny the possibility of
critical thought, of coming to see some practice as merely local or parochial, or as not warranting allegiance. However, he
takes such thought to be possible only after internalization has
taken place.)

We can take stock of Ilyenkov's position with the following
passage from *Dialectical Logic:*

A consistent materialist understanding of thought naturally
changes our approach to the central problems of logic in a
fundamental way. In particular, it alters our interpretation of
the nature of the logical categories. Above all, Marx and Engels held that the external world as it is in itself is not simply
and directly given to the individual in contemplation, but only in the process of its transformation by human agents, and
that both the *contemplating individual* and the *world contemplated*
are products of history.

Correspondingly, the forms of thought, the categories, were
also treated not as pure abstractions from sensuousness understood unhistorically, but primarily as universal forms of the
sensuously objective activity of social beings reflected in consciousness. The real, objective [*predmetnyi*] equivalent of logical forms was seen not simply as the abstract-general contours
of the object contemplated by the individual, but in the forms

of the real activity of human beings transforming nature in
accord with their ends ... The subject of thought becomes the
individual in the nexus of social relations, the socially defined individual, whose every form of life activity is given
not by nature, but by history, by the process of the coming-to-
be of human culture.

Therefore, forms of human activity (and the forms of
thought which reflect them) are laid down in the course of
history independently of the will and consciousness of separate persons, whom they confront as forms of the historically
developing system of culture. The latter develops not according to psychological laws, for the development of social consciousness is not a simple arithmetical sum of mental processes, but is a particular process controlled by the laws of development of the material life of society. And these laws not only
do not depend on the consciousness and will of particular individuals, but, on the contrary, actively determine consciousness and will. Isolated individuals do not and could not arrive
at [*vyrabotat'*] the universal forms of human activity, whatever
powers of abstraction they possessed. Rather, they assimilate
these forms ready made as they are themselves assimilated
into a culture, as they acquire language and the knowledge
expressed in it. (1974a: 207–8)

We have encompassed the full scope of Ilyenkov's theory of
the ideal. We shall now turn to its defence.

Ilyenkov, radical realism, and the critique of "two-worlds epistemology"

Earlier, we set out Ilyenkov's position in four theses:

1. Ideal phenomena may exist objectively.
2. They owe this objective existence to human activity.
3. Objectively existing ideal properties and relations comprise
   humanity's spiritual culture.
4. The emergence of this culture represents the idealization
   of nature as a whole.

We have now seen how Ilyenkov holds that these four theses
form the basis of a theory of the nature and possibility of
thought: A historical process, the idealization of nature by human activity, is the source both of a knowable world and of a
subject capable of knowing it.

We noted above that some of Ilyenkov's opponents suspect that the first thesis commits him to idealism, a suspicion fuelled by his expressed admiration for Hegel in his defence of the third. Indeed, despite Ilyenkov's insistence that his views are consistently materialist, his position undoubtedly provokes an objection that forces us to take this accusation of idealism seriously. The objection focuses on the fourth thesis, the idea that, through objectification, the *whole* of nature is idealized. Ilyenkov is committed to this thesis by his claim that for anything to be a possible object of thought it must be idealized, that is, brought within the compass of humanity's spiritual culture:

> ... Nature "in itself" is given to us if and only if it is transformed into an object, material, or means of production, of human life. Even the starry heavens, which human labour does not directly alter at all, becomes an object of human attention (and contemplation) when and only when it is transformed into natural "clock," "calender," and "compass," that is, into a means and an "instrument" of our orientation in space and time. (Ilyenkov 1964a: 42)

The objection is as follows: Ilyenkov claims that the mind has access to natural objects only insofar as they are incorporated into the practices that constitute our spiritual culture. There is, of course, a trivial sense in which this is true. We cannot, for example, perceive some object unless it, in some general sense, enters our lives (unless we bring ourselves into certain relations with it, or unless the object itself intrudes upon us). Ilyenkov, however, has something stronger in mind. He means that when objects are incorporated into our practices they are changed, and only in this changed state can the object stand in relation to a mind. However, if we are only acquainted with objects insofar as they are changed in this way, then surely we cannot be said to have access to them as they are "in themselves." In other words, if (as Ilyenkov himself puts it) the world is only given "refracted" through the "prism" of social consciousness, how can the mind reach out to the world as it is prior to that refraction (Ilyenkov 1960a: 41)? It seems that Ilyenkov is driven to the same unfortunate conclusion as the Kantian: Things in themselves are unknowable. He must therefore be committed either to agnosti-

cism about the nature and existence of a world independent
of us, or, like the Empiriocritics whom he so despises, to the
idealist view that the world is constructed out of our conceptual scheme. It seems that, by lifting the ban on anthropocentricity, Ilyenkov has let anthropocentricity run amok.

It is clear that Ilyenkov recognizes this problem. For example, he writes that

> The main difficulty, and therefore the main problem of phi-
> losophy, is not to distinguish and counterpose all that is "in the
> consciousness of each individual" to everything that is outside
> individual consciousness (that is in practice never difficult to
> do), but to differentiate the world of collectively acknowledged
> conceptions – that is, the whole socially organized world of
> spiritual culture, with all the stable and materially fixed uni-
> versal patterns of its structure and organization – from the real
> material world as it exists outside and independently of its ex-
> pression in these socially legitimized forms of "experience,"
> in the objective forms of "spirit." (1979a: 146)

It is also clear that Ilyenkov believes the problem to be soluble,
and that *activity* is the key to its solution. He claims that
though "the purely objective characteristics of natural material are given in contemplation in the form (*skvoz' tot obraz*)
which that natural material has acquired in the course of, and
as a result of, the subjective activity of social beings," it is nevertheless the case that "the very activity which transforms
(and sometimes also distorts) 'the genuine form' of nature is
also able to show how nature is without such 'subjective distor-
tions'" (1974a: 188; see also 1964a: 41, 1964b: 259).

It is unclear, however, exactly how Ilyenkov's appeal to activity is to explain how the world "in itself" can be accessible
to the mind. Ilyenkov offers no more than clues about how
this explanation might go. In what follows I shall attempt to
piece these clues together.

The alleged problem with Ilyenkov's position derives from
the fact that he agrees (in some sense) with the Kantian that
reality in its brute physicality, is not a possible object of
thought. Reality must in some way be changed, or "idealized," if it is to be "digestible" to minds. Once this is conceded, however, Ilyenkov's problem is to explain how the process
of "idealization" changes the world in a way that minds can

retrieve. This the Kantian conspicuously fails to do; why is Il-yenkov's position any better?

We must first diagnose exactly why the Kantian fails. Il-yenkov implies that this failure issues from the Kantian's commitment to a particular picture of the self. The "fundamental principle of Kantian dualism" is, he writes, the idea that

> The thinking soul [*dukh*] is, from the very beginning, set in absolute opposition to everything sensuous, bodily, and material. It is conceived as a special immaterial being, self-organizing and formed according to its immanent-logical laws and schemas, as something independent and self-sufficient. (1964a: 34, 1974a: 155)

Such a picture is, of course, not a feature of Kant's philosophy alone. By attributing the Kantian's failings to this conception of the self, we are indicting an entire philosophical tradition of which Kantianism is only one manifestation. This tradition has its origins in Descartes. The conception of the self Descartes introduced into modern philosophy dominates the thought of the Enlightenment; it forms the basis of classical empiricism, and, indeed, continues to exercise a powerful influence over both Soviet and Anglo–American philosophy. Il-yenkov's claim is that any philosopher who subscribes to this Cartesian conception will find it impossible to explain how the world "in itself" can be present to the mind. To see why this is so, we need a more comprehensive understanding of the Cartesian self than the above quotation provides.

Talk about the "self" is in fact already talk in Cartesian terms. By "the self," the philosopher usually means to refer, in the first instance, not to "persons" or "human beings," but to a distinctively philosophical subject, conceived primarily as a thinker of thoughts, a subject of consciousness.[10] For the Cartesian, the self is primarily a subject of consciousness in the sense that it is directly acquainted only with the contents of its own mind. By contrast, its contact with the "external" world is always indirect: It is acquainted with objective reality

10 The Cartesian tradition is so foreign to Russian thought that the Russian language contains no comfortable translation of the term "self." Russian philosophers usually resort to the first person pronoun, "*ya,*" enclosed in quotation marks.

only via its immediate acquaintence with its experiences and thoughts. The Cartesian self is therefore *self-contained*. It is the sole inhabitant of its own, "internal" mental world, the contents of which are revealed directly only to it. It is as if, to use Rorty's (1980) favourite metaphor, each mind is a great mirror, displaying images that the self alone surveys.

Each self-contained Cartesian self is *self-sufficient* in the sense that each is essentially independent of all others. Since nothing can affect the Cartesian self except by becoming an object of its thought, it can enter relations with others only insofar as it is already able to think. Therefore, its capacity to think cannot derive from its relations to others. It follows that what it is can, indeed must, be explained without reference to other selves. Indeed, Cartesianism encourages the view that the capacity to think is not something derived at all. Rather, Cartesian selves come *ready-made*, they spring into being with the essential apparatus for thought intact.

The Cartesian conception of the self as a self-contained and self-sufficient centre of consciousness is, of course, one side of the "two-worlds epistemology" described in Chapter 4. On this model, the subject–object relation is conceived as the interaction of two logically distinct worlds: the "internal world" of the subject's mental life and the "external world" of material things. This epistemological dualism issues from the Cartesian's radical distinction between mind and matter. For the Cartesian, mental and physical properties are utterly different in kind. While the physical is characterized primarily in terms of extension, mass, and mobility, the distinguishing feature of mental entities is that they possess "content" or meaning. In the case of many mental phenomena, this content is *representational* in nature: Mental states represent reality to the thinking subject. The mode of presentation of this representational content depends on the kind of mental entity that carries it. The content of such states as beliefs, desires, and intentions can be expressed in propositional form (the content of a subject's belief is *"that such-and-such is the case"*). In contrast, some states, such as sensations, convey their content through their distinctive phenomenology (e.g., by the fact that they *look, feel,* or *sound* a certain way). In addition, mental phenomena like occurrent thoughts, and some forms of memo-

ry, imagination, and perception, possess both a phenomeno-
logical and a propositional content.

The Cartesian position is defined by its commitment to two
crucial tenets:

1. that only *mental* entities have representational content, and
2. that minds can stand in direct relation only to entities
   with such content.[11]

It follows from these tenets that the subject's relation to the
physical world must necessarily be indirect. If the mind can
enter immediate relations with mental entities alone, then
thought may have access to the external world only insofar as
that world is presented to the subject in the form of "ideas," or
mental representations. For the Cartesian, the mind can never
be in direct contact with the physical world: "Thought," as Ilyenkov puts it, "is unable to encompass [*ogranichivat'*] an ex-
tented thing" (1964a: 26).

Thus, for the Cartesian, if the mind is to have access to
reality, reality must be presented in a mental idiom, a representation. "Idealization," the process in which the world becomes an object of thought, is construed as the *mentalization* of
the world: the translation of the object into an intrinsically
representational mental medium. For Ilyenkov, the doctrine
of idealization as mentalization is the fatal flaw of Cartesianism. For if we accept this idea, he suggests, we become prey to
a form of skepticism so catastrophic that we are robbed of any
conception of how a mind-independent world could be a possible object of thought.

In the Soviet philosophical tradition, skeptical attacks on the
two-worlds epistemological model are common. (The prece-
dent is Lenin [1909a], as we saw in Chapter 4.) The point of
departure of such attacks is usually the fact that the two-worlds
model invites us to treat the veracity of our ideas as a corre-

11   Descartes, of course, introduced the idea of the mind as a special
     substance. On the present analysis, however, the dualism of men-
     tal and physical substances is not the defining characteristic of a
     "Cartesian" position. Rather, Descartes's idea of a "mind-stuff" is
     simply an attempt to express, within the terms of seventeenth-
     century metaphysics, how the special, representational properties
     of the mental are possible (i.e., such properties require a special
     substance in which to inhere).

spondence between their content and the object they represent. To ascertain their truth therefore requires us to compare
idea and object. However, since the subject has direct access
only to ideas, and not to the objects themselves, it is argued
that there is no basis for the necessary comparison. On the
two-worlds model, as Descartes himself so clearly realized, it
always remains possible that the origin of our ideas is not the
object world we take to cause them. But if for all that we know
we might be wrong about the existence of the object world,
then we do not know that it exists: There might not be a mind-
independent world to be an object of thought.

This skeptical conclusion, however, is too weak for Ilyenkov's purposes, for it leaves us with a conception of what a
mind-independent world would be like if there was one. Ad-
mittedly, as we learn more about ourselves and (what we take
to be) the world, we realize that some of the properties that we
take to be "out there" in the world are in fact contributed by
our minds. Nevertheless, we can aspire to disentangle from
our conception of reality those properties our minds contribute, leaving a conception of the world as it is independently of
all minds. This, of course, is the project of constructing the
absolute conception of the world. The skeptical argument does
not conclude that such a conception is unintelligible, only
that we can never know whether there is such a world as the
absolute conception depicts. Therefore, the argument does not
show that such a mind-independent world could not be a possible object of thought.

However, a stronger skeptical argument (anticipated by Ilyenkov [1974a: 50]) can be formulated to yield the conclusion
Ilyenkov needs. The project of constructing an absolute conception of the world is, of course, the province of the empiricist. The real problem for the Cartesian framework becomes
clear once the empiricist's conception of experience is over-
turned. As we saw above, the Kantian, recognizing that sense
experience, as the empiricist understands it, has insufficient
structure to form the basis of judgment, argues that for experience to be possible, the deliverances of sense must be filtered
through our conceptual scheme. In other words, the Kantian's
reaction to empiricism is to deny that objects with representational content are simply given to the mind. Rather, the synthesizing power of the intellect *constitutes* or *creates* the object of

cognition as a representational entity. However, once we admit this, then it is no longer possible to argue that the subject grasps how an object is "in itself" by disentangling from its representation of the object those features that the mind itself contributes. For once we remove the mind's contribution to that representation, we are left with no representation at all. If we subtract the influence of our conceptual scheme from our picture of the world, we are left with nothing recognizable as a world because we are left with nothing recognizable as a picture. Thus, the Kantian ushers in a deadlier form of skepticism. On the Kantian position, the nature of a mind-independent reality becomes simply inconceivable.

We can now formulate the source of the Kantian's problem. In the grip of the two-worlds model, he or she construes idealization as mentalization. But, in response to the inadequacy of empiricism, the Kantian holds that, in the process of mentalization, the mind contributes to the direct object of cognition the very properties in virtue of which it exists as a representation. Thus, idealization changes the deliverances of the "external world" in a way that the mind cannot retrieve: For if the mind abstracts the results of idealization from its conception of the world, it leaves not a conception of a mind-independent world, but no conception at all.

Thus, if we are to defend Ilyenkov, we must establish a relevant difference between his conception of idealization and the Kantian's. As we noted above, there is a sense in which Ilyenkov agrees with the Kantian that reality in its brute physicality is not a possible object of thought. We can now see how this is so. Ilyenkov holds, first, that if something is to be a possible object of thought it must have "representational content," and second, that physical objects "in themselves" (i.e., independent of us) do not possess such content. In other words, if a thing T is to stand in some relation to a mind, then T must be something which can be *seen as* a T: It must "present itself" to the subject as a T. Ilyenkov holds that nothing about the physical nature of the thing explains how this is possible. The object's significance as an object is not part of its physical composition. Thus, something must be added to the object to make it accessible to a mind. However, Ilyenkov offers a radically different account from the Kantian of how the object acquires the representational content that transforms it into an object of

thought. For Ilyenkov, representational content is not something that minds contribute to the world. Idealization is not
mentalization, the creation of an intrinsically representational mental object by mental activity. Rather, Ilyenkov analyzes representational content as he does any ideal property: It
is a species of significance that objects acquire in virtue of
their incorporation into human practice. Thus, Ilyenkov's position diverges from the Kantian's in two crucial respects.
First, he treats representational content as a property that orig-
inates not in mental but in object-oriented activity. Second,
representational content is taken to exist as a property of the
physical object itself, rather than of any intermediary mental
object. It is as if the incorporation of the objects of the natural
world into human practice lends them a significance in virtue of which they present themselves to the subject *as* objects
of a certain kind.

By denying that only mental entities can possess representational content, Ilyenkov rejects the Cartesian thesis that the
mind can have direct access only to mental phenomena. For
him, the significance that makes an object accessible to the
mind is not conveyed by mental entities that threaten to come
between the subject and reality in itself. On the contrary,
mind-independent, material objects can be immediately present to the mind. Ilyenkov argues that the thinking subject
"is in immediate contact with the external world" (1964a: 43).
Thus, for Ilyenkov, the idealization of reality is not the translation of the world into a mental representation, but the process in which the natural world is made directly manifest to
the subject.

In Chapter 4, I suggested that the position Lenin develops in
Materialism and Empiriocriticism is ambiguous between two
forms of realism: first, an indirect, or "conservative," realism
constructed within the framework of "two-worlds epistemology," and second, a direct, or "radical," realism. It is now
clear which of the two interpretations of Lenin's text Ilyenkov would endorse. Ilyenkov offers us a radical realism, on
which the subject–object relation occurs not between two
worlds, but within *one:* the single, idealized natural environment in which the subject is immersed. To endorse such a
monism is, Ilyenkov claims, to subscribe to a theory in which
thought and being stand in a relation not of correspondence

but of identity. And this conception of the identity of thinking and being is, for Ilyenkov, the essential basis of materialism:

> Materialism recognizes the following fact: The world with which the mind is "in touch" [*umopostigaemiĭ mir*] and the [real, object] world we perceive [*chuvstvenno-vosprinimaemiĭ mir*] are one and the same, and not two different worlds between which we need to find a "bridge," an interchange, or interaction. (Ilyenkov 1964a: 41)

It is critical, however, that the theory of the ideal (completely absent in Lenin's writings) is the linchpin of Ilyenkov's radical realism. For him, the essence of materialism is the idea that minds can reach right out to the material world. Such a materialism, Ilyenkov argues, is impossible to develop if one believes, as many "materialists" do, that all objective reality contains are material phenomena.

For all that, however, Ilyenkov's opponent may yet doubt whether we have properly silenced the objection that Ilyenkov's position is prone to the same problem as the Kantian's. After all, by arguing that we have access to reality only insofar as it is idealized by human activity, Ilyenkov admits that the world our minds are "in touch" with is a world that has necessarily been changed. In what sense, then, can he claim that we have direct access to the world as it is independent of us?

The first stage of Ilyenkov's reply must be to remind his opponent that, though we have access to reality insofar as it is idealized, it is false that an idealized reality is mind-dependent (Ilyenkov 1964b: 257–8). The point of Ilyenkov's insistence that ideal properties are genuine, objectively existing properties of objects, and not mental projections, is to allow him to argue that, whereas the individual subject can only relate to an idealized environment, that environment is mind-independent (i.e., the physical properties of that environment are mind-independent per se, and its ideal properties, though anthropocentric, exist independently of any individual mind).

Ilyenkov's position would be endangered only by the admission that, in idealization, the world is changed in a way which the thinking subject cannot retrace. But Ilyenkov has no reason to admit that. On his view, to form a conception of

how the world exists independently of us, we are not required
to achieve the conceptually impossible. To conceive of an object as it exists independently of our minds does not require
that we subtract from an essentially mental entity, a "representation," that which the mind contributes to it, when what
the mind contributes to it are the very properties in virtue of
which it exists as a representation. Rather, on Ilyenkov's position, the question of what the world is like prior to idealization
is the question of what difference our activity makes to reality.
We must ask ourselves: What would the world be like had we
not acted, or were we not to act, on it? And this, for Ilyenkov,
is a question we can answer without transgressing the bounds
of sense. As Marx and Engels themselves put it:

> When we conceive things, thus, as they really are and hap-
> pened, every profound philosophical problem is resolved into
> an empirical fact. (1845–6: 62)

Of course, to say that the question of what the world is like
prior to idealization resolves into a matter of "empirical fact" is
not to say that it may be answered by observation. Ilyenkov
argues that we arrive at this knowledge by imagination and
by building theories. Sometimes, he suggests, we proceed by
what seem to be transcendental arguments (Ilyenkov 1964a:
32). We ask: How must things have been in order for our practices to have been possible? But the world we come to know by
answering such questions is neither transcendent nor transcendental. We seek neither to characterize a world in principle beyond our concepts from a position somewhere outside
them, nor to postulate an uncharacterizable world of *noumena*
as the necessary conditions of our experience. On the contrary, we seek only to determine "how things were and how
things are" in the only world there is. Ilyenkov holds that to
achieve such knowledge is simultaneously to achieve self-
consciousness, for to gain knowledge of the world as it is prior
to idealization is to learn the extent of our activity's influence
on reality, and thus to understand more about ourselves and
our place in nature (Ilyenkov 1964a: 33).[12]

12   It might be thought that Ilyenkov's approach, as I have presented it,
     is ambiguous, inviting two contrasting intepretations. On the one
     hand, Ilyenkov could be read as engaged in transcendental philos-

If this argument succeeds, then Ilyenkov's theory of idealization is not susceptible to the same objection as the Kantian

ophy, invoking the concept of activity as part of a philosophical theory designed to articulate the necessary conditions for the possibility of thought and experience. On such a reading, it would seem to follow from Ilyenkov's theory that the idea of the world as it is independent of our practices cannot be invoked as part of a *philosophical* explanation of how our practices are "anchored" on a world so conceived. Nevertheless, this reading would allow Ilyenkov to invoke an "empirical" distinction, drawn within the terms of our practices of representation, between the world as it is independent of us, and the world as it becomes through our agency – a distinction we constantly invoke in both our everyday and scientific modes of thinking and speaking. On such an interpretation, the resulting position, while different from the "two-worlds" Kantian, would be interestingly similar to (some readings of) the position of Kant himself.

Alternatively, Ilyenkov might be given a Wittgensteinian reading, on which his appeal to "activity" would be seen as an expression of hostility to the very project of building a philosophical theory of the relation between "subject" and "object." This view would hold that Ilyenkov invokes activity precisely as part of an argument that traditional philosophical explanations are misconceived. All explanation must ultimately end not in philosophical theory but in an appeal to human practices, to our "natural history," or our "form of life." Like the neo-Kantian approach, this Wittgensteinian reading would give no credence to the philosopher's notion of "the world as it is independent of our practices"; the distinction between reality "in itself" and the world as it becomes through our agency is just the ordinary "empirical" distinction we draw in our everyday and scientific practices.

Evidence may be found in Ilyenkov's writings to support either of these readings. For example, Ilyenkov certainly appears to invoke the concept of activity as a direct response to a problem he takes to have been posed by Kant. Nevertheless, his failure to develop this appeal to activity into a *systematic* theory of the conditions of thought and experience might be taken to suggest that the appeal is designed to reorientate the philosopher's project in ways to which a Wittgensteinian might be sympathetic. It could therefore be that Ilyenkov wished to be read in one of these two ways, but was perhaps hindered by the political climate from making this explicit. However, I believe it most likely that Ilyenkov would have resisted either interpretation, rejecting the conception of transcendental philosophy at the heart of the neo-Kantian reading, while fearing that a Wittgensteinian strategy ultimately robs us of the power to criticize those social practices in which all explanation ends. In consequence, I have (albeit at the risk of incoherence) resisted the temptation to resolve Ilyenkov's position into either of these readings, and presented him as striving to give sense to an alternative strategy.

position to which it is an alternative. And if so, Ilyenkov is innocent of the charge of idealism.

Materialism and the final refutation of idealism

We have defended Ilyenkov from what the Soviet tradition calls "subjective idealism," the view that we can make no sense of a mind-independent world existing beyond our forms of thought. What, though, is Ilyenkov's reponse to the "objective idealism" of his beloved Hegel, which, at least in some sense, admits the existence of a physical world independent of human minds? Unlike Dubrovsky, of course, Ilyenkov does not hold that materialism distinguishes itself from idealism by rejecting the objective idealist's belief in the objective existence of the ideal. Rather, Ilyenkov treats objective idealism as a mistaken theory of explanation:

> We consider idealist all those philosophical conceptions that take the ideal as the starting point of the explanation of history and cognition, however the concept of the ideal is decoded: as consciousness or as will, as thought or mind in general, as "soul" [dusha] or as "spirit" [dukh], as "sensation" or as "the creative principle," or even as "socially organized experience." (1962b: 128)

Ilyenkov argues that, by taking the ideal as the point of departure of historical and psychological explanation, objective idealism absolutizes the ideal. He accuses Hegel of turning categories, concepts, "forms of thought," norms, into an autonomous realm, a self-developing, highly structured reality set over and against human practices. For Hegel, it is not only that human practices are compelled to conform to the dictates of this reality; rather, they are seen as a vehicle through which this ideal realm manifests itself. The subject of history is reason, culture, the "world-spirit"; the human individual is the object of that spirit, its tool, its servant. Indeed, the entire edifice of material reality is presented as an expression of the grand design of self-developing thought thinking itself. Even the laws of nature are, for the objective idealist, "forms of a rational will acting in an aim-oriented way, as a stamp impressed on the substance of nature by this will, as a product of the 'alienation' of the forms of this will outside itself, in the material of nature" (Ilyenkov 1962b: 220).

Ilyenkov argues that the profound distortion, or "inversion," of objective idealism is that by absolutizing the ideal it robs itself of an explanation of the possibility of thought itself (1974a: 172–3). Idealism reverses the true direction of explanation, presenting "real, sensuous object-oriented activity," not as the source of an idealized world and, therefore, of the possibility of thought, but as the external manifestation of the cosmic subject. Hence, the first dimension of materialism's superiority over idealism is that it explains what the idealist takes as simply given: the possibility of thought. So doing, materialism completely reorientates our understanding of history, which can now be seen not as the unfolding of the design of some superindividual mind, but as an objectified expression of the collective activity of human individuals.

The second dimension of materialism's superiority is that it *explains objective idealism itself.* Ilyenkov follows Marx in holding objective idealism to be not simply false, but a complex distortion of the truth. How is this distortion possible? Ilyenkov argues that idealism, by treating the results of human activity as alien forces presiding over our existence, is a form of *fetishism.* For Ilyenkov, such fetishism is made possible by the kind of society in which objective idealism found its first modern expression: capitalism. Hegel's philosophy, he argues, represents an expression of the actual domination of human beings under capitalism by an ideal realm of their own making:

> The basic fact on which the classical systems of objective idealism grew up is the real fact of the independence of the total culture of mankind, and its forms of organization, from the individual; more broadly, it is the fact of the transformation of the universal products of human activity (both material and spiritual) into powers independent of the will and consciousness of people. (Ilyenkov 1962b: 219)

Where economic, political, and ideological structures exert an influence beyond the control of all individuals, rigidly allotting to each individual his or her role within the social whole, the fetishistic vision of the objective idealist seems overwhelmingly compelling (Ilyenkov 1963: 139–41).

Thus, for Ilyenkov, the very motivation for idealism will

wither away when the circumstances of life under capitalism are transformed by revolution. This revolution signifies human beings harnessing "the basic fact" of the objectification of their creative powers to create an environment in which they can flourish. It is this act, carried through, that represents the final refutation of idealism. As Marx puts it in the eighth "Thesis on Feuerbach":

> All mysteries which mislead theory to mysticism find their rational solution in human practice and in the comprehension of this practice. (1845: 30)

The theoretical dispute between materialism and objective idealism is thus ultimately resolved in practice (cf. Ilyenkov 1974a: 205–7).

It is an important feature of this Marxist position that the standard of human flourishing that humankind seeks to realize through socialism is not something given. For Ilyenkov, communist men and women do not simply strive to create an environment that conforms to some ideal conception of "human nature"; rather, they grasp the power to transform their environment, and through it, their own nature. A communist society, "where culture does not confront the individual as something given to him or her from without, something autonomous and alien," is one in which humanity, for the first time, is able to see itself clearly in the "mirror" human activity has created (Ilyenkov 1974a: 207). What we see there may lead us to judge that we cannot live with the image of ourselves offered by our surroundings. As we struggle to change ourselves, those changes too are objectified, offering us a new reflection of ourselves. The search for human perfection is thus a constant dialectic of objectification and perception.

It may seem that we have left far behind the discussion of the nature of moral value that opened this chapter. Yet, in fact, we have come full circle, for this picture of emancipated individuals asking whether they can identify with the historically forged social environment that constitutes their identity is a vision of human beings asking the Socratic question at the very basis of ethical thought: How should we live? Ilyenkov's admission that moral properties exist objectively is not to say that there is some final moral standard by appeal to which we can answer the Socratic question. Rather, the fact that moral requirements genuinely constitute part of the environment objectively confronting each human individual makes possible the dialectic of humanity's conception of itself and its expression in the world, the dialectic in which the search for perfection is realized.

Conclusion

In the first "Thesis on Feuerbach," Marx writes:

> The chief defect of all hitherto existing materialism – that of Feuerbach included – is that the thing [*Gegenstand*], reality, sensuousness, is conceived only in the form of the *object* [*Objekt*] or of *contemplation* [*Anschauung*], but not as *human sensuous activity, practice*, not subjectively. Hence it happened that the *active* side, in contradistinction to materialism, was developed by idealism – but only abstractly, since, of course, idealism does not know real, sensuous activity as such. Feuerbach wants sensuous objects, really differentiated from the thought objects, but he does not conceive human activity as *object-oriented* [*gegenständliche*] activity. (1845:28; translator's brackets)

Ilyenkov's theory of the ideal is an attempt (which he takes to be implicit in Marx's own writings) to remedy this defect. By giving sense to what it is to "conceive of the thing as human sensuous activity," Ilyenkov offers us a new, dialectical materialism in the form of a radical realism that treats the thinking subject as located in material reality, in direct contact with its objects.

As we noted above, Ilyenkov's account of the world as an object of thought includes a correlative theory of the nature of the individual subject. If we reject the Cartesian conception of the self as the foundation of the mistaken doctrine of idealization as "mentalization," we make room for a new idea of the individual, conceived not as a self-contained, self-sufficient, and ready-made subject of "inner" states, but as a socially formed being, essentially dependent on his or her ancestors and peers. We shall explore this idea in the next chapter.

7

THE SOCIALLY
CONSTITUTED INDIVIDUAL:
RETHINKING THOUGHT

The transformation of nature by human activity is the process of the idealization of the material world. In activity, human beings create and sustain an environment written through with significance; they nurture a world enriched with ideal properties, with value and meaning. This is the world we know. Indeed, only an idealized world can be known, for only such a world may be complemented by a subject able to reproduce it in thought and experience. In Marx's words:

> Only through the objectively unfolded richness of man's essential being is the richness of subjective *human* sensibility ... either cultivated or brought into being. For not only the five senses, but also the so-called mental senses, the practical senses (will, love, etc.), in a word, the *human* sense, the humanity of the senses, come to be by virtue of *their* object, by virtue of *humanized* nature. (Marx 1844: 103; quoted in Ilyenkov 1964b: 240)

On this view, the subjective and objective are not absolutely exclusive categories, but are unified by their common source in activity, which ever sustains their mutual opposition and interchange.

This, for Ilyenkov, is the essence of Marxism's solution to

the problem of the ideal. As we have observed, Ilyenkov believes this solution has radical consequences for our understanding of the mind, leading us to reject the abstract philosophical subject of classical epistemology for a conception of
the individual as a socially constituted being (see Chapters 5
and 6). He writes:

> The subject of thought becomes the individual in the nexus of
> social relations, the socially defined individual, whose every
> form of life activity is given not by nature, but by the coming-
> to-be of human culture. (Ilyenkov 1974a: 208)

Ilyenkov's conception of the individual is the focus of this
chapter.

Ilyenkov gives content to the idea of the "socially defined
subject" by advancing an account of the development of the
mind strikingly similiar to Vygotsky's theory.[1] Like Vygotsky, Ilyenkov holds that the human child at the early stages
of development lacks the system of higher mental functions
that constitutes consciousness.[2] Consciousness, he argues, is
something the child must *acquire*. Also like Vygotsky, Ilyenkov maintains that the higher mental functions do not
evolve "naturally" or "spontaneously" in a process analogous
to physical growth. Rather, the child's mind must be *created*
through the agency of the community. Children become
thinking subjects as they are socialized by their elders into
the community's forms of "life activity." As they appropriate,
or "internalize," those activities, so their minds are born.

Ilyenkov proceeds to supplement this "sociohistorical" theo-

---

1 Despite the similarity between their positions, it appears that Ilyenkov arrived at his conception of the individual some years before he
   studied Vygotsky's ideas and became the "philosophical mentor" of
   the Vygotsky School (see the opening of Chapter 3)
2 For Ilyenkov, "consciousness" (*soznanie*) is constituted by a system of
   psychological capacities (*sposobnost'*), which he treats as "higher
   mental functions" in Vygotsky's sense (e.g., Ilyenkov 1970: 89; see
   Chapter 3 [n4]). Of these capacities, Ilyenkov is concerned principally with the analysis of "thought" (*myshlenie,* which may also be translated as "thinking"), conceived as the capacity to form a conception
   of reality, the means by which the subject "finds his or her way in
   the world." Thus, by "thinking," Ilyenkov means all cognitive activity. In this chapter, I follow Ilyenkov's usage.

ry of the mind with two strong theses. First, he argues that if we accept that "all the specifically human mental functions without exception ... are, in their genesis and their essence, "internalized" modes and forms of man's external – sensuous, object-oriented – activity as a social being," then we are committed to the thesis that the higher mental functions are not genetically inherited capacities of the brain (Ilyenkov 1970: 89). This we can call Ilyenkov's *antiinnatism thesis:*

> This understanding [of internalization] – closely connected with the materialist foundation of Soviet psychology – holds that in the composition of the higher mental functions there neither is, nor can there be, absolutely anything innate or genetically inherited, that the human mind is formed during life as the result of up-bringing [*vospitanie*] in the broadest sense of the word; that is, it is passed from generation to generation not naturally [*estestvenno-prirodno*], but by an exclusively "artificial" route. (Ilyenkov 1970: 89)

Ilyenkov adds to this thesis a yet stronger claim. While he grants that the working of the brain is a necessary condition for the development and exercise of mental capacities, Ilyenkov argues that, for children with "normal" (i.e., healthy, undamaged) brains, genetic factors have no essential influence on the course of development of higher mental functions. Their development is, he maintains, wholly determined, and thus wholly explained, by social considerations (Ilyenkov 1968b: 149).

Second, Ilyenkov argues that the higher mental functions are not only social in origin, but that their exercise is also constantly mediated by society. This is so, he claims, because the mental states that issue from the operation of our psychological capacities are, in some sense, constituted in public space. For this reason, Ilyenkov contends that our mental capacities and mental states cannot be construed as capacities and states of the brain and that, therefore, analysis of individuals' brains, however comprehensive, cannot reveal either the character of their mental capacities or the content of their psychological states. Call this Ilyenkov's *antireductionism thesis:*

> It is impossible to "read off" the psychological definition of a human being from the anatomical-physiological structure of the human body. That isn't the book in which it is written.

> The psychological definition of man has its reality, its "being," not in the system of neurodynamic structures of the brain, but in a broader and more complex system – the system of relations of man to man, mediated by things created by man for man, that is, in the relations of production of the objective–human world and of the capacities that correspond to the organization of this world. (Ilyenkov 1964b: 240; cf. 1968b: 153, 1979c: 337)

Thus, when Ilyenkov says that we are "socially defined" individuals, he means more than that our personalities, intellectual abilities, and psychological states are formed under the influence of the societies in which we live. For Ilyenkov, the mind is essentially social in nature and origin. Nothing could be a subject of thought antecedently to, or independently of, participation in social forms of life, for our very mental capacities and mental states themselves are socially constituted phenomena.

Ilyenkov turns to Vygotsky and his followers for an account of the conditions in which the mind is formed in socialization; his own writings make no attempt to examine the development of the higher mental functions in detail. Nevertheless, Ilyenkov's contribution promises to strengthen Vygotsky's position. In Chapter 3, we observed that even scholars sympathetic to Vygotsky have expressed doubts about his extreme emphasis on the social determination of consciousness (e.g., Wertsch 1985a: 43–7). However, if Ilyenkov's antireductionism and antiinnatism theses can be defended in a way compatible with Vygotsky's thought, then Vygotskians will be justified in according biological factors no substantial explanatory role in the analysis of the higher mental functions.

Ilyenkov had every incentive to articulate a clear and compelling defence of his two radical theses. In the first place, his position provoked considerable controversy among his contemporaries. He voiced his vehement antiinnatism and antireductionism in a period of growing Soviet fascination about the prospects of cybernetic models of the mind and theories of the genetic inheritence of abilities (see Graham 1987: chaps. 6 and 8). Since cybernetics and genetics had suffered under Stalin, Ilyenkov's denial that either could explain the nature of the mind was easily misconstrued as yet another reactionary attempt by a dialectical materialist to restrict the autono-

my of the natural sciences (cf. Graham 1987: 286). Second, Ilyenkov held that the very possibility of communism turned
on the antiinnatism thesis. For him, communism's task is to
create the conditions in which the "all-round" [*vsestoronnyĭ*]
development and unqualified flourishing of each individual
is possible. Indeed, as we observed in Chapter 1, Ilyenkov held
that communism's vision of popular sovereignty could be fully realized only through the abolition of the division of labour
and the emergence of such "all-round" persons. Ilyenkov believed all this to be possible only if human individuals were,
in some sense, beings of infinite potential. He therefore resisted the idea that the direction and extent of a person's intellectual development might be constrained by the innate structures of the brain, and saw Soviet speculation about the genetic
basis of intelligence (e.g., Efroimson 1976) and antisocial behaviour (e.g., Efroimson 1971) as a symptom of the loss of faith
in communist ideals among Soviet thinkers of the post-Stalin
period (see Arsen'ev, Ilyenkov, and Davydov 1966: 281; Ilyenkov 1968b: 151).

Despite these incentives, Ilyenkov's discussion of "the socially defined subject" is among the least satisfactory aspects
of his legacy. Although he suggests that his concept of the individual is a consequence of his theory of ideality, his writings on the ideal appear only to present his position, elaborat-
ing no direct defence of the two problematic theses. Also, the
writings Ilyenkov devoted specifically to philosophical psychology are mainly popular and polemical in tone, and contribute little to the development of his arguments. Thus, once
again, our task is one of reconstruction. I shall begin by
considering two of Ilyenkov's most infamous popular writings, his discussion of Meshcheryakov's work with the blind-
deaf, and his polemic with Dubrovsky. While these works
fail to provide a defence of his conception of the individual,
their failure is revealing. I shall then return to Ilyenkov's
more scholarly writings in search of the means by which his
antireductionism and antiinnatism might be defended.

Meshcheryakov and the blind-deaf

Many of Ilyenkov's most enthusiastic descriptions of the social genesis of mind occur in his writings on an unusual, and

SOVIET PHILOSOPHY

222 SOVIET PHILOSOPHY

very stimulating, topic: Alexander Meshcheryakov's contribution to the education of the blind-deaf.[3] It is easy to understand why Ilyenkov, like many of his Vygotskian contemporaries, was fascinated by Meshcheryakov's work. Until the second half of this century, the treatment of the blind-deaf boasted only a few spectacular but isolated success stories, where children presumed uneducatable were brought to impressive levels of intellectual development through the untiring work of devoted teachers. While the story of Helen Keller is most famous in the West, the case best known in the Soviet Union is Olga Skorokhodova's education at the hands of Ivan Sokolyansky, the father of Russian "*tiphlosurdopedagogika*" and Meshcheryakov's mentor (see Skorokhodova 1972; Vasilova 1989). Meshcheryakov's contribution was to systematize and develop Sokolyansky's methods so that the education of the blind-deaf need no longer be confined to occasional "miracle" cases, but might proceed "on a mass scale." In 1963, a school for this purpose was founded in Zagorsk. In 1977, Meshcheryakov's four eldest charges graduated from Moscow University with degrees in psychology. Each went on to undertake research, and two, Alexander Suvorov and Sergei Sirotkin, have published significant articles in academic journals (Sirotkin 1979; Suvorov 1983, 1988, 1989).[4] These results conclusively show that, despite their catastrophic handicap, blind-deaf children may be made capable of leading fulfilling lives. This is possible, Meshcheryakov argues, because the course of the blind-deaf child's development is qualitatively identical to that of the "normal" child; its onset is merely inhibited by the fact that, in virtue of the absence of the primary senses, the blind-deaf child is isolated from normal social interaction. Howev-

3 Ilyenkov writes in praise of Meshcheryakov's work in Ilyenkov (1970, 1975, 1977a,d) and in Gurgenidze and Ilyenkov (1975), which reports the proceedings of a meeting of MGU's Faculty of Psychology at which several leading Soviet thinkers (e.g., Leontiev, Kedrov, Lifshits) commented on the significance of Meshcheryakov's achievements. Meshcheryakov describes his work in Meshcheryakov (1968, 1970, 1979). Other commentaries on the philosophical significance of Meshcheryakov's contribution, and on its place in the Vygotskian tradition of Soviet psychology, are Levitin (1975, 1982: 213–314); Mikhailov (1980: 258–66); Mikhailov and Kondratov (1982); and Bakhurst and Padden (in press).
4 Suvorov has also produced a remarkable short film, *Prikosnovenie* (*Touch*), broadcast recently on Soviet television.

er, once the appropriate forms of interaction have been established between blind-deaf children and their elders and peers, then the former's intellectual potential is as great as any normal child's.

Ilyenkov saw great theoretical significance in Meshcheryakov's achievements. Soon after he was introduced to Meshcheryakov's four star pupils in the late 1960s, he proclaimed that their successful education represented an "*experimentum crucis*" vindicating the sociohistorical theory of mental development (Ilyenkov 1970: 89). Ilyenkov's argument for this claim begins from Meshcheryakov's description of the "initial condition" of the blind-deaf child. According to Meshcheryakov, prior to their inclusion in a systematic pedagogical programme, children who are blind-deaf from birth or infancy (though with biologically normal brains) exhibit the following three features:

1. They do not engage in anything that might plausibly be called "end-orientated activity." Indeed, blind-deaf children fail even to exhibit many of the unconditional reflexes that form the basis of animal behaviour. Thus, prior to the intervention of the pedagogue, these children remain passive and immobile, their vegetable condition punctuated only by anarchic discharges of energy.
2. Blind-deaf children lack what Pavlovians would call the "search-orientation" reflex: They show no interest in manipulating objects and cannot orientate themselves. They do not have any sense of the identity of their own bodies, or of other entities.
3. They show no propensity to communicate, failing to display even those facial expressions that we deem most "natural": They must even be taught to smile.

Ilyenkov argues that these three features demonstrate that the blind-deaf child in his or her initial condition is a creature devoid of consciousness:

> ... The mind is not present at all, even in those elementary forms that any higher animal possesses almost from the moment of birth. This is a creature that, as a rule, is immobile and reminds one rather of a plant, of some kind of cactus or ficus, that lives only so long as it is in direct contact with food and water ... and dies without uttering a sound if it is forgot-

ten to feed, water, and protect it from the cold. It makes no attempt to reach for food, even if that food is half a meter away
from its mouth. It utters not a squeak when it is hungry, will
not cover itself from the draught with a warm blanket ... It is a
human plant in the full sense of the term, completely bereft of
mind. It will grow – increase in size – but the mind will still
not emerge. Not even the most elementary. (Ilyenkov 1977d:
23)

The conclusions Ilyenkov draws from this disturbing picture rest on the assumption that, far from constituting a paradigm of abnormality, the blind-deaf child's initial state represents the natural condition of any human child isolated from
the community. Thus, for Ilyenkov, the child's condition reveals the true nature of human individuals prior to society.
The blind-deaf child represents a modern-day *enfant sauvage*, a
measure of the true extent of our natural inheritence. On this
basis, Ilyenkov argues, first, that human beings are born without minds and, second, that the mind does not evolve spontaneously but must be created in socialization. This, Ilyenkov
claims, vindicates the antiinnatism thesis. Blind-deaf children show us, he argues, that mental capacities are not "built
in" to the structure of the brain and do not develop through the
unfolding of a biological programme:

The brain continues to develop according to the programme
encoded in the genes, in the DNA. However, there emerges
not one neurodynamical connection securing *mental* activity.
(Ilyenkov 1977d: 69)

Thus, Ilyenkov concludes, Meshcheryakov's "experiment"
conclusively shows that the mind is not a gift of nature, but a
product of society.

Ilyenkov stresses the theoretical significance of Sokolyansky and Meshcheryakov's pedagogical techniques. He argues
that their teaching methods provide essential data with which
we can pinpoint "with almost mathematical exactitude" the
conditions in which the internalization of the higher mental
functions takes place (Ilyenkov 1970: 89). The sighted and
hearing child is absorbed in so multivarious an environment,
and open to so many interwoven influences, that these conditions are greatly obscured. In the case of the blind-deaf child,

however, the very possibility of creating the child's mind depends upon deliberately determining and controlling the activities that precipitate internalization. Thus, as Leontiev put it, Meshcheryakov's work creates

> the conditions in which the key events in the process of the formation of the person and the coming-into-being (just think of it!) of human consciousness become *visible* – one wants to say, even touchable, and moreover drawn out in time as if in slow motion – conditions that, as it were, open a window upon the depths of consciousness's hidden nature. (cited in Gurgenidze and Ilyenkov 1975: 63)

The excitement Meshcheryakov's legacy generated within the Vygotsky school is easily understood, for his work appeared to promise insights into the process of internalization that would facilitate the education not just of the blind-deaf but of all children. Thus, the Vygotskians argued, Meshcheryakov's work helps us not only to understand the genesis of consciousness, but also to master it.

To sum up: Ilyenkov holds that Meshcheryakov's work with blind-deaf children shows

1. the human child at birth is not a thinking thing, and
2. the mind does not develop spontaneously in a process analogous to physical growth.

From this it follows that

3. human mental capacities are not genetically inherited but are created in socialization.

Finally, Ilyenkov claims that

4. analysis of the process in which of the blind-deaf child is brought to conscious life may reveal the conditions in which the internalization of the higher mental functions takes place.

However, for all its eloquence and passion, Ilyenkov's argument is unpersuasive. As the Soviet biologist Malinovsky was quick to point out, Ilyenkov writes as if, were the higher mental functions genetically inherited, the mind would develop merely in virtue of the organic maturation of the brain, regardless of the child's relation to his surroundings (1970: 92). No one, however, would endorse such a view. A thinker who, like Malinovsky, maintains that the child's higher mental functions are inborn capacities of the brain, will nonetheless admit that those capacities may be exercised, and may develop, only if the child interacts with the environment in an appropriate way. Innatism about mental faculties is clearly compatible with the obvious truth that the right sort of interaction between brain and environment is a necessary condition of the development and functioning of the mind.

Let us call Malinovsky's innatism "bioenvironmental interactionism." Philosophers who endorse this position will offer an alternative interpretation of the results of Meshcheryakov's "experiment." First, they will propose a different explanation of the blind-deaf child's initial state. They will argue that the child's woeful condition is caused, not because the child "has no mind," but because the child's innate mental capacities cannot spontaneously develop in the absence of the primary senses. For example, without the information yielded by these senses, the child cannot begin to form concepts. Therefore, the child's mind remains frozen in a primitive condition (a condition no doubt exacerbated by the trauma of his or her isolation). Second, interactionists will redescribe the role of the pedagogue in the child's development. For them, the pedagogue's task is to secure that the necessary interaction between brain and environment can take place despite the child's disabilities. This is achieved by establishing alternative ways of presenting the child with the information normally yielded by sight and hearing. To do so, however, is merely to bring about the fulfilment of certain necessary conditions of mental development. It is not, as Ilyenkov suggests, literally to "create" the child's mind.

Despite Ilyenkov's confidence, nothing in Meshcheryakov's work decides between his interpretation and that of his interactionist opponent. Thus, to rescue Ilyenkov's reading of Meshcheryakov, we must find independent reasons why Ilyenkov rejected bioenvironmental interactionism. We thus turn to Ilyenkov's exchange with an opponent we encountered in Chapter 6, and whose work he took to encapsulate the trend toward bioenvironmental interactionism in Soviet thought: David Dubrovsky.

"Brain and Mind": Dubrovsky versus Ilyenkov

In 1968, Dubrovsky published "Mozg i psikhika" ("Brain and Mind"), an article directly attacking Ilyenkov and his colleague Felix Mikhailov, a philosopher who, in his book *The Riddle of the Self,* had independently advanced a conception of the individual similiar to Ilyenkov's (Mikhailov 1964, 1976, 1980).[5] Dubrovsky opens his article by challenging Mikhailov's claim that the mind–body problem is a pseudoproblem (see Mikhailov 1980: 115–42). For Dubrovsky, such a "nihilistic attitude" to the mind–body problem is a fundamental departure from the principles of Marxist philosophy (1968: 125). For Dubrovsky, as every textbook of dialectical materialism states on page 1, Marxists believe that the basic question of philosophy is the "opposition and relation between matter and consciousness, the material and the ideal, being and thought" (Dubrovsky 1983: 8). The mind–body problem, Dubrovsky argues, is clearly a dimension of this question. Dubrovsky then proceeds to attack Ilyenkov's claim (referring to Ilyenkov 1964b) that the study of the brain has nothing to contribute to a materialist answer to the basic question of philosophy. Surely, Dubrovsky claims, as the existence of a necessary connection between brain states and mental states is beyond doubt, the primacy of matter over consciousness must be explained, at least in part, in terms of the primacy of the neurophysiological over the mental. Dubrovsky argues that, since such an explanation cannot be derived a priori, the findings of brain science are obviously relevant to the philosophy of mind (Dubrovsky 1968: 126). Thus, he concludes, materialists must address the mind–body problem, and must do so in a way that, on the basis of empirical data, explains how "psychological phenomena are a product of the material activity of the brain" (1968: 126).

In "Brain and Mind," Dubrovsky suggests a solution to the mind–body problem that he has developed in all his later work (e.g., 1971, 1980, 1983). In these writings, Dubrovsky rep-

5 Like Ilyenkov, Mikhailov collaborated with Meshcheryakov in the 1960s and 1970s. It was in Mikhailov's laboratory at the Institute of General and Pedagogical Psychology, Moscow, that Meshcheryakov's four eldest pupils conducted their research after graduating from MGU (see Bakhurst and Padden 1990).

resents the relation between mind and body as a relation of
two "realities." He argues that each individual mind represents a "subjective reality," an "internal, spiritual world" (Dubrovsky 1971: 203). Subjective reality, or consciousness, is constituted by a series of episodic mental phenomena – occurrent
thoughts, sensations, images, and so on – with which only
the subject of consciousness is directly acquainted, and in virtue of which the subject is aware of the "objective reality" beyond the mind (see, e.g., 1971: 202–3). Dubrovsky holds that
the phenomena of subjective reality are nonmaterial, or ideal,
in nature. Indeed, as we saw in Chapter 6, Dubrovsky takes
the episodic states of individual consciousness to be the only
ideal phenomena. The objective reality "outside our heads"
contains nothing ideal: It is matter in motion (e.g., Dubrovsky
1971: 186, 195; 1983: 14–20; see Chapter 6 above).

Thus, for Dubrovsky, the core of the basic question of philosophy becomes the problem of how the ideal, "subjective reality" of individual consciousness is related to the material, "objective reality" of the physical world. Dubrovsky holds that
the two realities are "necessarily connected" in three ways:

1. *Epistemically:* Subjective reality is a *reflection* of objective reality; that is, it represents objective reality to the subject.
   This representation is possible, Dubrovsky claims, because
   the phenomena that comprise subjective reality are *informational* in nature.
2. *Ontologically:* The ideal states of subjective reality possess a
   material "substratum" or "bearer" independently of which
   they cannot exist: This substratum is the brain. While the
   informational content of mental states is presented to the
   subject "in pure form" (i.e., the subject is aware only of the
   information and not of its material bearer), the content of
   these states is simultaneously "encoded" in the structures
   of the brain.
3. *Informationally:* The states of subjective reality are "informationally isomorphic" with the brain states in which
   they are encoded; that is, for any particular mental state,
   the information as presented to the subject "in pure form"
   and as encoded in the brain has the same structure (see
   Dubrovsky 1971: 284–93).

Thus, for Dubrovsky, the sense in which the brain "produces

subjective phenomena" (1971: 18) is that, as a result of the interaction between brain and environment, and within the brain itself, the physical structures of the brain encode information that is presented to the subject "in pure form." Information in this mode of presentation is consciousness, "subjective reality." In "Brain and Mind," Dubrovsky illustrates his position with the example of a simple case of perception:

> Of course one cannot say that when I see a tree there is an image of a tree in my brain. In the brain at that moment there objectively exists a certain neurodynamical system caused by the activity of the tree and responsible for the image of the tree I am now experiencing; the latter is not a material, but an *ideal image* of the object. This ideal image is a subjective reality, it is information, acting for me in pure form, in seeming independence from its material bearer – the neurodynamical system that is activated at the given moment by external influences. (1968: 126)

Dubrovsky's solution to the mind–body problem brings him into direct conflict with Ilyenkov. First, Dubrovsky's view that mental states are informationally isomorphic with brain states leads him to argue that analysis of an individual's brain could, in principle, reveal both the nature of that individual's mental capacities and the content of his or her mental states. Hence, he flatly contradicts Ilyenkov:

> The psychological definition of man (to adopt Ilyenkov's terminology) has its reality, its being, exactly "in the system of neurodynamic structures of the brain." It is the "book" in which they are recorded. (Dubrovsky 1968: 131, quoting Ilyenkov 1964b: 240)

Second, Dubrovsky construes mental capacities as capacities to manipulate (encode, transmit, decode) information. Since he holds that the information presented to consciousness may be manipulated only by altering the brain states in which it is encoded, he is led to represent mental capacities as capacities of the brain itself. On such a view, it becomes inviting to argue that the brain possesses these capacities in virtue of its physical organization, the basis of which is determined by genetic considerations. Reasoning in this way, Dubrovsky challenges Ilyenkov's antiinnatism thesis, suggesting that mental capacities, and even tendencies to exercise and develop those capacities in specific ways, are genetically inherited:

> To think that the morphological peculiarities of the brain of a given individual make no difference to the functioning of that brain is to deny the principle of the unity of function and structure, and to deny the principle of evolution in general. The genetic, structural characteristics of the brain of a given individual must to an essential degree determine those ontological, structural characteristics of the brain (which still, for the moment, escape direct analysis) that are directly responsible for the individual's psychological states. Many weighty facts and conclusions of contemporary science speak in favour of this conclusion. (Dubrovsky 1968: 129)

Before examining Ilyenkov's reply to "Brain and Mind," we should briefly observe that the style of Dubrovsky's philosophy recalls the Soviet Mechanism of the 1920s (see Chapter 2). First, like the Mechanists, Dubrovsky holds that philosophy must construct its theories by generalizing the results of the natural sciences. While dialectical materialism proclaims that matter is primary to consciousness, it is genetics, neurophysiology, and cybernetics that discover exactly how that primacy is realized. The philosopher's project is then to weave the results of these sciences into a single theory of the mind. Second, at least in his early writings, Dubrovsky shares the Mechanists' optimism that it is, in principle, possible to reduce all phenomena to entities explicable by appeal to natural scientific laws. He suggests that, since mental states are informationally isomorphic with brain states, science may eventually formulate a single set of principles governing the flow of information in both material and ideal forms of expression (see Dubrovsky 1971: 279–317). As Dubrovsky holds that consciousness is the sole province of the ideal, such principles would bring all nonmaterial phenomena within the compass of scientific explanation. And third, like the Mechanists, Dubrovsky deplores

> that tendency to scholastic theorizing . . . [which] results from tearing philosophy from science, from the attempt to disappear into the lofty heights of philosophical abstraction, where the voice of real life, social practice and scientific enquiry is not heard. Such a tendency is displayed by those who play

with dialectical categories in the Hegelian manner and make oracular pronouncements devoid of precise analysis, scientific argumentation, and the bearing of real life. (Dubrovsky 1980: 8)

Thus, once again in Soviet philosophy we find a form of Mechanism railing against the excesses of Hegelian Marxism. This time, however, it is Ilyenkov, rather than Deborin, who is the target.

"Mind and Brain": Ilyenkov's reply to Dubrovsky

Perceiving "Brain and Mind" as an expression of a growing trend in Soviet thought, Ilyenkov replied immediately with "Mind and Brain" ("Psikhika i mozg"), a typical Ilyenkov polemic, witty and indignant, but ultimately enigmatic and inconclusive. Ilyenkov's principal targets are two claims about explanation that he attributes to Dubrovsky:

1. Since our "psychological characteristics" (*psikhologicheskaya osobennost'*) are all "in one way or another fixed" in the "neurodynamic organization" of our brains, science will eventually be able to explain and predict the mental states and character traits of an individual on the basis of an analysis of his or her brain.

2. Since the development of our intellectual abilities and character is influenced by the innate properties of our brains, science will eventually be able to produce (what Ilyenkov calls) a "genetic horoscope" for each individual child; that is, a profile of the innate microstructure of the child's brain on the basis of which we can determine the directions in which his or her intellect and character are predisposed to develop (e.g., whether the child is musically or mathematically "gifted," whether he or she will be prone to aggressive or antisocial behaviour).

Ilyenkov sets out to show these claims to be unfounded. His tactics, however, are curious. He makes no attempt to elaborate the theoretical basis of his own position, simply reasserting his view that psychological characteristics are neither "written" in the brain, nor determined, even in part, by its innate structures (Ilyenkov 1968b: 155, 149). Nor does he attempt to undermine the philosophical foundation of Dubrovsky's stance. Instead, Ilyenkov attacks the scientific credibility of Dubrovsky's claims and their moral and political standing.

Ilyenkov opens by reminding Dubrovsky that, at present, science cannot even begin to construct explanations and predictions of the kind promised in (1) and (2), for we know nothing of the supposed correlations between brain structures and psychological phenomena:

> ... With respect to the connection between microstructural properties [of the brain] and various "instincts" (let alone "abilities," which should never be confused with instincts!) Dubrovsky and I, and the whole of world science, can say absolutely nothing genuinely reliable. Here we stand with both feet on the shaky ground of pure hypothesis, assumption, and even guesswork. (Ilyenkov 1968b: 146)

Thus, Ilyenkov concludes, claims (1) and (2) are based on pure speculation.

Ilyenkov then proceeds to argue that our ignorance of correlations between neurophysiological and mental phenomena is insuperable. Thus, even if it were true that our psychological characteristics were encoded in our brains, and partly determined by genetic factors, (1) and (2) would still be false. This is because, he claims, it is impossible to establish the relevant correlations by empirical means for two reasons. First, to determine the relation between (a) the microstructure of the brain and (b) mental states and behavioural dispositions would require knowledge of a web of causal relations too complex to be analyzed in a finite time (Ilyenkov 1968b: 146). Second, the research necessary to produce a genetic horoscope would require that the subject be killed and the brain dissected, thus rendering the theory impossible to verify (148). Hence, the explanations Dubrovsky promises will never be forthcoming.

Ilyenkov suggests that this conclusion in fact places no constraint on the explanation and prediction of psychological characteristics. First, he argues that even if personality traits were genetically inherited, and correlations between these traits and innate features of the brain could be identified, it would still be true that a complete account of the microstructure of a child's brain would reveal nothing about the future development of his or her abilities and personality. This is so,

Ilyenkov claims, because innate behavioural dispositions would "cancel each other out," thus rendering all inherited character types psychologically equivalent. Satirically associating his opponent's views with the medieval physiology of the four humours, Ilyenkov writes that

> ... from the point of view of "specifically human functions," nervous systems of various types are completely equal in value. Although the phlegmatic person loses out to the sanguine when it come to quickness, he compensates for this by his solidity, avoiding the need to correct blunders made in haste, and so on, so that in the end and on the whole the two turn out just the same. Each type has its "pluses" and "minuses" that cannot be separated from each other, and these "pluses" and "minuses" extinguish and neutralize each other. (1968b: 148)

For this reason, Ilyenkov argues, "a healthy brain of any type is able to assimilate any specifically human ability" (148) and that, therefore, "everyone born with a biologically normal brain is potentially talented, able, gifted" (151).

Second, in a rather obscure passage, Ilyenkov suggests that we suppose that genetics and neurophysiology must play a substantial role in the explanation of psychological phenomena because we attribute to "genetic contingency" those of an individual's psychological characteristics that we fail to explain by other means. If we cannot account for the origin of some ability or character trait, we suppose that the individual who possesses it does so simply in virtue of his or her "nature," and, in our naturalistic culture, we construe that nature biologically. But, Ilyenkov claims, as our understanding of the social and historical origins of the mental increases, so the role played by "unknown genetic factors" in our psychological explanations will eventually diminish to nothing (Ilyenkov 1968b: 146–7). Thus, the fact that science cannot deliver on Dubrovsky's promises is of no concern to psychology.

Having poured scorn on Dubrovsky's speculations about the explanatory relevance of brain science to psychology, Ilyenkov challenges the political motivation of his opponent's claims. At the end of Chapter 2, I suggested that Ilyenkov would have seen political dangers in the Mechanists' utopian conception of technology's potential contribution to economic and social planning, and in their picture of the individual as a mechanism, the operations of which science will eventually render transparent. For Ilyenkov, these two themes converge in Dubrovsky's neo-Mechanism. Ilyenkov suggests that behind Dubrovsky's idea that a child's "genetic cerebral features" may be "strictly and exactly classified . . . and correlated with various mental qualities, 'instincts,' and even 'abilities'" lies the dream that brain science may eventually facilitate the rational allocation of human resources by establishing which individuals are predisposed to which vocations (Ilyenkov 1968b: 147).[6] Such a dream, Ilyenkov argues, is morally repugnant:

> It is a very bad thing if we put the responsibility onto neurophysiology to define (even worse onto the genetic code!) by which "social-biographical trajectory" a child must be directed: who from the cradle should be given the career of a musician, who a mathematician, who a cosmonaut, who should be allowed to become a ballerina, who a dressmaker.
> Let us frankly admit that we are very skeptical about the idea of drawing up such horoscopes, about the idea of fortune-telling on the basis of the as yet undeveloped seeds of a nervous system ... And we are all the more skeptical about the hope that such horoscopes will aid the progress of the human race ... In general, to turn neurophysiology into a tool for the division and selection of children is justified – even in fantasy – only in a society built on the model of Aldous Huxley's *Brave New World.* (1968b: 147–8)

The suggestion that the Soviet education system should be designed to preselect children for special educational programmes on the basis of their supposedly innate talents is, Ilyenkov argues, a betrayal of Marxism's commitment to the universal flourishing of all (Ilyenkov 1968b: 151). By encouraging children to specialize in areas where they were supposedly naturally gifted, such preselection would perpetuate the division of labour that communism is pledged to destroy (cf. Arsen'ev, Ilyenkov, and Davydov 1966: 281). Furthermore,

6 As Ilyenkov admits (1968b: 147), it is probably unfair to accuse Dubrovsky himself of entertaining this dream. However, such ideas (together even with speculations about a "humane" Soviet eugenics) were certainly voiced by some neo-Mechanists in the 1960s and 1970s (see Graham 1987: chap. 6, esp. 225). Ilyenkov is not, therefore, attacking a straw man.

since the gifted in fact owe their talents to social advantage rather than to nature, an education system explicitly devoted to nurturing those talents would reinforce inequality of opportunity in Soviet society (cf. Ilyenkov 1977a: 45, 1977d: 77). Dubrovsky's philosophy is thus a rationale for social conservatism. Therefore, Ilyenkov concludes, Dubrovsky's views are as morally dangerous as they are scientifically unfounded.

However, Ilyenkov's arguments are once again unconvincing. For example, he fails to show that our ignorance of the correlations between neurophysiological structures and "psychological characteristics" is insuperable, for his claims that the relevant causal relations are too complex to investigate, and that brain science cannot be conducted on live subjects, are false. Moreover, Ilyenkov does not establish that knowledge of these correlations would in any case be irrelevant to psychological explanation. He offers no grounds for his confidence that a full understanding of the sociohistorical basis of the mind would show that psychological explanations need make no appeal to biological factors, and his suggestion that inherited personality traits would "cancel each other out" is manifestly absurd. Furthermore, the failure of these arguments seriously undermines Ilyenkov's attack on the politics of his opponent's position. Dubrovsky can reply that his motive for adopting his position is its truth, and that if Ilyenkov is suggesting that communism should obscure the truth, then it is he who is the reactionary. In any case, Dubrovsky would contest the implication that his position conflicts with the ideals of communism. On the contrary, he might argue, if communism seeks to realize universal human flourishing, then the genetic horoscopes Ilyenkov fears might be used to determine how best to promote the flourishing of each unique individual.

Thus, like his writings on the blind-deaf, Ilyenkov's response to Dubrovsky fails to establish his idea of the socially defined subject. Indeed, so weak are his arguments in these writings that the reader might be led, like Dubrovsky, to dismiss Ilyenkov's position as an empty expression of Marxist faith, as a piece of pure ideology. In what follows, I shall endeavour to salvage Ilyenkov's position. Since Ilyenkov suggests that his conception of the individual is a consequence of his theory of the ideal, we shall return to that theory in search, first, of a more plausible case against Dubrovsky and, second, for a philosophical defence of the antiinnatism and antireductionism theses. Finally, we must explain why, if Ilyenkov had such a defence, it is conspicious by its absence in his polemical writings.

Ilyenkov on the ideal: The dismissal of Dubrovsky

In Chapter 6, we saw that Ilyenkov's theory of the ideal is a response to the problem of how it is possible for the world to be an object of thought and experience. The problem is this: Minds, it seems, may stand in direct relations only to entities that possess meaning or "content." Semantic or representational properties are not, however, properties of material objects as they are independently of human beings: Nature, in its brute physicality, is devoid of meaning. How, then, do minds gain access to mind-independent objects? Ilyenkov proposes an explanation of the following form. Drawing on Marx's conception of objectification, Ilyenkov argues that it is through their incorporation into social forms of activity that mind-independent objects attain the significance, or "ideal form," in virtue of which they may enter immediate relations with minds. Nature becomes an object of thought, or is "idealized," though the "real, sensuous-objective" activity of human beings.

We contrasted Ilyenkov's position with the account of the mind's access to reality offered by philosophers who subscribe to an epistemological dualism owed ultimately to Descartes. This is the dualism of "two-worlds epistemology," the framework that defines many of the "empiricist" positions we have encountered in this work: the Lockean or "conservative" realism and the Empiriocriticism of Chapter 4, and the empiricism discussed in Chapter 5. To recapitulate, this Cartesian framework presents the relation between subject and object as a relation between two logically independent "worlds": the "external" world of extended, mind-independent, material objects and the "inner" world of the thoughts and experiences of the conscious subject. Like Ilyenkov, the Cartesian maintains that minds may deal directly only with phenomena that possess semantic or representational properties.[7] However, unlike Ilyenkov, the Cartesian holds that only mental entities may possess such properties: The world beyond the mind is bereft of meaning. Thus, for the Cartesian, the mind's access to mind-independent objects is necessarily indirect: The mind is acquainted with material objects only insofar as such objects are presented to the mind by mental intermediaries (classically called "ideas"). Thus, in contrast to Ilyenkov's conception of the idealization of the world by activity, the two-worlds dualist portrays idealization as the "mentalization" of reality, its translation into an intrinsically representational mental medium.

Ilyenkov's writings suggest two reasons why he holds the doctrine of idealization as mentalization to be untenable. First, the doctrine has disastrous consequences. For example, the thesis that the subject is acquainted directly only with mental entities forces the philosopher into methodological solipsism: The philosopher must explain how the subject constructs a conception of the world out of material to which the subject alone has access. Ilyenkov, as we noted in Chapter 5, thinks such an explanation doomed to failure. Moreover, even if such an explanation could be given, the subject's conception of reality would be haunted by skepticism (see, e.g., Ilyenkov 1964a: 23, 1974a: 11–12). For if we have access to mind-independent objects only via ideas, we may never compare our ideas with the objects they supposedly represent. How, then, can we be sure that our ideas are accurate representations, or even that there is an external world to be represented?

Such moves are familiar in Soviet philosophy. Ilyenkov's second reason for rejecting the doctrine of idealization as mentalization is more unusual. For the doctrine to work, the Cartesian must explain how our ideas succeed in representing a mind-independent reality. However, as Ilyenkov remarks (1974a: 16), at least on "classical" versions of the two-worlds model, it is by no means clear how this representation is achieved. In Chapter 6 we traced how, treating idealization as mentalization, the Kantian is led to the view that mind-independent objects cannot be objects of experience, thus in-

---

7   In this chapter, I shall refer to philosophers who adopt the two-worlds model as "Cartesians." On this usage, one may be a Cartesian without holding that the mind is a special substance. This follows my presentation of Cartesianism in Chapter 6.

Practice as experiment whereby ideas are tested

troducing what, for Soviet philosophers, is a yet more potent skepticism than the form expressed above: Now the problem is not that it is possible that our ideas do not represent objects as they are independently of us, but that our ideas could not so represent objects. While, as we saw, the Kantian's position emerges as a response to the classical empiricists' conception of experience, Ilyenkov's writings imply that such skepticism is not endemic to Kantianism alone: There are further, general reasons why any position framed within the two-worlds model will find it impossible to explain how our ideas could represent mind-independent objects (see esp. 1974a: 11–16).

What account of representation is available on the two-worlds model? Consider visual perception. The two-worlds theorist must hold that the subject's visual experience E of mind-independent object O represents O in virtue of some special relation R obtaining between E and O. How is R to be conceived? At first sight, it seems plausible to follow Locke and construe R as a relation of resemblance. For Locke, to resemble something is to share (some of) its properties. Thus, on this view, we can think of E as a kind of mental portrait of O, a portrait that, perhaps like any picture, depicts its object in virtue of attributes it shares with that object. This account of representation, however, will not do. On the Cartesian model, the objects of the external world possess only primary qualities, that is, properties that can be characterized without essential reference to human subjects: shape, size, mass, and so on. Our mental representations, however, are nonspatial, nonmaterial entities. They thus have no size, shape, or mass to share with the objects they represent.

The problematic relation R cannot therefore be construed in terms of a resemblance between the intrinsic properties of E and O. What other kind of property might E and O be thought to share? It seems inviting to hold that, where E is an experience *of a square object*, E represents O not because E possesses the intrinsic property of squareness, but because it possesses the *representational* property of being of a square object. Once again, however, the representational properties of E are not properties that it may share with O, for the Cartesian holds that the world beyond the mind has no representational properties. In short, it seems the Cartesian makes E and O too unlike one another for R to be conceived as a relation of resemblance.

As Ilyenkov puts it, for the Cartesian, experience resembles object in the way that "the taste of steak" resembles "the diagonal of a square" (1974a: 12).

If R cannot be understood in terms of resemblance, how else might it be analyzed? One alternative is to treat R as a relation of *isomorphism*: E represents O in virtue of sharing the same structure as O. Various accounts might be given of the "structure" of experience. For example, as we noted in Chapter 6, the content of some mental states, such as beliefs, desires, and intentions, may be given in propositional form. Since propositions are structured entities, we can identify the structure of such mental states with the structure of the propositions that convey their content. And it seems plausible that the structure of at least some kinds of perceptual experience might be analyzed in the same way. We can represent the experience of O as an experience that p (e.g., that there is an object of such-and-such a kind at such-and-such a location in the visual field), and think of the structure of the experience as the structure of p. However, the Cartesian who ventures such an analysis of the structure of experience cannot claim that experience and object may stand in a relation of isomorphism. For if mind-independent reality is devoid of meaning, it could not share a structure that is propositional in form. For the Cartesian, the external world is a totality of material things, not of facts, and the relations such things bear to one another are in no way analogous to the relations between the parts of a proposition. Moreover, it seems that no alternative analysis of the structure of experience will rescue the Cartesian. For the structure of mental entities, however construed, must surely be taken to derive from their status as carriers of meaning, and is therefore not a structure that could be shared by the material world as the Cartesian understands it. Thus, on the Cartesian picture, isomorphism between experience and object is impossible.

Without a plausible account of R, the Cartesian cannot make sense of the notion of mental representation: The Cartesian two-worlds model, therefore, cannot explain how a mind-independent reality can be an object of experience.

Ilyenkov holds that to escape the Cartesian predicament we must admit that ideal properties have objective existence. To make this admission, however, is not to save the two-worlds model. On the contrary, once we allow that the world beyond the mind embodies semantic and representational properties, it becomes open to us to hold that minds may enter immediate relations with the world; in Ilyenkov's terms, the relation between thought and reality may now be seen as one of identity, rather than correspondence. There is therefore no longer an incentive to endorse the central tenet on which the two-worlds model rests: the idea that the mind is in touch with objective reality only through its awareness of mental intermediaries.

This reading of Ilyenkov, I believe, explains his dismissive attitude to Dubrovsky's philosophy. For Ilyenkov, Marx's great philosophical achievement is that, by advancing the idea that human agency invests objective reality with ideal properties, he laid the foundation for a radical alternative to the unsatisfying conception of the relation between thought and reality at the heart of the Cartesian tradition. Dubrovsky, however, though he takes pains to present his position as consistently Marxist, is oblivious to Marx's contribution as Ilyenkov understands it (see, e.g., Dubrovsky 1968: 135, 1983: chap. 1, esp. 39–42). Dubrovsky poses his solution to the mind–body problem in strikingly Cartesian terms. He explicitly adopts a "two-worlds" model, describing the relation between subject and object as a relation of two "realities." Moreover, his account of those realities preserves many features of the Cartesian picture. First, like the Cartesian, Dubrovsky portrays "objective reality" as an exclusively material phenomenon: The world as it exists independently of our minds contains no ideal phenomena. Second, Dubrovsky's idea of "subjective reality" reproduces the principal features of the Cartesian conception of the self.

In Chapter 6 I argued that three characteristics define the Cartesian self: It is a "ready-made," "self-sufficient," and "self-contained" thinker of thoughts. Dubrovsky's conception of the subject of consciousness inherits each of these properties. First, the idea that the self is ready-made appears in Dubrovsky's view that the capacity to engage in mental activity is the brain's innate capacity to process information. The capacity to think is something with which any creature possessing a functioning brain of sufficient complexity is endowed. For Dubrovsky, there is simply no story to be told about how this capacity might come to be in the course of an individual's development. Second, by representing mental activity as information processing occurring in the head of each individual through the exercise of an innate capacity, Dubrovsky presents the self as self-sufficient. Each subject's capacity to think may, at least in principle, function independently of all others, and may therefore be understood without essential reference to other selves. And third, by arguing that the subject is aware of objective reality only indirectly, in virtue of a direct awareness of the ideal phenomena of subjective reality, Dubrovsky reproduces the Cartesian idea that the conscious subject inhabits a self-contained world of mental states, the contents of which are revealed "in pure form" to the subject alone. Dubrovsky therefore subscribes to the problematic doctrine of idealization as mentalization: The world becomes an object of conscious experience by being translated into an intrinsically representational, nonmaterial medium.

Thus, viewed from Ilyenkov's perspective, Dubrovsky's position represents just one more form of supposedly Marxist empiricism framed within the terms of an epistemological dualism long since exploded by Marx himself. As such, Ilyenkov deems Dubrovsky's theory unworthy of serious refutation; its failings "will be obvious," he writes in a late work, "to anyone remotely acquainted with the critique of empiricism developed by the German classical tradition," the tradition that, for Ilyenkov, culminates in the Marxist theory of the ideal (Ilyenkov 1979a: 130). This helps us understand why, in "Mind and Brain," Ilyenkov pays such scant attention to the philosophical credentials of his opponent's position.

However, even someone sympathetic to Ilyenkov might suggest that his dismissal of Dubrovsky's position is premature. For while Dubrovsky clearly operates within the two-worlds framework, his position differs from "classical" Cartesianism in at least one significant respect. Dubrovsky, while denying that objective reality contains ideal properties, holds that "information," conceived as a *material* phenomenon, may be a property of the world beyond the mind. As we have seen, Dubrovsky construes perception as a process in which our brains encode information presented to us by the states of affairs we perceive. By admitting semantic properties into objective reality, Dubrovsky seems to gain immunity from the problem about representation that we raised for the Cartesian. For by holding that both our mental states and the states of affairs they represent contain information, Dubrovsky gives sense to the idea that thought and reality may share the same content or structure. He can thus argue that mental representation is possible in virtue of an informational isomorphism, or of a sameness of content, between the ideal states of subjective reality and the material states of the world beyond the mind. Therefore, Ilyenkov cannot dismiss Dubrovsky's position for simply reproducing the malignant aspects of the Cartesian framework.

Ilyenkov would, I believe, have rejected this plea on Dubrovsky's behalf. First, Ilyenkov would have argued that Dubrovsky's appeal to the existence of informational states in objective reality takes us no closer to understanding the nature of mental representation. Dubrovsky offers no explanation of how it is possible for material phenomena to possess semantic properties, simply asserting that material systems of sufficient complexity possess informational states. However, to state that there is information in the world, the brain, and the mind is not to solve the problem of representation but to announce that it has been solved. Second, Ilyenkov would have held that Dubrovsky's attempt to admit meaning into objective reality while preserving the two-worlds model is deeply confused. As we have seen, Ilyenkov believes that the only plausible explanation of the origin of meaning in the material world – the Marxist theory of the ideal – undermines the very foundation of two-worlds dualism. However, even disregarding that argument, Dubrovsky's strategy seems odd. A philosopher who can give sense to the idea that mental phenomena are informational processes materially encoded in the brain has little to gain by persisting, as Dubrovsky does (see esp. 1983: chap. 3), with a picture of consciousness as a relation between a self and a continuum of immaterial states. Though such a picture might be thought to capture the subjectivity of the mental by grounding the intuition that our mental states are noncontingently inaccessible to others, it raises a host of philosophical problems. Not least among them is the question of how it is possible for the information materially encoded in the brain to be given to the subject in an ideal mode of presentation. This, however, is another phenomenon for which Dubrovsky offers no explanation. For him, that such a mode of presentation is possible is just "a cardinal fact of our mental organization ... usually doubted by no one" (Dubrovsky 1983: 140). Thus, from Ilyenkov's perspective, Dubrovsky's appeal to "material" information is unexplanatory and confused.

This explanation of Ilyenkov's dismissal of Dubrovsky is in harmony with the "nihilistic attitude" to the mind–body problem that Dubrovsky deplores in Mikhailov. For Mikhailov, the mind–body problem, as traditionally conceived, is the problem of the relation of being and consciousness posed as the problem of the ontological relation of the two worlds of the Cartesian model. A materialist who accepts this formulation of the basic question of philosophy will thus inevitably be led, like Dubrovsky, to project the properties of the Cartesian self onto the brain and to argue that, through the physical interaction of its parts, the brain "produces" the subjective phenomena of consciousness (Mikhailov 1980: 136–8). For Ilyenkov and Mikhailov, however, if materialism is to explain the relation of being and consciousness, it must jettison the mind–body problem along with the Cartesian framework that lends the problem its sense:

> As soon as we ask how an immaterial, nonspatial thought is transformed into a spatially expressed movement (the movement of the human body) or, conversely, how the movement of the human body, under the influence of some other body, is transformed into an idea, we have already started from absolutely false premises. (Ilyenkov 1964a: 27)

> There are not two different and fundamentally opposed objects of research – body and thought – but only one, single object: the thinking body of real, living man ... Real, living man, the only thinking body we know, does not consist of two Cartesian halves, an "incorporeal mind" and an "unconscious body." In relation to the real man both are equally false abstractions. (Ilyenkov 1974a: 22)

As we have seen, Ilyenkov holds that it is by recognizing the idealization of reality by activity that we overcome the false abstractions of Cartesianism. However, while it may now be clear why Ilyenkov's understanding of a Marxist theory of the ideal leads him to hold Dubrovsky's philosophy in such contempt, we have yet to examine how such a theory supports Ilyenkov's conception of the socially defined subject.

The defence of the antireductionism and antiinnatism theses

The first step toward understanding Ilyenkov's idea of the individual is to grasp his conception of thought. As we have seen, Ilyenkov argues that, in activity, human agents endow their physical environment with a complex realm of ideal properties and relations. This realm, which Ilyenkov calls "humanity's spiritual culture," is said to embody the totality of normative demands on the action of each individual, including the requirements of logic, language, and morality. Ilyenkov thus argues that the objectification of humanity's spiritual culture represents the transformation of nature into a qualitatively different environment. Objective reality now confronts humanity "refracted through the prism" of our spiritual culture, and we relate to each object as to something that has significance for us: Each object is seen as an object *of a certain kind*. Thus, once idealized, the "external world" no longer exercises a purely physical influence over the subject. Rather, objectification makes possible a new mode of interaction between human agents and their surroundings: a norm-governed interaction mediated by meanings, values, and reasons.

The crucial feature of Ilyenkov's philosophy of mind is that thought (*myshlenie*) is analyzed primarily in terms of this norm-mediated mode of interaction with the world. For Ilyenkov, the definitive characteristic of a thinking being is that its movements are not dictated by the physical influence of its surroundings, but are built (*stroit'*) in conformity to the ideal form, or "logic," of the situation in which it finds itself (1974a: 33, 36). Thus, Ilyenkov maintains, something is a thinking thing only if it has the ability to orientate itself within, and to respond to, an idealized environment. Indeed, he holds this ability to be not only necessary but sufficient for thought. The capacity to think is just the capacity to inhabit an idealized environment.

Identifying the "higher mental function" of thought with the ability to enter a specific mode of interaction with the environment, Ilyenkov argues that the activity that constitutes the exercise of that function should primarily be understood not as a succession of happenings in a private "inner realm" (or, as Dubrovsky would say, in a "subjective reality"), but as the "spatially expressed" activity of the human body itself (Ilyenkov 1964a: 44). This understanding of thought, he claims, must form the basis of any materialist philosophy that seeks to transcend the logic of Cartesianism:

> Materialism is, in this case, the categorical recognition that thought is a mode of the active existence of a material body, the activity of the thinking body in real space and time, in the real material (sensually perceptible) world. (Ilyenkov 1964a: 41)

> [As Spinoza correctly believed,] Thought prior to and outside of its spatial [external] expression in appropriate material forms simply does not exist. (Ilyenkov 1974a: 31)

Thus we see that Ilyenkov's theory of the ideal leads him to hold that the life of the mind is lived only in and through its embodiment in the public, outward activity of the human subject within an idealized environment. This idea must guide our attempt to piece together Ilyenkov's defence of his two problematic theses.

The antireductionism thesis claims that although the occurrence of certain neurophysiological processes is a necessary condition of mental activity, our mental capacities and mental states cannot be reduced to capacities and states of our brains; therefore, analysis of an individual's brain, however exhaustive, can reveal neither the character of his or her psychological capacities nor the nature of his or her mental states. Ilyenkov sometimes writes as if this thesis follows directly from his claim that thought is "the mode of activity of the thinking body" (1974a: 32; cf. 1964a: 29). For if thought is essentially embodied in its expression in external activity, then it cannot be represented as a process that occurs inside the subject, in the brain. On the contrary, thought is "on the surface," manifest in the interchange between individual and environment:

> In order to understand thought as a function, as a mode of activity of a thinking thing in the world of other things, we must go beyond what is going on inside the thinking body

(be it in the brain or in the human body as a whole – it makes no difference) and consider the real system in which that function is realized – the real system of relations between the thinking body and its object. (Ilyenkov 1974a: 38; cf. Ilyenkov 1979c: 347)

Therefore, Ilyenkov concludes, to describe the brain events "with the help of which thought is realized ... has no direct bearing on the question 'What is thinking?'" (1974a: 32).

This argument, however, does not succeed in vindicating Ilyenkov's antireductionism. If we grant Ilyenkov that the process of thinking must be understood primarily as a species of public activity, it would seem natural to construe particular mental states in terms of the contribution they make to that activity. (After all, we explain people's actions by appeal to their mental states.) Thus, Ilyenkov's view invites us to characterize particular mental states in terms of their causal role in interacting with other states to produce the activity that constitutes "thinking." So far, however, Ilyenkov has offered us no reason why mental states, thus understood, should not be identified with brain states, and further, why the capacity to possess such states should not be portrayed as a capacity of the brain.

Ilyenkov does not address this counterargument directly. However, passages in his own writings, and in Mikhailov's, suggest how he might have done so. In *The Riddle of the Self*, Mikhailov argues that mental states are irreducible to brain states because no description of the brain will capture the content of mental states:

> One may study physiological processes, but the content of the sensation will be the very thing that is not covered in such a study. (Mikhailov 1980: 116)

Here, Mikhailov is not just contending that the study of the brain's physical structures does not reveal anything recognizable as a "content"; rather, the basis of his argument is the claim that the content of psychological states (i.e., what the subject is thinking, feeling, seeing, etc.) is determined by factors that obtain outside the subject's head. As Ilyenkov puts it:

> The real composition of mental acts (including the logical composition of thought) is determined not by the structure and

distribution of parts of the body and the brain of man, but only by the external conditions of universal–human actions in the world of other bodies. (Ilyenkov 1974a: 53; see also Ilyenkov 1964a: 44)

From the fact that the content of the subject's mental states is determined by the states of the "external" world, and by the psychological history of the subject him- or herself, both Mikhailov and Ilyenkov conclude that brain states do not fix the content of mental states. On this basis, they argue that mental states are neither identical to, nor "informationally isomorphic" with, physical states. Indeed, Mikhailov even suggests that mental states are not supervenient on brain states, arguing that the content of a subject's thoughts may vary independently of changes in his or her brain (Mikhailov 1980: 116).

In "Brain and Mind," Dubrovsky expresses his puzzlement over this argument as it finds expression in Mikhailov. Dubrovsky replies that no one would deny that the content of our mental states is determined by factors that obtain "outside the head," in the sense that what mental states we have depends causally on the external world. But such considerations about the causal antecedents of our mental states show nothing about whether those states are realized by processes in the brain (Dubrovsky 1968: 125–7). However, once we read Ilyenkov and Mikhailov's argument in the light of the former's theory of the ideal, it becomes clear that Dubrovsky's objection misses the point. Their argument, I believe, rests on an Ilyenkovian answer to a question Dubrovsky ignores: How is meaning possible in the material world? As the first premise of the argument observes, mental states have content, content that they possess in virtue of representational and semantic properties. Indeed, it might be said, mimicking Dubrovsky, that mental states are pure content, pure meanings (cf. Mikhailov 1980: 118). Thus, for Ilyenkov, mental states are quintessentially ideal phenomena. His theory of the ideal, however, dictates that human activity is the sole source of ideality: Configurations of matter are endowed with ideal properties only in virtue of their incorporation into human forms of life activity. Mental states, therefore, can derive their content only from the incorporation of their material substratum into the practices of the community.

From this, two considerations follow. First, the substratum of the mental must be conceived not as the brain but as the person. It is the person, not his or her brain, that is a possible object of incorporation into those of the community's activities that constitute mental activity; and it is the behaviour of the person, not of the brain, that the community seeks to render intelligible by the ascription of mental states. These considerations are behind the slogan that frequently appears in both Ilyenkov's and Mikhailov's writings: The brain itself does not think – the person thinks with the help of the brain (see, e.g., Ilyenkov 1964a: 232, 1974a: 183; Arsen'ev, Ilyenkov, and Davydov 1966: 265; Mikhailov 1986: 63). If this is so, then the capacity to think cannot be seen as a capacity of the brain. Second, it follows that the content of an individual's mental states is fixed not by the physical condition of his or her body or brain, but by the mode of his or her participation in the life activity of the community. Therefore, when Ilyenkov and Mikhailov say that the content of mental states is "determined" by factors "outside the head," they mean that the mental is semantically constituted, and not just caused, in virtue of the "location" of the subject of those states in the social environment.[8]

Ilyenkov's position invites us to think of the social environment in either of two ways. First, we can see it as constituted by the community of thinking subjects who, by incorporating the individual into their life activity, confer upon the individual's actions the ideal properties that make them manifestations of thought (cf. Mikhailov 1980: 182). On this view, the content of an individual's thoughts may be represented as a

8 Interestingly, a similar position is advanced in V. N. Voloshinov's classic *Marxism and the Philosophy of Language* (1929) (a work that may in fact have been authored by Mikhail Bakhtin). In this work, Voloshinov may be read as arguing that all conscious mental happenings are essentially semiotic phenomena, and that, since the meaning of such phenomena is determined in public space by the interpretative practices of the community, we must think of the mind as "on the surface," on the "borderline ... between the organism and the outside world" (Voloshinov 1929: 26). While Ilyenkov would have resisted the identification of the mental with the semiotic, claiming that thought has modes of expression other than the linguistic (cf. 1977b), he would have applauded the idea that the meaning that makes our actions expressions of thought is constituted in the public realm. I give an account of Voloshinov's position, and of its relation to Ilyenkov and Vygotsky, in Bakhurst (1990).

function of the "interpretative practices" of the community, where those practices comprise the entire gamut of activities that involve treating the individual as a subject whose behaviour is meaningful in the broadest sense. Alternatively, we can think of the social environment as "humanity's spiritual culture," the environment of ideal properties to which individuals must mould their behaviour. As children learn to respond to the requirements of this "concrete-historical" environment, so their movements are seen as products of thought. However, these two ways of representing the environment in which bodily movements become expressions of thought are not distinct, for it is precisely the activity of the community – including its interpretative practices – that engenders and sustains the ideal properties that demand of each individual an appropriate response, a thinking response.

Thus, Ilyenkov's theory of the ideal provides the basis of an argument for his antireductionism. If we take that theory seriously, we are led to hold that mental capacities are not properties of the brain and that the content of mental states is not fixed by the states of the brain. Moreover, the theory of the ideal supports the antireductionism thesis in a way that gives substance to Ilyenkov's conception of the socially defined individual, for thinking becomes an activity in which the subject may engage only in a social context:

> Human beings think only in unity with society, in unity with a sociohistorical community reproducing its material and spiritual life. An individual, extracted from the social relations, within and by means of which he or she realizes human contact with nature (i.e., exists in human unity with nature), thinks just as much as a brain extracted from) the human body. (Ilyenkov 1974a: 183)

The mind may live its life only in a social world.

This defence of the antireductionism thesis immediately yields an argument for part of Ilyenkov's antiinnatism: his claim that the higher mental functions are not genetically inherited capacities of the brain. For if psychological functions are capacities of persons and not brains, then they could not be innate capacities of brains. To establish his antiinnatism thesis in full, however, Ilyenkov needs to show further that persons cannot be held to possess psychological functions solely

in virtue of facts about their genetically inherited neurophysiological organization. On what grounds, then, does Ilyenkov
hold that the activity that constitutes thought is of a kind that
"the thinking body" could in no way be genetically predisposed to undertake?

A number of isolated passages in Ilyenkov's writings indi-
cate how an argument might be constructed (e.g., Ilyenkov
1964a: 232–5, 1974a: 33–6, 1977a: 13–15). The argument turns
on whether the activity characteristic of thinking beings can
be formalized. In Chapter 5 I argued that Ilyenkov, in harmony with Akselrod and Vygotsky, offers a particularist account
of dialectical method; that is, he holds that the dialectical
method cannot be understood as a set of principles that may
be applied in any domain, but must be conceived as a non-
codifiable technique for following the specific logic of the object of inquiry. Thus, scientists engaged in the theoretical cognition of reality through the application of dialectical method
cannot be portrayed as following a procedure governed by
rules, adherence to which somehow guarantees that they will
arrive at an adequate conception of their object. Now, Ilyenkov
suggests that it is a characteristic not just of scientific but of all
cognitive activity that it cannot adequately be represented as
the outcome of following rules. No statable procedure can determine how the thinking body is to find its way through its
idealized environment.

In his discussion of Spinoza in *Dialectical Logic*, Ilyenkov advances the following account of the nature of thinking activity:

> The cardinal distinction between the mode of action of a
> thinking body from the mode of movement of any other
> body – fairly clearly noticed, but not understood by Descartes
> and the Cartesians – is that the thinking body actively builds
> (constructs) the form (trajectory) of its movement in space in
> accordance with the form (the configuration or the state) of
> *another body,* making the form of its movements (its actions)
> agree with the form of this other body, and moreover, with
> the form of *any* other body. Therefore, the genuine, specific
> form of the action of a thinking body is its *universality...*
>   ... *Man – the thinking body – builds his movements according to
> the form of any other body.* He does not wait until the insur-
> mountable opposition of other bodies forces him to swerve

from his path; the thinking body freely negotiates any obstacle of the most complex form. *The ability actively to build one's action according to the form of any other body,* actively to make the form of a spatial movement agree with the form and disposition of all other bodies, Spinoza considers the distinguishing feature of the thinking body, the specific mark of those actions that are called "thought," "reason." (Ilyenkov 1974a: 33–4)[9]

Thus, though he construes thought on the model of activity, Ilyenkov does not reduce the capacity to think to the ability to undertake certain *specific* operations. Rather, Ilyenkov presents thought as a capacity to undertake any movement, according to the logic of the object of thought. It is this ability to conform to the dictates of no particular situation, but of any, that Ilyenkov calls thought's *universality.*

Ilyenkov's rhetoric is slightly misleading. He does not intend to imply that thinking bodies are, in the actual world at least, capable of all and every activity. Indeed, his emphasis on spatial movement must be read metaphorically. His point is that the thinking subject can conform his or her activity to the dictates of novel situations, that is, situations that have never before been encountered and that demand responses never before executed (Ilyenkov 1977a: 14). Thought embodies the permanent possibility of transcendence; it may always go beyond what it took to be its own limits.

The universality of thought, Ilyenkov argues, makes it impossible to represent thinking as an activity wholly dictated by rules, for there cannot be rules that determine in advance what will count as an appropriate response to a genuinely new situation (1977a: 14). The rules will always be outrun by the world. Thus, Ilyenkov claims, since the capacity to think resists formalization, this capacity cannot be contained in the physical structure of the organism "in the form of a rule or algorithm" (1977a: 15). The ability to conform one's activity to the logic of *any* circumstances cannot be "built in" if the content of those circumstances is in principle unforeseeable:

9 Just as Ilyenkov presents much of his theory of the ideal in the course of a sympathetic exposition of Hegel, so his conception of thought largely emerges during his treatments of Spinoza (in Ilyenkov 1964a, 1974a: chap. 2) and, to a lesser extent, Feuerbach (in Ilyenkov 1964a).

Since the forms of things and the circumstances of action
are in principle infinite in number, the "soul" (i.e., "reason")
must be capable of an infinite number of actions. An infinite
number of actions cannot, however, be anticipated in the form
of a ready-made, bodily programmed formula [*skhema*]. (Ilyenkov 1974a: 36)

Thus, Ilyenkov concludes, the thinking body is able to "act in
accord with any pattern of activity that, at a given time, is dictated by the form and composition of other bodies" (1974a: 37)
precisely because it is not "*structurally–anatomically* predisposed
in advance" (33) to undertake any particular action.

Read as an empirical argument, Ilyenkov's suggestions
would fail to persuade. There exist machines capable of learning from their mistakes, and of making "decisions" about
how to treat cases they have not been directly programmed to
confront. However, such a reading misses Ilyenkov's point.
Once again, his argument depends on his conception of the
nature of the environment human beings inhabit. For Ilyenkov, human beings have a way of adapting to their surroundings that neither animals nor machines exhibit. He holds that
whereas the animal lives in a purely physical habitat that is
qualitatively unchanging, human beings adapt to their idealized environment, itself a product of transformation, by transforming it, by creating properties, relations, and norms that
previously did not figure in its structure. For Ilyenkov, since
the dictates ideality places on activity are constantly developing, the physical structure of the subject's body or brain cannot, prior to socialization, be genetically "fit" to adapt to a
specific historical environment. The development of our "spiritual culture" proceeds on a different time scale from the biological evolution of the central nervous system. The mode of
inheritance of psychological capacities must, therefore, be sociohistorical and not biological. Thus, Ilyenkov invites us to
see the human child as entering the world with the forms of
thought contained not in the physical structures of his of her
brain but in the modes of activity of the community that constitute the social environment. To appropriate those activities is
not to grasp a body of rules or procedures but to enter a specific
mode of life. As this occurs, so the child inherits humanity's
greatest achievement, the capacity to think:

Nature, reconstituted by human labour (what Marx called "the inorganic body of man"), and not nature as such (including the physiological organization of the body of the individual) is the "body," the "organism" that conveys the forms of thought and forms of contemplation from one generation to another. (Ilyenkov 1964a: 235)

Thus, for Ilyenkov, our biological inheritence is one of undifferentiated potentiality. We are beings that nature leaves fundamentally incomplete. We are finished by culture, in a process in which some part of our potential is realized in concrete form, and the possible trajectories of our development are fashioned. Ilyenkov held this fact to express a profound truth about humanity's creative powers: We are beings who create ourselves through the creation of culture. Furthermore, he believed this to be a truth of great political significance, for to recognize it was to acknowledge society's power, and hence its responsibility, to facilitate the development of all, so that each of its members might flourish as "whole persons" (*tselostnaya lichnost'*).

Conclusion: The polemical and the political

I have argued that, notwithstanding the impression created by his polemical writings, Ilyenkov's philosophy does contain resources to develop a philosophical critique of Dubrovsky's neo-Mechanism, and the beginnings of a defence of his antiinnatism and antireductionism. The character of that defence casts light on the intimate relation between Ilyenkov's conception of the individual and his commitment to Marxism. For not only does Ilyenkov hold that the possibility of communism depends on the antiinnatism thesis, he also believes that the truth of that thesis may be seen only once we countenance Marx's contribution to philosophy. If my reading is correct, Ilyenkov would argue that we can understand the true extent of our social being only if we heed the "Theses on Feuerbach" and conceive of the relation between subject and object as mediated not by contemplation (i.e., by the self's awareness of intrinsically representational mental entities) but by "real, sensuous activity" (i.e., by the subject's active transformation of the physical environment) (Marx 1845: 28).

And for Ilyenkov, the Marxist theory of the ideal, properly understood, is the sole possible foundation for such a position.

However, a puzzle remains: If Ilyenkov had the means to defend his vision of the socially constituted individual, why did he not develop that defence in his writings on the blind-deaf and in his reply to Dubrovsky? The answer, I believe, differs in each case. Ilyenkov was drawn into the polemic with Dubrovsky principally because of the political dangers he perceived in Soviet neo-Mechanism. His main objective was thus to discredit this trend in Soviet thought. With this as his agenda, there are two reasons why Ilyenkov might have chosen to attack the scientific and moral standing of Dubrovsky's position rather than its philosophical content. First, Ilyenkov was concerned that the growing support for innatist theories of the mind frequently found expression not only in Soviet academic literature but also in Soviet popular culture, and he set out to counter those theories in a way that would be accessible to an audience comprised not simply of academics (see Ilyenkov 1968b: 154–5). However, Ilyenkov's philosophical defence of his conception of the individual is not only technical, but focuses on issues – such as the objectivity of meaning and value, and the nature of a "humanized" environment – that at first sight seem very distant from the question of the genetic inheritability of intelligence, a question construed by his opponents to be a matter of empirical fact. Moreover, Ilyenkov might have worried that those tutored on "textbook" dialectical materialism would read his acknowledgement of the objective status of ideal phenomena as an expression of idealism. Thus, Ilyenkov had reason to believe that a philosophical assault on Dubrovsky might be misunderstood by the readers he most wanted to convince.

Second, he might have feared that to attack Dubrovsky on philosophical grounds would precipitate a theoretical stalemate of the kind that beset the original Deborinite–Mechanist controversy. The debate was likely to have degenerated into a squabble over the concept of explanation, with Dubrovsky (in harmony with the tenor of "Brain and Mind") complaining that Ilyenkov was attempting to dictate the possible limits of scientific explanation on a priori grounds. Ilyenkov would not have wished to be drawn into such an argument because, in the aftermath of Lysenkoism and in a period of optimism about the liberating power of science and technology, the majority of Ilyenkov's readers would have been instantly suspicious of a thinker accused of meddling with the autonomy of science. Thus, by ignoring the philosophical substance of the dispute, Ilyenkov could avoid the accusation that he was erecting philosophical barriers to science, while ensuring that his criticisms would remain accessible to a wide readership.

However, while these considerations may explain Ilyenkov's strategy, they do not improve his arguments. "Mind and Brain" remains a mistake, its pseudoscientific assertions and moral posturing contributing nothing to Ilyenkov's credibility as a philosopher. It is a great irony that a philosopher who so valued the Bolshevik ideal of the unity of theory and practice should have allowed the practical significance of his position to result in the impoverishment of its presentation in theory.

Different considerations account for the character of Ilyenkov's writings on the blind-deaf. Ilyenkov was so impressed by Meshcheryakov's work that he became personally involved in the project, befriending Meshcheryakov's four eldest charges and taking an active role in their education. He believed that the experience of these blind-deaf students showed that even individuals whom nature had treated so ruthlessly might come to lead flourishing intellectual lives in a society prepared to take proper responsibility for the education of its citizens. As such, he saw Meshcheryakov's "experiment" as a model for the Soviet education system as a whole. Not everyone, however, shared Ilyenkov's enthusiasm. Like many innovators in special education, Meshcheryakov's plans were expensive to instigate, demanding not only plentiful material resources but also the reeducation of caretakers and teachers. As a result, Meshcheryakov's career was beset by bureaucratic obstacles. Ilyenkov and others therefore sought to propagandize their friend's work in order to generate resources, intensifying their efforts after Meshcheryakov death in 1974 so that his work might be continued. At this time, however, no article on "defectology" would be accepted for publication in either the popular or party press unless it proclaimed the successes of the Soviet education system and argued that these achievements conclusively verified Soviet educational and psychological theory. This explains the character of Ilyenkov's writing on "the Meshcheryakov experiment."

Ilyenkov's writings on the blind-deaf backfired in an even more damaging way than his polemic against neo-Mechanism. Not only did he fail to stimulate adequate resources for Meshcheryakov's project, but by idealizing his friend's contribution, Ilyenkov laid himself open to the charge that he was deliberately distorting the data to vindicate his own sociohistorical theory of consciousness. This charge has been made recently by a number of Ilyenkov's enemies, including David Dubrovsky himself, at a symposium on Meshcheryakov's legacy (Dubrovsky 1988). In an attack simmering with personal animosity, Dubrovsky portrays Ilyenkov as the Lysenko of the Brezhnev era, manipulating the party press to ensure that his own views went unchallenged. It is ironic that this attack on Ilyenkov's integrity is conducted under the banner of *perestroĭka*, since Ilyenkov's opponents conveniently ignore the political conditions in which he was writing. True advocates of *glasnost'* would ask how these conditions might have influenced Ilyenkov's choice of arguments. Instead, Ilyenkov's opponents remain faithful to the methods they supposedly deplore, presenting him as an opportunist whose actions conflict with the present "party line" of democracy and openness.[10] It is to be hoped that Ilyenkov's reputation will not be tarnished by these accusations. However, the incident certainly casts doubt on the wisdom of Ilyenkov's strategy of cheapening his theoretical views in his efforts to fight political causes.

We may observe that this discussion highlights the difficulties facing the Western scholar confronting the Soviet philosophical literature. Ilyenkov's polemical writings on the individual are among the best known in his corpus. However, were we to have judged Ilyenkov on these texts alone, we might easily have portrayed him as just a cavalier contributor to the nature–nurture debate, his position ideologically motivated and unsupported by genuine arguments. Yet, when these texts are read in light of the rest of Ilyenkov's philosophy, the political context in which they were produced, and the history of the Soviet philosophical tradition, we find not only that

10   See Bakhurst and Padden (in press) for a fuller discussion.

Ilyenkov was equipped with arguments for his position, but that there are reasons why he might have suppressed those arguments in his polemics. Significantly, neither fear of censorship, nor of political retribution are among these reasons.

It is a matter of considerable regret that Ilyenkov chose to expound his conception of the individual in fruitless polemics rather than to elaborate the philosophical ideas from which his position derives its sense. For although we have established that Ilyenkov's conception of the ideal is the foundation on which his theory of the socially defined subject rests, it is still unclear exactly how that theory is to be developed. Consider, for example, Ilyenkov's contribution to our understanding of the Vygotskian theory of internalization. On the one hand, Ilyenkov's conception of mental activity seems the perfect complement to Vygotsky's theory: A Vygotskian who follows Ilyenkov and construes thought as a mode of "external" activity within an idealized environment cannot be accused of representing the development of the higher mental functions as a mysterious process in which the child's participation in social activities somehow causes his or her mind to spring into being. For, on Ilyenkov's view, participation in the relevant forms of activity is literally constitutive of the behaviour of a thinking thing; therefore, to master such activities is just to acquire the capacity to think. On the other hand, however, Ilyenkov's conception of thought as activity seems to leave us with no means to make sense of the metaphor of "internality" at the centre of the concept of internalization. Self-consciousness, introspection, the privacy of thought, and "inner speech" are all phenomena that need to be reconceptualized within the terms of Ilyenkov's position. Ilyenkov's writings, however, offer few clues about how this reconceptualization is to be achieved. We learn only that each of these phenomena must be understood as a relation between the subject and the modes of his or her "object-oriented" activity.

Ilyenkov thus leaves us with a glimpse of a non-Cartesian conception of the self, a vision of thinking subjects whose mental lives, born and sustained only in social intercourse, place them in immediate cognitive contact with the natural world of which they are part. He also leaves us with an enormous project of reconstruction. To give real content to his idea of the socially constituted subject, we must rebuild the philoso-

phy of mind, placing the concept of activity at its core. I hope
this book has shown that Ilyenkov's contribution, and the Vygotskian tradition of which it is part, are insightful enough to
make this a project worth pursuing.

8

IN CONCLUSION

Our study of consciousness and revolution in Soviet philosophy began at the very outset of the Soviet philosophical tradition; it proceeded through the controversies of the 1920s and the stagnant orthodoxy of the Stalin era to the contribution of one of the most important of contemporary Soviet philosophers, Evald Ilyenkov. The purpose of this concluding chapter is twofold: First, it briefly considers how the various philosophical themes of this work converge in Ilyenkov's thought. Second, it offers some tentative suggestions about how we should interpret Ilyenkov's life and work in light of the forces unleashed by *glasnost'* in the USSR today.

In Chapter 5 we saw how Ilyenkov sought to develop and defend a conception of dialectical method drawn from Marx. Ilyenkov, like Akselrod and Vygotsky before him, understands dialectical method as a technique for following the specific nature, or "logic," of the object of inquiry. Ilyenkov's conception of the individual may be seen as the outcome of his application of this dialectical method to what the Soviet tradition considers the "basic question of philosophy": the problem of the relation of thinking and being, subject and object.

Ilyenkov's approach to this problem, we may now observe, is strikingly analogous to Vygotsky's attempt to apply Marx's

method to the analysis of thought and speech. Ilyenkov treats
the subject–object relation as Vygotsky treats the relation between the higher mental functions of thought and speech: as
an "internal" relation of mutual determination. Ilyenkov recognizes that, just as the subject is formed through the influence of the object world, so the object world itself is moulded
by the agency of the subject; the nature of each evolves in interaction with the other. Ilyenkov concurs with Vygotsky that
such internal relations cannot be satisfyingly explained either by treating the two relata as logically independent phenomena, or by reducing one relatum to the other. Ilyenkov
argues that, uninformed by dialectics, philosophy will find
itself compelled to adopt either of these two erroneous approaches to the analysis of subject and object. That is, if nondialectical philosophers do not follow Descartes and construe
subject and object as logically distinct realms, then they will
try to collapse the two realms into one, either by reducing the
subject to an entity intelligible in physical terms alone (phys-
icalism, behaviourism), or by representing the object world as
a construction of the mind (subjective idealism).

Ilyenkov advances an alternative strategy. He argues that
the philosopher must not take the opposition between subject
and object as simply given, but must reveal how their opposition has its basis in a single source. Thus, again like Vygotsky, Ilyenkov maintains that the essence of an internal relation is revealed by identifying the "genetic root" of the two
relata, a third phenomenon that explains both the origin of the
relata and the possibility of their special relation. Whereas
Vygotsky takes "meaning" as the genetic root of thought and
speech, Ilyenkov follows Marx's counsel in the first "Thesis
on Feuerbach" and treats "object-oriented activity" (*predmetnaya deyatel'nost'*) as the root of the relation between subject and
object.

Drawing on Marx's concept of objectification, Ilyenkov argues that it is the idealization of nature by human activity that
simultaneously transforms the material world into a possible
object of thought and the human agent into a thinking subject. In this sense, both subject and object owe their very possibility to activity. Moreover, Ilyenkov portrays activity not only
as the source of subject and object but as the permanent basis of their interaction. In Ilyenkov's view, the ideal realm of

"humanity's spiritual culture," the medium through which the object world is presented to the subject, is ultimately constituted by the practices of the community whose existence it mediates; in turn, the mental life of each individual member of the community is born and sustained through his or her appropriation of, and participation in, those social practices. The concept of activity is therefore the "concrete universal" of the subject–object relation – the key concept that explains their initial bifurcation and their subsequent mutual interpenetration and determination.

Ilyenkov offers his conception of the relation between subject and object as a radical alternative to epistemological dualism at the heart of the Cartesian tradition, the "two-worlds dualism" that defines the various empiricist positions we have encountered in this work: the positivism of the Mechanists, the overt dualism of the "conservative realist" of Chapter 4, the idealism of the Empiriocritics, and Dubrovsky's neo-Mechanism. In place of the Cartesian framework, Ilyenkov offers a vision of the subject and object of thought as two dimensions of a single world, a "unity in diversity." Here, thought is conceived not as a barrier or interface between the self and the world beyond the mind, but as the means by which the individual enters into immediate cognitive contact with the material world. Thought, the mode of activity of the socially defined subject, reaches right out to reality itself. Thus by applying his dialectical method to the relation of thinking and being, Ilyenkov provides a framework for a "radical realism," the seeds of which we found in Lenin's contribution to philosophy.

Ilyenkov is adamant that his philosophy is materialist. It represents, however, a species of materialism we might not have expected to encounter at the outset of this work. Ilyenkov is not a materialist who believes that objective reality is composed exclusively of material entities. Indeed, it is a central tenet of Ilyenkov's thought that ideal phenomena, though irreducible to the physical, are genuine constituents of objective reality. Neither is Ilyenkov a materialist who holds that "being always determines consciousness." On the contrary, the starting point of his philosophy is the recognition of the mutual determination of subject and object. Ilyenkov considers himself a materialist because he holds that the very possibility of ideal phenomena, and of the mutual determination of subject and object, has its basis in a single material source: the transformation of nature by social, object-oriented activity.

In taking the ideas of Soviet philosophers seriously as philosophy, this book has frequently been forced to address the complex relation between the development of the Soviet philosophical tradition and the checkered political history of the USSR. It would be misleading to say that the Soviet tradition has been *influenced* by politics, for Soviet philosophy is and always has been an essentially political phenomenon. The political has been the very medium of Soviet philosophy, its driving force and ultimate rationale. As such, the quest to bring philosophical theory to bear on political reality, and on our practical lives in general, has motivated the best of Soviet philosophy, as well as the worst.

It is difficult, however, to offer a definitive judgment on the political character of the life and work of this book's main protagonist, Evald Ilyenkov. When I began research on Ilyenkov at the very end of the sluggish Brezhnev era, the West's characterization of Soviet intellectual life was understandably dismissive. The politically engaged Soviet intellectual was typically portrayed by means of one of the following images: the docile conformist, who parrots the party line in order to survive; the cynical opportunist, who takes advantage of the paranoid conditions of Soviet life to advance himself and his ends; and the dissident, who completely rejects the ideology and practices of the Soviet state. The dawn of the Gorbachev era reawakened Western curiosity in the Soviet Union, stimulating in particular an interest in Soviet art, politics, and popular culture of the 1920s, which were thought to bear parallels to the exciting events of the 1980s. With this, a fourth image of the Soviet intellectual came back into fashion after years of suppression during the Cold War. This is the image of the romantic revolutionary, the courageous visionary who struggles against the old order to bring a new utopia in which the establishment of social justice will secure universal human flourishing.

Each of these stereotypical images has been argued, at one time or another, to apply to Evald Ilyenkov. His contemporaries among the "critical Marxists" portray him as the inspired revolutionary, challenging the oppressive orthodoxy of the Stalin era in order to return Soviet philosophy to its original project. Yet, as we saw in Chapter 7, some of his enemies take the opposite view, repesenting him as an unscrupulous opportunist who exploited the political climate to ensure that his own views would go unchallenged. Ilyenkov's supporters might argue that, as a critical Marxist, Ilyenkov was the ultimate dissident, an oppositional figure of the kind most feared by the Soviet establishment. His detractors, however, could counter that, by couching his work in the rhetoric of "true" dialectical materialism, Ilyenkov was in fact a conformist, helping to legitimize and perpetuate the very orthodoxy he pretended to despise.

It is hard to achieve a coherent picture of Ilyenkov so long as we continue to see him in terms of these traditional stereotypes. In many ways, Ilyenkov should be seen as a modest figure, out of place in the usual angelology or demonology of Soviet intellectual history. He was primarily an intelligent philosopher, more learned than most of his peers, who sought to advance his discipline and to hold Soviet philosophy to its original values. Paramount among these values was the idea that philosophy, particularly in its theories of the self and of the nature of scientific inquiry, was not a politically neutral subject. Ilyenkov therefore urged Soviet philosophers to defend and develop a Marxist philosophy that, he thought, would facilitate the flowering of a new and just society in the Soviet Union. Of course, many of Ilyenkov's contemporaries shared such ideas. But what made his contribution special was the excellence of his early philosophical writings. These works did much to inject new impetus into Soviet philosophy after Stalin, stimulating philosophers to take a more responsible and sophisticated attitude to the classics of Marxism. Furthermore, as we have seen, Ilyenkov helped to preserve the continuity of the Soviet tradition, by raising once again issues that had dominated Soviet debates of the 1920s and early 1930s, but that had been swept aside in the Stalin years. This he may have done unconsciously, for Stalinism did much to destroy the Soviet tradition's memory of its own history. Nevertheless, the logic of Soviet philosophical culture demanded that these questions be addressed once more, and Ilyenkov's writings served, not only to resurrect, but to advance the discussion. It would be naïve to claim that Ilyenkov succeeded in returning Soviet philosophy to the original Bolshevik ideal. Nevertheless, we should not underestimate his power as a teacher and colleague to inspire his contemporaries to keep faith in the idea of a progressive unity of philosophical theory and political practice, even when the post-Stalin reforms floundered.

I believe these considerations best express Ilyenkov's political significance for the Soviet philosophical tradition. It is true that he wrote many works that directly addressed political issues, such as his polemic with Dubrovsky and his essay on Lenin's philosophy. Moreover, he also took up specific political causes, such as his support for Meshcheryakov's work with the blind-deaf. However, as we have seen, these writings are his least successful. In all these works, Ilyenkov rails against the fetishism of science and technology, and stresses communism's responsibility to enable the flourishing of each human individual, but his dogmatic language often smacks of the empty rhetoric of the Soviet orthodoxy. Whether he wrote in this way through political necessity, failure of imagination, or even, as his own theory might predict, because the culture he had appropriated lent him no other resources with which to make his case, the result is a series of writings that seem to serve the ideology that he allegedly wished to reform. It is to be hoped that the new political climate in the Soviet Union will facilitate a better understanding of these problematic writings by elucidating the circumstances in which they were produced. Let us hope also that, following the Soviet publication of Ilyenkov's interesting "Marx and the Western World" (1965), further hitherto unpublished writings will emerge that cast a more subtle light on Ilyenkov's political sensibilities.

Just as recent changes in the Soviet Union may allow us to reach a better appreciation of Ilyenkov, so the study of intellectuals of his kind is crucial to understanding the character of *glasnost'* itself. The revolution now occurring in the USSR was begun "from above," precisely by critical intellectuals of Ilyenkov's generation. Indeed, there are several interesting parallels between Ilyenkov and Gorbachev himself. Both may be seen as seeking, in their respective domains, to promote reform from within. Both are Marxists of a critical persuasion, though both are capable of resorting to dogmatism in pursuit of certain political causes. Just as Gorbachev began his call for *perestroĭka* with the slogan, "The Party and the people are one – the Party's plan is the people's plan," so Ilyenkov appealed to the authority of Lenin to win acceptance in his efforts to challenge the status quo. Thus, neither Gorbachev nor Ilyenkov are fully intelligible in terms of our traditional images of the *dramatis personae* of the Soviet scene. They are neither revolutionaries, nor opportunists, neither dissidents, nor conformists, though there is something of each of these figures in both of them.

In these fast-changing times, Western analysts find it hard to imagine what reform could amount to in the Soviet Union, if not the gradual emergence of a liberal democracy and a free market economy. We lack a sense of what a genuinely democratic form of Russian socialism might look like. If the idea of such a socialism is still alive in Russia, then it can only be because it has been preserved and developed by the intellectuals of Ilyenkov's generation and their immediate successors. If the idea is dead, then the reasons for its demise lie in the circumstances that robbed Ilyenkov and his contemporaries of an authentic political culture. In either event, the story of intellectuals like Ilyenkov will represent an important chapter in the history of the Soviet Union.

REFERENCES

Abbreviations:
PZM = Pod znamenem marksizma [*Under the Banner of Marxism*]
VF = Voprosy filosofii [*Questions of Philosophy*]

Afanasyev, V. G. (1980), *Marxist Philosophy*, trans. D. Fidlin, 4th ed., rev. Moscow: Progress.

Ahlberg, René (1962), The Forgotten Philosopher: Abram Deborin. L. Labedz (ed.), *Revisionism.* London: George, Allen and Unwin: 126–41.

Akademik (1922), Kakoĭ dolzhna byt' vysshaya laboratoriya marksizma? [What must the highest laboratory of Marxism be like?]. *PZM*, no. 3: 119–20.

Akselrod, L. (Ortodoks) (1909), review of *Materialism and Empirio-criticism* by N. Il'in' [Lenin]. Lenin (1927–35: vol. 13, 328–9). Originally published in *Sovremenniĭ mir* [*The Contemporary World*], 29 September.

(1927a), Nadoelo! [I've had enough!]. *Krasnaya nov'* [*Red Virgin Soil*], no. 3: 171–81.

(1927b), Otvet na "Nashi raznoglasiya" A. Deborina [Reply to A. Deborin's "Our Differences"]. *Krasnaya Nov'* [*Red Virgin Soil*], no. 5: 136–63.

Alekseev, I. S. (1983), Nauka [Science]. *Filosofskiĭ éntsiklopedicheskiĭ slovar'*: 403–6.

Anderson, Perry (1976), *Considerations on Western Marxism.* London: New Left Books.

Armstrong, D. M. (1961), *Perception and the Physical World*. London: Routledge & Kegan Paul.

(1968), *A Materialist Theory of the Mind*. London: Routledge & Kegan Paul.

Arsen'ev, A. S., E. V. Ilyenkov, and V. V. Davydov (1966), Mashina i chelovek, kibernetika i filosofiya [Machine and Man, Cybernetics and Philosophy]. *Leninskaya teoriya otrazheniya i sovremennaya nauka* [*Lenin's Theory of Reflection and Contemporary Science*]. Moscow: Politizdat: 265–85.

Avineri, Shlomo (1968), *The Social and Political Thought of Karl Marx*. Cambridge: Cambridge University Press.

Bakhurst, D. J. (1985a), Deborinism versus Mechanism: A Clash of Two Logics in Early Soviet Philosophy. *Slavonic and East European Review 63*(3): 422–8.

(1985b), Marxism and Ethical Particularism: A Response to Steven Lukes's *Marxism and Morality*. *Praxis 5*(2): 209–23.

(1986), Thought, Speech and the Genesis of Meaning: On the 50th Anniversary of Vygotsky's *Myshlenie i rech'*. *Studies in Soviet Thought 31*: 103–29.

(1990), Social Memory in Soviet Thought. David Middleton and Derek Edwards (eds.), *Collective Remembering*. London: Sage Publications: 203–26.

Bakhurst, David, and Carol Padden (in press), The Meshcheryakov Experiment: Soviet Work on the Education of Blind-Deaf Children. *International Journal of Educational Research*.

Batishchev, G. S., and Yu. N. Davydov (1961), Problema abstraktnogo i konkretnogo i trudnosti eë issledovaniya [The Problem of the Abstract and the Concrete and the Difficulties of its Research]. *VF*, no. 8: 161–5.

Bennett, Jonathan (1971), *Locke, Berkeley, Hume. Central Themes*. Oxford: Oxford University Press.

Berdyaev, Nikolai (1933), The "General Line" of Soviet Philosophy. *The End of Our Time*, trans. Donald Atwater. London: Sheed and Ward: 209–58.

Berestnev, V. (1938), Men'shevistvuyushchiĭ idealizm [Menshevising Idealism]. *Bol'shaya sovetskaya ėntsiklopediya* [*Great Soviet Encyclopaedia*], vol. 38. Moscow: Sovetskaya ėntsiklopediya: 827–30.

Besançan, Alain (1981), *The Intellectual Origins of Leninism*, trans. Sarah Matthews. Oxford: Basil Blackwell.

Blackburn, Simon (1984), *Spreading the Word*. Oxford: Oxford University Press.

Bocheński, J. M. (1961), On Soviet Studies. *Studies in Soviet Thought 1*: 1–11.

(1963a), *Soviet Russian Dialectical Materialism (Diamat)*, trans. Nicolas Sollohub, rev. T. J. Blakeley. Dordrecht: Reidel.

(1963b), Why Studies in Soviet Philosophy? *Studies in Soviet Thought* 3: 1–10.

(1963c), Research at the Fribourg Institute of East-European Studies 1958–1963. *Studies in Soviet Thought* 3: 294–313.

Bogdanov, A. A. (1904a), *Iz psikhologii obshchestva* [*From the Psychology of Society*]. Petersburg: Pallada-Delo.

(1904b), Filosofskiĭ koshmar [A Philosophical Nightmare]. *Pravda* (monthly), June: 225–59 (reprinted in Bogdanov 1904, 1906).

(1905–6), *Émpiriomonizm* [*Empiriomonism*], 3 bks. (bk. 1 in 2nd ed.). Moscow: Dorovatorskiĭ and Charushnikov (Delo).

(1906), *Iz psikhologii obshchestva* [*From the Psychology of Society*], 2nd ed., enlarged. Petersburg: Pallada-Delo.

(1908), *Red Star*. Bogdanov (1984: 17–140).

(1910), *Vera i nauka* [*Belief and Science*]. Moscow.

(1913), *Engineer Menni*. Bogdanov (1984: 141–233).

(1921), *Essays in Tektology*, trans. George Gorelik. Seaside, Calif.: Intersystems Publications, 1980.

(1925–9), *Vseobshchaya organizatsionnaya nauka (Tektologiya)* [*Universal Organizational Science (Tektology)*], 3rd ed., rev., 3 vols., Leningrad-Moscow: Kniga.

(1984), *Red Star. The First Bolshevik Utopia*, trans. Charles Rougle, ed. Loren R. Graham and Richard Stites. Bloomington: Indiana University Press.

Bosse, G. G. (ed.) (1925), *Mekhanisticheskoe estestvoznanie i dialekticheskiĭ materializm* [*Mechanistic Science and Dialectical Materialism*]. Vologda.

Bukharin, Nikolai (1921), *Historical Materialism. A System of Sociology*. Ann Arbor: University of Michigan Press, 1969.

Bulgakov, M. (1909), review of *Materialism and Empiriocriticism* by N. Il'in' [Lenin]. Lenin (1927–35: vol. 13, 327). First published in *Kriticheskoe obozrenie* [*The Critical Review*], nos. 7–8 (May).

Campbell, Tom (1983), *The Left and Rights: A Conceptual Analysis of the Idea of Socialist Rights*. London: Routledge & Kegan Paul.

Cole, Michael (1988), Cross-Cultural Research in the Socio-Historical Tradition. *Human Development 31*: 137–57.

Colletti, Lucio (1969), Marxism: Science or Revolution. From Rousseau to Lenin. *Studies in Ideology and Society*. London: New Left Books: 229–36.

Dahm, Helmut, Thomas J. Blakeley, and George L. Kline (eds.) (1988), *Philosophical Sovietology: The Pursuit of a Science*. Dordrecht: Reidel.

Dancy, Jonathan (1988), Contemplating One's Nagel. *Philosophical Books 29*(1): 1–16.

Davidson, Donald (1985), *Inquiries into Truth and Interpretation*. Oxford: Oxford University Press.

Davydov, V. V. (1986), *Problemy razvivayushchego obucheniya* [*The Problem of Developmental Education*]. Moscow: Pedagogika.

Deborin, A. M. (1925), Éngels' i dialekticheskoe ponimanie prirody [Engels and the Dialectical Understanding of Nature]. Deborin (1961: 212–50). First published in *PZM*, nos. 10–12.

(1926a), Nashi raznoglasiya [Our Differences]. Deborin (1961: 303–45). First published in *Letopisi marksizma* [*Annals of Marxism*], no. 2.

(1926b), Predmet filosofii i dialektika [The Subject of Philosophy and Dialectics]. Deborin (1961: 166–83). First published in *PZM*, no. 11.

(1961), *Filosofiya i politika* [*Philosophy and Politics*]. Moscow: Akademiya Nauk.

Dialektika v prirode [*Dialectics in Nature*]. Five vols. Vologda: Severnyĭ pechatnik, 1926–9.

Dubrovsky, D. I. (1968), Mozg i psikhika [Brain and Mind]. *VF*, no. 8: 125–35.

(1971), *Psikhicheskie yavleniya i mozg* [*Mental Phenomena and the Brain*]. Moscow: Nauka.

(1980), *Informatsiya, soznanie, mozg* [*Information, Consciousness, Brain*]. Moscow: Vyshchaya shkola.

(1983), *Problema Ideal'nogo* [*The Problem of the Ideal*]. Moscow: Mysl'.

(ed.) (1988), *Slepoglukhonemota: istoricheskie i metodologicheskie aspekty. Mify i realnost'* [*Blind-deafness: Historical and Methodological Aspects. Myths and Reality*]. Moscow: Filosofskoe obshchestvo SSSR.

Efroimson, V. P. (1971), Rodoslovnaya al'truizma [Genealogical Altruism]. *Novyĭ mir* [*New World*], no. 10: 193–213.

(1976), K biokhimicheskoĭ genetike intellekta [Towards a Biochemical Genetics of the Intellect]. *Priroda* [*Nature*], no. 9: 62–72.

Elster, Jon (1985), *Making Sense of Marx*. Cambridge: Cambridge University Press.

Engels, Frederick (1873–83), *Dialectics of Nature*, trans. Clemens Dutt. Moscow: Progress, 1976.

(1878), *Anti-Dühring*, trans. Emile Burns. Moscow: Progress, 1978.

Filosofskaya éntsiklopediya [*Philosophical Encyclopedia*] (1960–70), five vols. Moscow: Sovetskaya éntsiklopediya.

Filosofskiĭ éntsiklopedicheskiĭ slovar'. [*Philosophical Encyclopedic Dictionary*] (1983). Moscow: Sovetskaya éntsiklopediya.

Filosofskiĭ slovar' [*Philosophical Dictionary*] (1975). Under the editorship of M. M. Rozental', 3rd ed. Moscow: Politizdat.

Frolov, I. T., V. S. Stepin, V. A. Lektorsky, and V. Zh. Kelle (1988). O zamysle knigi *Vvedenie v filosofiyu* [On the design of the book *Introduction to Philosophy*]. *VF*, no. 9: 3–11.

Fundamentals of Marxist-Leninist Philosophy, The (1982). Under the General Editorship of F. V. Konstantinov, trans. Robert Daglish. Moscow: Progress. Translation of *Osnovy Marksistsko-leninskoĭ filosofii*, 5th ed. Moscow: Politizdat, 1980.

Goldstick, D. (1980), The Leninist Theory of Perception. *Dialogue* 19(1): 1–19. First published in *Filosofskie nauki* [*Philosophical Sciences*], 1978, no. 3.

Graham, Loren R. (1987), *Science, Philosophy and Human Behaviour in the Soviet Union.* New York: Columbia University Press.

Gurgenidze, G. S., and E. V. Ilyenkov (1975), Vydayushcheesya dostizhenie sovetskoĭ nauki [A Magnificent Achievement of Soviet Science]. *VF*, no. 6: 63–84.

Hecker, Julius (1933), *Moscow Dialogues.* London: Chapman and Hall.

Hegel, G. W. F. (1807), *Phenomenology of Spirit,* trans. A. V. Miller. Oxford: Oxford University Press, 1977.

(1812–16), *Science of Logic,* trans. A. V. Miller. London: Allen and Unwin, 1969.

(1830a), *Logic. Being Part One of the Encyclopaedia of the Philosophical Sciences (1830),* trans. William Wallace. Oxford: Oxford University Press, 1975.

(1830b), *Philosophy of Nature. Being Part Two of the Encyclopedia of the Philosophical Sciences (1830),* trans. A. V. Miller. Oxford: Oxford University Press, 1970.

History of the Communist Party of the Soviet Union (Bolsheviks). Short Course (1938), ed. by a Commission of the Central Committee of the CPSU (B). Moscow: Foreign Languages Publishing House, 1943.

Hume, David (1739), *Treatise of Human Nature,* ed. L. A. Selby-Bigge. 2nd ed. rev. by P. H. Nidditch. Oxford: Oxford University Press, 1978.

"E. V. Ilyenkov" (1979). *Filosofskie Nauki,* no. 4.

Ilyenkov, E. V. (1955), O dialektike abstraktnogo i konktretnogo v nauchno-teoreticheskom poznanii [On the Dialectics of the Abstract and the Concrete in Scientific-Theoretical Cognition]. *VF,* no. 1: 42–56.

(1957), K voprosu o protivorechii v myshlenii [On the Question of Contradiction in Thought]. *VF,* no. 4, 63–72. Republished in Ilyenkov (1974a: 232–49; 1984a: 257–70).

(1960a), *The Dialectics of the Abstract and the Concrete in Marx's "Capital,"* trans. Sergei Syrovatkin. Moscow: Progress, 1982.

(1960b), Vseobshchee [The Universal]. *Filosofskaya éntsiklopediya,* vol. 1: 301–4.

(1962a), Ponimanie abstraktnogo i konkretnogo v dialektike i formal'noĭ logike [The Understanding of the Abstract and Concrete in Dialectics and Formal Logic]. *Dialektika - logika. Forma myshleniya [Dialectics - Logic. Forms of Thought].* Moscow: Politizdat: 172–210. Amended version of Ilyenkov (1960a: chap. 1).

(1962b), Ideal'noe [The Ideal]. *Filosofskaya éntsiklopediya,* vol. 2: 219–27. Republished, amended, in Ilyenkov (1974a: 183–210; 1984a: 164–88).

(1962c), Logika *Kapitala* [The Logic of *Capital*]. From "Kapital" ["Capital"], *Filosofskaya éntsiklopediya,* vol. 2: 436–9.

(1962d), Problema ideala v filosofii [The Philosophical Problem of Ideals], part 1. *VF,* no. 10: 118–29. Abridged version of Ilyenkov (1968a: 59–117).

(1963), Problema ideala v filosofii [The Philosophical Problem of Ideals], part 2. *VF,* no. 2: 132–44. Abridged version of Ilyenkov (1968a: 117–52).

(1964a), Vopros o tozhdestve myshleniya i bytiya v domarksistskoĭ filosofii [The Question of the Identity of Thinking and Being in pre-Marxist Philosophy]. *Dialektika – teoriya poznanie [Dialectics – the Theory of Cognition].* Moscow: Politizdat: 21–54.

(1964b), Ob ésteticheskoĭ prirode fantasii [On the Aesthetic Nature of Fantasy]. Ilyenkov (1984b: 224–77). First published in *Voprosy éstetiki [Questions of Aesthetics],* no. 6.

(1965), Marks i zapadnyĭ mir [Marx and the Western World]. *VF,* 1988, no. 10: 99–112. Early version of Ilyenkov (1967c).

(1967a), Problema abstraktnogo i konkretnogo v svete "Kapitale" Marksa [The Problem of the Abstract and the Concrete in the light of Marx's *Capital*]. *"Kapital" K. Marksa. Filosofiya i sovremennost' [Marx's "Capital": Philosophy and The Present].* Moscow. Republished, abridged, as Ilyenkov (1967b).

(1967b), Problema abstraktnogo i konkretnogo [The Problem of the Abstract and the Concrete]. *VF,* no. 9: 55–65.

(1967c), From a Marxist–Leninist Point of View. Lobkowicz (1967: 391–407). Amended version of Ilyenkov (1965).

(1968a), *Ob idolakh i idealakh [Of Idols and Ideals].* Moscow: Politizdat.

(1968b), Psikhika i mozg. [The Mind and The Brain]. *VF,* no. 11: 145–55.

(1968c), Ponyatie "abstraktnogo" ("ideal'nogo") ob"ekta [The Concept of an "Abstract" ("Ideal") Object]. *Problemy dialektiches-*

Problemy dialekticheskoĭ logiki [*Problems of Dialectical Logic*]. Alma Ata: 62–77. Republished, amended, as part of Ilyenkov (1971a) and in Ilyenkov (1984a: 223–30).

(1968d), Pochemu mne eto ne nravitsa [Why I don't like it]. Ilyenkov (1984a: 277–300). First published in *Kul'tura chustv* [*The Culture of the Senses*]. Moscow. Also published, abridged, in Ilyenkov (1968a: 11–28).

(1968e), Dumat', myslit' [To think, to reason]. *Obshchestvo i molodëzh'* [*Society and Youth*]. Moscow.

(1970), Psikhika cheloveka pod "lupoĭ vremeni" [The Mind of Man under the "Magnifying Glass of Time"]. *Priroda* [*Nature*], no. 1: 87–91.

(1971a), Dialcktika abstraktnogo i konkretnogo [The Dialectics of the Abstract and the Concrete]. *Ot vozniknoveniya marksizma do leninskogo ètapa* [*From the Origin of Marxism to the Leninist Stage*]. Moscow: 236–64. Includes an amended version of Ilyenkov (1968c). Republished in Ilyenkov (1984a: 216–38).

(1971b), Logicheskoe i istoricheskoe [The Logical and the Historical]. *Ot vozniknoveniya marksizma do leninskogo ètapa* [*From the Origin of Marxism to the Leninist Stage*]. Moscow: 265–88. Republished in Ilyenkov (1984a: 238–57).

(1973), Gegel' i problema predmeta logiki [Hegel and the Problem of the Subject of Logic]. *Filosofiya Gegelya i sovremennost'* [*The Philosophy of Hegel and the Present*]. Moscow: 120–44.

(1974a), *Dialekticheskaya logika. Ocherki istorii i teorii* [*Dialectical Logic. Essays in Its History and Theory*]. Moscow: Politizdat. Translated as Ilyenkov (1977e).

(1974b), Leniniskaya ideya sovpadeniya logiki, teorii poznaniya i dialektiki [The Leninist Idea of the Coincidence of Logic, the Theory of Cognition and Dialectics]. *Filosofiya i estestvoznanie* [*Philosophy and Natural Science*]. Moscow: 39–61. Republished in Ilyenkov (1974a: 211–32; 1984a: 188–206).

(1975), Aleksandr Ivanovich Meshcheryakov i ego pedagogika [Alexander Ivanovich Meshcheryakov and His Pedagogy]. *Molodoĭ kommunist* [*The Young Communist*], no. 2: 80–4.

(1977a), Uchites' myslit' smolodu. [Learn to think when you are young]. Moscow: Znanie. Includes Ilyenkov (1968e); partly translated as Ilyenkov (1978).

(1977b), Soobrazheniya po voprosu ob otnoshenii myshleniya i yazyka (rechi) [Considerations on the Question of the Relation of Thought and Language (Speech)]. *VF*, no. 6: 92–6.

(1977c), The Concept of the Ideal. *Philosophy in the USSR: Problems of Dialectical Materialism*. Moscow: Progress: 71–99. Trans. (abridged and amended) by Robert Daglish of Ilyenkov (1979a).

(1977d), Stanovlenie lichnosti: k itogam nauchnogo éksperimenta [The Genesis of the Person: on the Results of a Scientific Experiment]. *Kommunist (Communist)*, no. 2: 68–79.

(1977e), *Dialectical Logic. Essays in Its History and Theory*. Trans. by H. Campbell Creighton of Ilyenkov (1974a). Moscow: Progress.

(1978), Learn to think while you are young. *Sputnik 3*: 76–9. Excerpt from Ilyenkov (1977a).

(1979a), Problema ideal'nogo [The Problem of the Ideal]. *VF*, no. 6: 145–58, no. 7: 128–40. Republished as Dialektika ideal'nogo [The Dialectic of the Ideal], Ilyenkov (1984b: 8–77); partly trans. as Ilyenkov (1977c).

(1979b), Materializm voinstvuyushchiĭ – znachit dialekticheskiĭ [Militant Materialism is Dialectical Materialism]. Ilyenkov (1984a: 286–304). First published in *Kommunist*, 1979: no. 6.

(1979c), Chto zhe takoe lichnost'? [What is Personhood?]. *S chego nachinaetsa lichnost'* [*Where Personhood Begins*]. Moscow: Politizdat, 1st ed.: 183–237; 2nd ed. (1984): 319–58.

(1979d), Problema protivorechiya v logike [The Problem of Contradiction in Logic]. *Dialekticheskoe protivorechie* [*Dialectical Contradiction*]. Moscow: Politizdat: 122–43.

(1979e), O material'nosti soznaniya i o trantsendental'nykh koshkakh [On the Materiality of Consciousness and on Transcendental Cats]. *Dialekticheskoe protivorechie* [*Dialectical Contradiction*], Moscow: Politizdat: 252–71.

(1979f), Dialektika i mirovozzrenie [Dialectic and Worldview]. Ilyenkov (1984a: 304–17). First published in *Materialisticheskaya dialektika kak logika* [*Materialist Dialectics as Logic*]. Alma-Ata, 1979.

(1980), *Leninskaya dialektika i metafizika positivizma* [*Leninist Dialectics and the Metaphysics of Positivism*]. Moscow: Politizdat.

(1982), *Leninist Dialectics and the Metaphysics of Positivism*. Trans. of Ilyenkov (1980). London: New Park.

(1984a), *Dialekticheskaya logika. Ocherki istorii i teorii*. 2nd ed. (rev. and enlarged) of Ilyenkov (1974a). Moscow: Politizdat.

(1984b), *Iskusstvo i kommunisticheskiĭ ideal* [*Art and the Communist Ideal*]. Moscow: Iskusstvo.

Il'in, I. A. (1909), review of *Materialism and Empiriocriticism* by N. Il'in' [Lenin]. Lenin (1927–35: vol. 13, 328–9). Originally published in *Russkie vedomosti* [*The Russian Gazette*], no. 222, 29 September.

Inwood, M. J. (1983), *Hegel*. London: Routledge & Kegan Paul.

Istoriya filosofii v SSSR [*The History of Philosophy in the USSR* (1985)], vol. 5, bk. 1. Moscow: Nauka.

Joravsky, David (1961), *Soviet Marxism and Natural Science.* London: Routledge & Kegan Paul.

Kammari M., and P. Yudin (1932), Tov. Stalin o razrabotke Leninym materialisticheskoǐ dialektiki [Com. Stalin on Lenin's working out of Materialist Dialectics]. *PZM,* nos. 11–12: 95–117.

Kant, Immanuel (1788), *The Critique of Pure Reason,* trans. Norman Kemp Smith. London: MacMillan, 1929.

(1790), *The Critique of Judgement,* trans. J. H. Bernard. New York: Hafner Publishing, 1951.

Kapustin, Mikhail (1988), Dialectics by Command: Revolutionism in Philosophy and the Philosophy of Revolutionism. *Studies in Soviet Philosophy 28*(2) (Fall): 6–29.

Karev, Nikolai (1926), Neskol'ko zamechaniǐ po povodu stat'i professora Samoǐlova [Some remarks on Professor Samoǐlov's article]. *PZM,* no. 4–5: 82–7.

Kedrov, B. M. (1961), Kak izuchat' knigu V. I. Lenina "Materialism i émpiriocrititsizm" [*How to Study Lenin's "Materialism and Empiriocriticism"*]. Moscow: Gospolitizdat.

Kelly, Aileen (1981), Empiriocriticism: a Bolshevik Philosophy? *Cahiers du monde russe et soviétique 22:* 89–118.

Kolakowski, Leszek (1978), *Main Currents of Marxism,* trans. P. S. Falla. 3 vols. Oxford: Oxford University Press.

Kozulin, Alex (1984), *Psychology in Utopia.* Cambridge, Mass.: MIT Press.

(1986), Vygotsky in Context. Vygotsky (1986: xi–lvi).

Kripke, Saul (1980), *Naming and Necessity.* Oxford: Basil Blackwell.

(1982), *Wittgenstein on Rules and Private Language.* Oxford: Basil Blackwell.

Ksenofontov, V. I. (1975), *Leniniskie idei v sovetskoǐ filosofskoǐ nauke 20-kh godov.* (*Diskussiya "dialektikov" s mekhanistami*) [*Leninist Ideas in Soviet Philosophical Science of the 1920s (The discussion between the "Dialecticians" and the Mechanists)*]. Leningrad: Izdatelstvo leningradsckogo universiteta.

Lecourt, Dominique (1983), Avant le déluge. Zapata (1983a: 9–24).

Lee, Benjamin (1985), "Intellectual Origins of Vygotsky's Semiotic Analysis." Wertsch (1985b: 66–93).

(1987), Recontextualizing Vygotsky. Maya Hickmann (ed.), *Social and Functional Approaches to Language and Thought.* Orlando: Academic Press: 87–104.

Lenin, V. I. (1895–1916), *Philosophical Notebooks,* trans. Clemence Dutt. Lenin (1960–78, vol. 38).

(1902), *What Is to Be Done?* Lenin (1975, vol. 1: 92–241).

(1909a), *Materializm i émpiriocrititsizm* [*Materialism and Empiriocriticism*]. Lenin (1958–69, vol. 18).

(1909b), *Materialism and Empiriocriticism,* trans. Abraham Fineberg. Lenin (1960–78, vol. 14).

(1917), *State and Revolution.* Lenin (1975: vol. 2, 238–327).

(1922), O znachenii voinstvuyushchego materializma [On the Significance of Militant Materialism]. *PZM,* no. 3: 5–12. Trans. in Lenin (1975: vol. 3, 599–606).

(1927–35), *Sochineniya* [*Works*], 2nd ed., ed. N. I. Bukharin et al. Moscow: Institut Lenina.

(1958–69), *Polnoe sobranie sochinenii* [*Collected Works*], 5th ed. Moscow: Institut marksizma-leninizma pri Ts-K KPSS, Gospolitizdat.

(1960–78), *Collected Works.* 4th English ed. Moscow and London: Lawrence and Wishart.

(1975), *Selected Works.* 3 vols. Moscow: Progress.

Leontiev, A. N. (1981), The Problem of Activity in Psychology. Wertsch (1981: 37–71).

Levitin, Karl (1975), Luchshiĭ put' k cheloveku [The Best Path to Man]. *Vsë, naverno, proshche* [*Everything, it seems, is simpler*]. Moscow: Znanie: 85–143. Trans. in *Soviet Psychology 18*(1) (Fall 1979): 85–143.

(1982), *One Is Not Born a Personality,* trans. Yevgeni Filippov. Moscow: Progress.

Liebmann, Marcel (1975), *Leninism under Lenin,* trans. Brian Pearce. London: Merlin Press.

Lifshits, M. A. (1984), Pamyati Eval'da Il'enkova [Recollections of Evald Ilyenkov]. Ilyenkov (1984b: 3–7).

Lobkowicz, Nicholas (ed.) (1967), *Marx and the Western World.* Notre Dame and London: University of Notre Dame Press.

Locke, John (1689), *An Essay Concerning Human Understanding,* ed. Peter H. Nidditch. Oxford: Oxford University Press, 1975.

Lovibond, Sabina (1983), *Realism and Imagination in Ethics.* Oxford: Basil Blackwell.

Luria, A. R. (1979), *The Making of Mind: A Personal Account of Soviet Psychology,* ed. Michael and Sheila Cole. Cambridge, Mass., and London: Harvard University Press.

McDowell, John (1978), Are Moral Requirements Hypothetical Imperatives? *Proceedings of the Aristotelean Society Suppl. 52:* 13–29.

(1981), Non-Cognitivism and Rule-Following. Steven Holtzman and Christopher Leich (eds.), *Wittgenstein: To Follow a Rule.* London: Routledge & Kegan Paul: 141–62.

(1983), Aesthetic Value, Objectivity and the Fabric of the World. E. Schaper (ed.), *Pleasure, Preference and Value.* Cambridge: Cambridge University Press: 1–16.

(1985), Values and Secondary Qualities. Ted Honderich (ed.), *Morality and Objectivity*. London: Routledge & Kegan Paul: 110–29.

Mach, Ernst (1900), *Die Analyse der Empfindungen und das Verhältnis des Physischen zum Psychischen* [*The Analysis of Sensations and the Relation of the Physical to the Mental*]. 2nd ed., enlarged. Jena: Gustav Fischer.

(1914), *The Analysis of Sensations and the Relation of the Mental to the Physical*, trans. C. M. Williams. Rev. and suppl. from the 5th German ed. by Sydney Waterlow. Chicago and London: Open Court.

(1976) *Knowledge and Error*, trans. T. J. McCormack and P. Foulkes. Dordtrecht: Reidel.

MacIntyre, Alistair (1981), *After Virtue*. London: Duckworth.

(1988), *Whose Justice? Which Rationality?* Notre Dame: University of Notre Dame Press.

Mackie, John (1976), *Problems from Locke*. Oxford: Oxford University Press.

(1977), *Ethics: Inventing Right and Wrong*. Harmondsworth: Penguin.

McNaughton, David (1988), *Moral Vision*. Oxford: Basil Blackwell.

Malinovsky, A. A. (1970), Nekotorye vozrazheniya E. V. Il'enkovu i A. I. Meshcheryakovu [Some Objections to E. V. Ilyenkov and A. I. Meshcheryakov]. *Priroda* [*Nature*], no. 1: 92–5.

Marx, Karl (1844), *Economic and Philosophic Manuscripts of 1844*, Moscow: Progress, 1977.

(1845), Theses on Feuerbach. Marx and Engels (1968: 28–30).

(1857), Introduction to a Critique of Political Economy. Marx and Engels (1845–6: 124–51).

(1865), *Wages, Price and Profit*. Marx and Engels (1968: 185–226).

(1867), *Capital. A Critique of Political Economy*, trans. Ben Fowkes. Penguin: Harmondsworth, 1976.

(1873), Postface to the Second Edition of *Capital*. Marx (1867: 94–103).

Marx, Karl, and Frederick Engels (1845–6), *The German Ideology*, ed. C. J. Arthur. London: Lawrence and Wishart, 1970.

(1968), *Selected Works in One Volume*. London: Lawrence and Wishart.

Materialist (1922), Zapros redaktsii "Bibliot. kommun." [An Inquiry of the Editors of "The Library of Communism"]. *PZM*, nos. 7–8: 169.

Meikle, Scott (1985), *Essentialism in the Thought of Karl Marx*. London: Duckworth.

Meliukhin, S. T. (1966), *Materiya v eë edinstve, beskonechnosti i razvitii* [*Matter in its Unity, Infinity and Development*]. Moscow: Mysl'.

Mepham, John (1979), From the *Grundrisse* to *Capital:* The Making of Marx's Method. John Mepham and David-Hillel Ruben (eds.), *Issues in Marxist Philosophy. Volume 1. Dialectics and Method.* Brighton: Harvester: 145–73.

Meshcheryakov, A. I. (1968), Kak formiruetsa chelovecheskaya psikhika pri otsutstvii zreniya i slukha [How the Human Mind is Formed in the Absence of Sight and Hearing]. *VF,* no. 9: 109–18.

(1970), Poznanie mira bez slukha i zreniya [The Cognition of the World Without Sight and Hearing]. *Priroda [Nature],* no. 1: 78–87.

(1974), *Slepoglukhonemye deti [Blind-Deaf Children].* Moscow: Pedagogika.

(1979), *Awakening to Life,* trans. by Katherine Judelson of Meshcheryakov (1974). Moscow: Progress.

Mikhailov, F. T. (1964), *Zagadka chelovecheskogo "ya" [The Riddle of the Self].* Moscow: Politizdat.

(1976), *Zagadka chelovecheskogo "ya" [The Riddle of the Self].* 2nd. ed., rev. and enlarged. Moscow: Politizdat.

(1980), *The Riddle of the Self,* trans. by Robert Daglish of Mikhailov (1976). Moscow: Progress.

(1986), Preemstvennost' v razvitii soznaniya Progression in the Development of Consciousness]. *Priroda [Nature],* no. 5: 63–72.

(1990), Slovo ob Il'enkove [A Word on Ilyenkov], *VF,* no. 2: 56–64.

Mikhailov, F. T., and R. Kondratov (1982), Spasitel'noe tvorchestvo [Saving Creativity]. *Znanie – sila [Knowledge Is Strength],* no. 3: 11–13.

Minin, S. K. (1922a), Filosofiya za bort! [Philosophy Overboard!]. *PZM,* nos. 5–6: 122–7.

(1922b), Kommunizm i filosofiya [Communism and Philosophy]. *PZM,* nos. 11–12: 184–98.

Mitin, M. B. (1930), K itogam filosofskoĭ diskussii [The Results of a Philosophical Discussion]. *PZM,* nos. 10–12: 25–59.

(1931), Gegel' i teoriya materialisticheskoĭ dialektiki [Hegel and the Theory of Materialist Dialectics]. *PZM,* nos. 11–12: 23–52.

(1932), O filosofskoĭ nasledstve V. I. Lenina [On the Philosophical Legacy of V. I. Lenin]. *PZM,* nos. 3–4: 13–38.

Mitin, M. B., V. Ral'tsevich, and P. Yudin (1930), O novykh zadachakh marksistsko–leninskoĭ filosofii [On the New Tasks of Marxist–Leninist Philosophy]. *Pravda,* 7 June: 5–6.

Nagel, Thomas (1986), *The View from Nowhere.* Oxford: Oxford University Press.

Novokhat'ko, A. G. (1988), Predislovie k publikatsii [Preface]. *VF,* no. 10: 98–9.

O raznoglasii na filosofskom fronte [*On a Disagreement on the Philosophical Front*] (1930), Meeting of the Presidium of the Communist Academy, 18 and 20 October. *Vestnik kommunisticheskoĭ akademii*, bks. 40–1: 12–165 (part I), bk. 42: 20–89 (part II).

O zhurnale "Pod znamenem marksizma" [On the Journal *Under the Banner of Marxism*] (1930). *PZM*, nos. 10–12: 1–2. Also published in *Pravda*, 26 January 1931.

Pannekoek, Anton (1938), *Lenin as Philosopher*. London: Merlin Press, 1975.

Partiets (1922), O kursakh po izucheniyu marksizma pri Sotsialisticheskoĭ Akademii [On the Courses in Marxism run by the Socialist Academy]. *PZM*, nos. 1–2: 66–9.

Pashukanis, E. (1924), The General Theory of Law and Marxism. Piers Beirne and Robert Shartlet (eds.), *Pashukanis: Selected Writings on Law and Marxism*. London: Academic Press, 1980: 40–131.

Pearson, Karl (1900), *The Grammar of Science*. 2nd ed. London: A. and C. Black.

Proekt plana programmy po kursu dialekticheskogo i istoricheskogo materializma dlya sotsial'no-ėkonomicheskikh i pedagogicheskikh vysshikh uchebnikh zavedeniĭ [Projected Plan for the Programme of a Course on Dialectical and Historical Materialism for Socio-Economic and Pedagogical Institutions of Higher Education] (1937). *PZM*, no. 6: 130–75. Also published (abridged) in *Bolshevik*, 1937, no. 16: 85–9.

Psikhologicheskiĭ slovar' [*Dictionary of Psychology* (1983)], ed. V. V. Davydov et al. Moscow: Pedagogika.

Putnam, Hilary (1962), Dreaming and Depth-Grammar. *Mind, Language and Reality*. Cambridge: Cambridge University Press, 1975: 304–24.

(1973), Meaning and Reference. S. P. Shwartz (ed.), *Naming, Necessity and Natural Kinds*. Ithaca, N.Y.: Cornell University Press, 1977.

Quarterly Newsletter of the Laboratory of Comparative Human Cognition, LCHC, University of California, San Diego.

Quine, W. V. O. (1960), *Word and Object*. Cambridge, Mass.: Harvard University Press.

(1961), Two Dogmas of Empiricism. *From a Logical Point of View*. 2nd ed., Cambridge, Mass.: Harvard University Press: 20–46.

Rogoff, Barbara, and James V. Wertsch (eds.) (1984), *Children's Learning in the "Zone of Proximal Development." New Directions for Child Development*, no. 23. San Fransisco: Jossey-Bass.

Rorty, Richard (1980), *Philosophy and the Mirror of Nature*. Oxford: Basil Blackwell.

(1982), The World Well Lost. *Consequences of Pragmatism.* Brighton: Harvester.

Rosdolsky, Roman (1968), *The Making of Marx's "Capital,"* trans. Pete Burgess. London: Pluto Press, 1977.

Rosental, M. (1960), Preface. Ilyenkov (1960a: 7–8).

Rubin, I. I. (1928), *Ocherki po teorii stoĭmosti Marksa* [*Essays on Marx's Theory of Value*]. 3rd ed. Moscow–Leningrad: Gosizdat.

(1972) *Essays on Marx's Theory of Value,* trans. by Milos Samardzija and Fredy Perlman of Rubin (1928). Detroit: Black & Red.

Rumiĭ, V. (1922a), Filosofiya za bort? [Philosophy Overboard?]. *PZM,* nos. 5–6: 127–30.

(1922b), Az-Buki-Vedi [The A. B. C.]. *PZM,* nos. 11–12: 210–42.

Russell, Betrand (1948), *Human Knowledge: Its Scope and Limits.* London: George, Allen and Unwin.

Samoĭlov, A. F. (1926), Dialektika prirody i estestvoznanie [The Dialectics of Nature and Natural Science]. *PZM,* nos. 4–5: 61–81.

Sandel, Michael (1982), *Liberalism and the Limits of Justice.* Cambridge: Cambridge University Press.

(1984), Introduction. Michael Sandel (ed.), *Liberalism and Its Critics.* Oxford: Basil Blackwell: 1–11.

Sarab'yanov, V. (1922), Dialektika i formal'naya logika [Dialectics and Formal Logic]. *PZM,* no. 3: 64–76.

Scanlan, James P. (1985), *Marxism in the USSR. A Critical Survey of Current Soviet Thought.* Ithaca, N.Y., and London: Cornell University Press.

Scribner, Sylvia (1985), Vygotsky's Uses of History. Wertsch (1985b: 146–61).

Service, Robert (1985), *Lenin: A Political Life. Volume 1: The Strengths of Contradiction.* London: MacMillan.

Sirotkin, S. A. (1979), The Transition from Gesture to Symbol. *Soviet Psychology 17*(3): 46–59.

Skorokhodova, O. I. (1972), *Kak ya vosprinimayu, predstavlayu i ponimayu okruzhayushchiĭ mir* [*How I Perceive, Represent and Understand the Surrounding World*]. Moscow: Pedagogika.

Smith, Peter, and O. R. Jones (1986), *The Philosophy of Mind.* Cambridge: Cambridge University Press.

Sokolyansky, I. A., and A. I. Meshcheryakov (eds.) (1962), *Obuchenie i vospitanie slepoglukhonemykh* [*The Instruction and Upbringing of the Blind-Deaf*]. Moscow.

Spinoza, Benedictus de (1677), "Treatise on the Correction of the Understanding." *Ethics,* trans. Andrew Boyle. London: Dent/Heron, n.d.: 225–63.

Spirkin, Alexander (1983), *Dialectical Materialism.* Moscow: Progress.

Spirkin, A. G., and M. G. Yaroshevskiĭ (1983), Kategorii [Categories]. *Filosofskiĭ éntsiklopedicheskiĭ slovar'*: 251.

(Skvortsov-)Stepanov, I. I. (1925), Éngel's i mekhanicheskoe ponimanie prirody [Engels and the Mechanistic Conception of Nature]. *PZM*, nos. 8–9: 44–72.

(1928), *Dialekticheskiĭ materializm i deborinskaya shkola* [*Dialectical Materialism and Deborin's School*]. Moscow–Leningrad: Gosizdat.

Suchting, W. A. (1985), *Marx and Philosophy*. London: MacMillan.

Suvorov, A. V. (1983), Problema formirovaniya voobrazheniya u slepoglukhonemykh deteĭ [The Problem of the Formation of the Imagination in Blind-Deaf Children]. *Voprosy psikhologii* [*Questions of Psychology*], no. 3: 62–72. Trans. as "The Formation of Representation in Blind–Deaf Children" in *Soviet Psychology* 22(2) (1983–4: 3–28).

(1988), Muzhestvo soznaniya [The Fortitude of Consciousness], *VP*, no. 4: 68–79.

(1989), The Blind-Deaf and Those Who See and Hear. Unpublished paper presented at the World Congress for the Blind-Deaf, Stockholm, 1989.

Sypnowich, Christine (1990), *The Concept of Socialist Law*. Oxford: Oxford University Press.

Taylor, Charles (1979), Atomism. Taylor (1985, vol. 2: 187–210).

(1985), *Philosophy and the Human Sciences. Philosophical Papers, Volume 2*. Cambridge: Cambridge University Press.

Timpanaro, Sebastiano (1975), *On Materialism*, trans. Lawrence Garner. London: New Left Books.

Tiukhtin, V. S. (1972), *Otrazhenie, sistemy, kibernetika* [*Reflection, Systems, Cybernetics*]. Moscow: Nauka.

Tolstykh, V. I. (1981), Soznanie (dukhovnoe) kak predmet sotsial'no-filosofskogo analiza [Consciousness (the Spritual) as a Subject of Philosophical Analysis]. V. I. Tolstykh (ed.), *Dukhovnoe kul'tura* [*Spiritual Culture*]. Moscow: Nauka: 21–70.

Trotsky, L. D. (1922), Pis'mo redaktorstvu *Pod znamenem marksizma* [Letter to the editors of *Under the Banner of Marxism*]. *PZM*, nos. 1–2: 5–7.

(1942), *In Defence of Marxism*. 2nd ed. New York: Pioneer, 1973.

Valsiner, Jaan (1987), *Developmental Psychology in the Soviet Union*. Bloomington: Indiana University Press.

Vasil'ev, S. (1927), K kharakteristike mekhanicheskogo materializma [Toward a Characterisation of Mechanistic Materialism]. *Dialektika v prirode* [*Dialectics in Nature*], bk. 2.

Vasilova, T. A. (1989), Ivan Afanas'evich Sokolyansky. *Defektologiya* [*Defectology*], no. 2: 71–5.

Vercors (1952), *Les animaux dénaturés*. Paris: Michel.

Volodin, A. I. (1982), *"Boĭ absolyutno neizbezhen"* [*"An Absolutely Un-avoidable Battle"*]. Moscow: Politizdat.

Voloshinov, V. N. (1929), *Marxism and the Philosophy of Language*, trans. Ladislav Matejka and I. R. Titunik. Cambridge, Mass.: Harvard University Press, 1986.

Vygotsky, L. S. (1925a), *Psikhologiya iskusstva* [*The Psychology of Art*]. Moscow: Isskustvo, 1st ed., 1965; 2nd ed. (enlarged), 1968. Trans. 1st ed. as Vygotsky (1971).

(1925b), Soznanie kak problema psikhologii povedeniya [Consciousness as a Problem in the Psychology of Behaviour]. Vygotsky (1982a: 78–98).

(1927a), *Istoricheskiĭ smysl psikhologicheskogo krizisa* [*The Historical Meaning of the Crisis in Psychology*]. Vygotsky (1982a: 291–436).

(1927b), Biogeneticheskiĭ zakon [Biogenetic Law]. *Bol'shaya sovetskaya ėntsiklopediya* [*Great Soviet Encyclopedia*], 1st ed. Moscow: Sovetskaya ėntsiklopediya: 275–9.

(1929), The Problem of the Cultural Development of the Child. *Journal of Genetic Psychology 36*: 415–34.

(1931a), *Istoriya razvitiya vysshikh psikhicheskikh funktsiĭ* [*The History of the Development of the Higher Mental Functions*]. Vygotsky (1983a: 5–328).

(1931b), The Genesis of the Higher Mental Functions. Wertsch (1981: 145–88).

(1934), *Myshlenie i rech'* [*Thought and Speech*]. Vygotsky (1982b: 5–361).

(1960), *Razvitie vysshykh psikhicheskikh funktsiĭ* [*The Development of the Higher Mental Functions*]. Moscow: Pedagogika.

(1962), *Thought and Language*. Abridged trans. by E. Hanfmann and G. Vakar of Vygotsky (1934). Cambridge, Mass.: MIT Press.

(1971), *The Psychology of Art*, trans. Scripta Technica. Cambridge, Mass.: MIT Press.

(1978), *Mind in Society. The Development of Higher Psychological Processes*, ed. M. Cole, V. John-Steiner, S. Scribner, and E. Souberman. Cambridge, Mass.: Harvard University Press.

(1982a), *Sobranie sochineniĭ, tom 1: Voprosy teorii i istorii psikhologii* [*Collected Works, vol. 1: Problems in the Theory and History of Psychology*]. Moscow: Pedagogika.

(1982b), *Sobranie sochineniĭ, tom 2: Problemy obshcheĭ psikhologii* [*Collected Works, vol. 2: Problems of General Psychology*]. Moscow: Pedagogika.

(1983a), *Sobranie sochineniĭ, tom 3: Problemy razvitiya psikhiki* [*Collected Works, vol. 3: Problems in the Development of Mind*]. Moscow: Pedagogika.

(1983b), *Sobranie sochineniĭ, tom 5: Osnovy defektologii* [*Collected*

Works, vol. 5: The Foundations of Defectology]. Moscow: Pedagogika.

(1984a), *Sobranie sochineniĭ, tom 4: Detskaya psikhologiya* [*Collected Works, vol. 4: Child Psychology*]. Moscow: Pedagogika.

(1984b), *Sobranie sochineniĭ, tom 6: Nauchnoe nasledstvo* [*Collected Works, vol. 6: Scientific Legacy*]. Moscow: Pedagogika.

(1986), *Thought and Language*. Enlarged ed. of the 1962 trans. of Vygotsky (1934). Rev., ed., and introduced by Alex Kozulin. Cambridge, Mass.: MIT Press.

Wertsch, James V. (ed.) (1981), *The Concept of Activity in Soviet Psychology*. Armonk, New York: M. E. Sharpe.

(1985a), *Vygotsky and the Social Formation of Mind*. Cambridge, Mass. and London: Harvard University Press.

(ed.) (1985b), *Culture, Communication and Cognition. Vygotskian Perspectives*. Cambridge: Cambridge University Press.

Wetter, Gustav A. (1958), *Dialectical Materialism. A Historical and Systematic Survey of Philosophy in the Soviet Union*, trans. Peter Heath. London: Routledge & Kegan Paul.

Wiggins, David (1976), Truth, Invention and the Meaning of Life. *Proceedings of the British Academy 62*: 331–78.

Williams, Bernard (1978), *Descartes. The Project of Pure Enquiry*. Harmondsworth: Penguin.

Wittgenstein, Ludwig (1953), *Philosophical Investigations*. Oxford: Basil Blackwell.

(1980), *Remarks on the Philosophy of Psychology. Vol. 2*. Oxford: Basil Blackwell.

Wolff, Christian (1730), *Philosophia prima, sive ontologica*. Frankfurt.

Wood, Allen (1981), *Karl Marx*. London: Routledge & Kegan Paul.

Yakhot, Jehoshua (1981), *Podavlenie Filosofii v SSSR-e: 20–30 gody* [*The Suppression of Philosophy in the USSR: 1920–30*]. New York: Chalidze.

Yakubinsky, L. P. (1923), *O dialogicheskoĭ rechi* [*On Dialogic Speech*]. Petrograd: Trudy foneticheskogo Instituta Prakticheskogo Izucheniya Yazykov.

Yudin, P. (1932), God raboty [A Year's Work]. *PZM*, nos. 1–2, 115–27.

Zapata, René (ed.) (1983a), *Luttes philosophiques en URSS 1922–1931*. Paris: Press Universitaires de France.

(1983b), La formation de la philosophie soviétique, 1922–1931. Zapata (1983a: 25–44).

Zelený, Jindřich (1962), *The Logic of Marx*, trans. Terrell Carver. Oxford: Basil Blackwell, 1980.

Zinchenko, V. P. (1985), Vygotsky's Ideas about Units for the Analysis of Mind. Wertsch (1985b: 94–118).

INDEX

[handwritten at top: Thereas, closs with the Rest - a posture are incorporated into lucrature - cultural form-activity (practical)]

[handwritten at bottom: There is no one standpoint from which a homogeneous collective subject views the world as a meaningful, collectively-created object open to recuperation. On the contrary capitalist constitutes atomistic subjects who by virtue of their atomistic nature are psychically impoverished -]